Someone's in the Kitchen
with

Melanie

Happy Cooking!

by

MELANIE REID SOLES

Melanie Soles
2006

Edited by Martha J. Long
2004

ISBN: 0-9758642-0-3

First Printing   3,000 copies
Second Printing   2,000 copies

WIMMER
COOKBOOKS

A CONSOLIDATED GRAPHICS COMPANY

800.548.2537   wimmerco.com

Introduction

Melanie Reid Soles

As I have just typed my 800th recipe into this laborious cookbook effort, I have had ample time to reflect upon the true intent and meaning of this four-year project. As I look back at my earliest intentions, they began eighteen years ago, the year I was married, and I truly did not know how to cook.

Since then, I have become an accomplished home cook and have enhanced my knowledge with dozens of cooking classes and a cooking tour in Bordeaux, France with the well known chef Jean Pierre Moulle, head chef at Chez Pannise in Berkeley, California for over 20 years. Recently, I took a four week apprenticeship in the kitchen of Mark's on Westover in Greensboro, working with chef/owner Mark Freedman, who was very patient with my "home cooking" techniques. Within that four week period, I quickly eliminated any thoughts I had ever had of opening a restaurant!

However, back in 1987, I asked my grandmother, Ava Heritage Faulconer of Burlington, North Carolina, a very good old-fashioned cook, to write some of her recipes down for me so that I could prepare them for my new husband. Many of her meals were prepared without recipes, but she managed to present to me for my 27th birthday in 1988, a handmade cookbook with her favorite dishes either handwritten on the journal pages or old recipes were cut and glued in the fabric covered journal.

She was 89 years old when she gave me her treasured gift. Bubba, as I always called her, lived to be 101½ years old. Thus, my accumulation of old family recipes began.

Shortly after my husband Bill and I were married, his mother, Majelle Morris Soles, of Greensboro, died. Majelle had also been raised by a mother who was nearly the same age as my grandmother and who had been taught to cook in similar ways. I inherited most of my mother-in-law's recipes, which were geared towards entertaining. My father-in-law retired that year as CEO and President of Jefferson-Pilot Corporation, after serving 27 years in that position. Decades of company entertaining taught my mother-in-law how to entertain effortlessly and without too much fuss.

A year after my mother-in-law died, her 99 year old mother, Blanche Ingram Morris from Salisbury, North Carolina passed away. We called her Mom Morris. While we were cleaning out her house, I discovered all of her old recipes which she had written with a lead pencil on scraps of parchment paper. Years later, the recipes and the handwritings were so similar to my own grandmother's that I had a hard time determining which grandmother the recipes had come from.

My collection was growing. At that time I began to have an interest in preserving this part of my family's heritage and history for our children. At the turn of the century (2000 that is), I began to realize that many of these recipes had begun even two centuries before – with our grandmothers learning many of their recipes from their mothers in the 1800s.

Guarding these treasures carefully, I began to sort through and accumulate hundreds of old fashioned, simple, family recipes. I raided my own mother's boxes and files, taking many of them with me. My children think their grandmother, June Faulconer Reid of Burlington, North Carolina (my mother) is the best cook in the world. My collection was growing faster by the month.

Then, in 2001, my mother's sister, Catherine Faulconer Farriss of New York City, died after a short illness. My aunt always fashioned herself not as a Southern, old fashioned, country cook – but as a gourmet cook in New York City. She was an Emmy-award winning writer with NBC and when she had a free weekend in her younger days, would fly off to Paris for Cordon Bleu cooking school classes.

Catherine has a shelf in her name at the James Beard House and was a member of that society for many years. She had many of her original recipes printed in Southern Living and I found lots of them in my grandmother's files thirty years later.

Aunt Pal, the name I always called her, may have well been a gourmet cook, but she loved her southern classics and oooohed and aaaahed every time she would come home and eat one of my mother's summer vegetable plates with cornbread or biscuits. Pal was an accomplished cook with a sophisticated palate and we enjoyed eating out in New York the many times I was there for work. She loved entertaining her friends in her corner apartment on Fifth Avenue in New York's trendy Greenwich Village neighborhood, and I found many of her menu plans in her recipe files which I inherited.

Then in 2003, when I was cleaning out my husband's godmother's house for her move into a retirement home, I came across another batch of treasures, hundreds of old, Southern recipes. When her good friend, Woodley Martin, passed away in 2000, our godmother, Lenora Jackson, inherited everything her friend owned. Woodley's recipes were tucked away in a large old box, and after a quick review, I realized what wonderful gems they were; a little more sophisticated than my grandmother's recipes, but truly grounded in southern, old fashion virtues. I was ecstatic. My collection was nearly complete.

In the summers of my childhood, we spent a lot of time visiting cousins on my father's side in Staunton, Virginia. My aunt and uncle had a hunting camp in the George Washington National Forest in the Shenandoah Valley. Some of my fondest memories revolved around the meals that were served for large crowds gathered around their picnic-style dining table. My aunt, Betty Lee Beam, passed away in late

2003 and I recently spent a weekend with my Beam cousins – Becky, Lee and Tommy and his wife Diana, collecting our family's favorite childhood recipes, many of which I have included in this collection.

Lastly, my friend Katie Redhead of Greensboro, shared with me many recipes that her mother, Ida Lawrence from Dunn, NC and mother-in-law, the late Virginia Potts Redhead, wife of the renowned Presbyterian minister Dr. John Redhead, Jr., had given her over the years. Other friends and family members may recognize some of their old favorites that we have shared around for years. I have tried to identify sources when they were specific, but most of the recipes represent all of our family favorites passed on from generation to generation, from friend to friend, from their kitchen to mine.

When I am in the kitchen preparing a meal for my family or a treat for a friend, I always feel as if there is someone in the kitchen with me – memories of days gone by, family members passed on, or my mother's current guidance advising me along the way. This book contains treasured family favorites, lovingly preserved for others to remember and enjoy.

It is my hope that the younger generation will cherish this timeless recipe collection, tweaked and guarded over the many years that they have changed hands. When their children ask them what kinds of food they grew up with, or what their mothers and grandmothers cooked, they'll be able to find it in this collection.

I finish with the words that my grandmother wrote in my first recipe book that she penned for me in 1988 and I dedicate this book to her memory, and in honor of my mother, my current cooking inspiration.

As I looked over all these recipes,
I pictured myself trying to cook a meal for my husband.
I was married in the year 1923
and was only twenty-three years old.
With his help, we made it and going to cooking schools,
I must say, I pleased my family.

I wish I could once again cook those big meals,
But time will tell and
I think I cooked enough, don't you?

With my love,
Bubba
1988

Acknowledgments

To my mother, June Reid, who helped me research many of the family recipes, especially my grandmother's, and for editing and testing many of the recipes.

To my father, Nelson Reid, who always believed that I could successfully complete this cookbook project and to both parents for providing the necessary capital for the initial printing.

To my teenage children, Reid and Roger, for enduring many weird meal combinations, especially during the testing period, and for raving about the dishes that succeeded. I always love it when my children tell their friends, "My mom is a really good cook."

To my husband, Bill, for having to look at all of my recipes, cookbooks, binders, papers and laptop computer spread all over the house for four years while I was working on the cookbook and for not complaining about the strange dinners I prepared. The worst was when we had eight barbeque sauces, two barbequed chickens and rice for dinner.

To Katie Redhead, my greatest cheerleader, for helping me get started on this ambitious project; for sharing many of her family's old fashioned, Southern recipes; for enthusiastically testing many of the dishes and lastly, for naming the title of the book. I am grateful for your friendship and love of good food and wine that we share.

To Ella Barham, I will always treasure the day we spent together, with you teaching me how to make your famous ham biscuits and yeast rolls. What a treat it was. Thank you for allowing me a peak at your 60 year tradition of making the best party biscuits in Greensboro and possibly the entire South. I promise to perpetuate your legacy by making Ella's famous ham biscuits for the rest of my life and sharing them with my friends like you have done for over half a century. Greensboro loves you – and your biscuits.

To Mark Freedman, owner of Mark's on Westover in Greensboro, for allowing me to work in your kitchen and learn the basics of restaurant preparation. You're the best chef in town and most chefs would not want a novice under their feet in their kitchen. I had a great time and learned much from the master.

To Martha Long, former food editor and lifestyles editor of the Greensboro News and Record, for editing this cookbook and writing my Foreword. It was a pleasure to work with such a beautiful writer and fellow foodie.

To Julie Knight of J. Knight Photography for the jacket cover photograph.

And to all my friends and family members whose recipes wound up in this Southern compilation of timeless, treasured recipes – recipes that are just as good today as they were forty or fifty years ago. Feel free to change them around, experiment with low fat options, vary the ingredients and make them your own. My greatest hope is that you will rediscover some of your childhood favorites in this cookbook and remember all the good times that you shared with your family and friends around the dinner table. Bon Appétit!

Melanie

Recipe Contributors

Becky Anhold

Ann Hall Banks

Ella Barham

Diana Beam

Lee Ann Beam

Beth Jones Carpenter

Betsy Flowers

Mark Freedman

Jeannie Fuller

Betsy Hayes Gaefell

Joann and David Grimes

Ross Harris

Lois Hill

Melinda Holt

Ruth Hope

Margaret Isley

Sarah Jasperse

Dina Jennings

Melanie Ketner

Gayle Koonce

Martha Long

Emily Reid McDonald

Barbara McNeely

Mary Nahser

Jane Pearce

Elizabeth Pitts

Day Redhead

Katie Redhead

June Reid

Barbara Shank

Arlene Simonton

Dorothy Singleton

Kim Stump

Toccoa Switzer

Dorothy Whitfield

BJ Williams

Foreword

By Martha J. Long

Once upon a time in the real world mealtime was a major player in family life. Whether the family gathered around the kitchen table or the dining room table, it was the setting for family bonding, for conversation that both enlightened and amused, for adults to teach by word and example and for children to learn from both. At times, at least, it included three or more generations, which added to the treasures and pleasures gleaned at mealtime from both the palate and the participants.

Melanie Reid Soles is a forty-something woman who is old enough to remember such family tables and young enough to live a thoroughly modern lifestyle as a wife, mother, civic leader and businesswoman. Those memories formed the yeast that gave rise to inspiration when faced with recipes written on the backs of envelopes or clipped from magazines and newspapers that had been lovingly used by her grandmother and other older family members. With the knowledge that friends, too, were the owners of such a rich heritage, Melanie set out on a journey to capture the culinary flavor of an earlier, though far from primitive time.

She tested and tested, and tested some more, until her heritage loaf was ready for the "oven." And now here it is golden brown, crusty and yeasty. Ready to savor not only for this generation, but also for that of her children – and for yours.

Martha Long
June 28, 2004

Table of Contents

 Denotes Personal Favorites

In Memory
of
Ava Heritage
Faulconer
(Bubba)
1899-2000

appetizers and beverages

SAUSAGE CHEESE COCKTAIL BITES

1 lb. sausage (hot)
1 lb.
1/2/aged cheddar - grated
2 pkgs. 10¢ biscuit mix
(cheese if possible; other-
wise plain)

Combine all ingredients,
mixing thoroughly. Using
a teaspoon, dip up just that
amount of mixture and roll
into a ball and place on a
cookie sheet. (Some like to
use ice tea_spoon instead
of regular teaspoon).

Bake at 400º about 10 to 12
minutes or until brown.
Serve hot.

Cheese Spread:

1 Large Phil. cream cheese
1 5 oz. jar Kraft Old English
Sharp cheese
1 5 oz. jar Kraft Roka Bluechew
1/2 cup chopped pecans
1/8 t garlic powder

Soften cheese - room
Temperature - Blend
(over)

Well in bowl.
Add nuts and garlic powder - Blend -
may be frozen in plastic container
and defrosted in refridgerator overnight
before serving.
You may use 5 oz. of blue cheese instead
of Roka cheese which gives a thicker
consistency -
The dip we had at Point Clear was
made with blue cheese.

For Ham Delights — Serves —

1/4 lb butter - room temp.
2 ts prepared mustard
2 tbs poppy seeds
2 tsp Worcestire
1 sm. onion grated
1 pkg. party rolls
1 4-8oz pkg ham
1 4oz pkg sliced swiss

Mix together butter, mustard, poppy
seeds, worcestire, onion. Use tiny day-
old party rolls. Open them & spread
mixture on both sides of roll; top
each half w/ a small piece of ham.
Put a small piece of swiss cheese
between halves before closing. Heat in
350º oven until cheese is melted.
Makes 30 sand.

appetizers and bev~

From the Ki...

Percolato
30-3½

1 64 oz. bottle apple juic
1 64 oz. bottle cranberr

Pour into large coffee

Add the following to the
basket:
   1 c. brown sugar
   4 cinnamon sticks
   2 T. whole cloves

Plug in the percolator and perk.

2 8oz cream
cheese, soft.
1 med onion
chopped & sautéd
1 lg tom chopped
1 can green
chiles, drained

To June
Here's What's Cookin'   Screw Drivers   Yield: about 4 qts   Serves 4 qts

  3 qts. orange juice
  3 cups Vodka
  ¼ c. lime juice (this really helps)
  Lime slices (op)
    Combine juice, vodka, and
lime juice. Mix well, and
pour into punch bowl or picher.
Serve over ice.

A tasty tidbit from   B. Flowers

©Carson-Dellosa Pub. RC-101

 # Vidalia Onion Dip

2	cups Vidalia onions, finely chopped, drained	2	cups Cheddar cheese, finely shredded	
2	cups mayonnaise (Hellmann's)		Paprika	

Preheat oven 375°. Let the onions drain after chopping. (I use a mini food processor/chopper.) Mix the mayonnaise with the Cheddar cheese. Add the drained onions. Fold and mix well. Pour into a 2-quart baking dish. Sprinkle with paprika. Bake 20 minutes until bubbly.

This Vidalia Onion Dip is my most requested dip to bring to people's houses. My good friend John Redhead likes it so much, that I renamed it John Redhead's Favorite Onion Dip for the Greensboro Day School Cookbook. People are always asking me for the recipe and it's a little embarrassing to tell them there's only three ingredients! If you have a convection oven, this will puff up like a dream.

Shrimp Butter

A classic low-country spread!

1	(8-ounce) package cream cheese, softened	1	pound shrimp, cooked and chopped
1	stick butter, softened		Juice of 1 lemon
¼	cup mayonnaise		Salt and pepper to taste
1	small onion, grated		Garlic salt to taste

Combine all ingredients. Refrigerate until chilled. Remove mixture from refrigerator and allow to soften before serving. Serve on crackers or toast points.

Spinach Dip

1-1½	packages frozen chopped spinach	2	cups sour cream
1	package Knorr's vegetable soup mix	4	tablespoons mayonnaise
		3	chopped green onions

Drain spinach and squeeze dry. Add other ingredients. Chill and serve.

Variation: 1 package spinach, 1 package Knorr's vegetable soup mix, 1 cup mayonnaise, 1 cup sour cream, 1 medium onion, 1 (8-ounce) can of water chestnuts, chopped.

This Spinach Dip was a stand-by dip in the seventies and eighties. Although you don't see it much anymore, it's still a good classic. Hollow out a round bread loaf and mound dip in the center.

Over the years, we dropped the clams in this recipe and used all shrimp. When I was getting married, in the eighties, this Shrimp-Clam Dip was always a staple on my mother's dining room table during our parties. I made this dip for years, as well. Feel free to use 1 pound of shrimp instead of shrimp and clams. This recipe can easily be doubled.

As the wife of a successful CEO of a large insurance company, my mother-in-law was always entertaining for company agents and clients and this Shrimp Dip was a staple. Perfect for a large party, it can easily be cut in half.

Shrimp-Clam Dip

½	pound shrimp, cleaned, shelled and deveined	5	tablespoons mayonnaise
1	small can clams, drained	1	cup diced celery
11	ounces cream cheese, softened	½	cup chopped onions
		1½	tablespoons lemon juice
			Dash of garlic salt
		1	cup sour cream
			Salt and pepper to taste

Cook shrimp in boiling water for approximately 2 minutes until done. Do not overcook. Cool and chop. Mix all ingredients well, adding a splash of ketchup to give the dip a pink color. Chill thoroughly. Serve with Fritos or crackers.

Shrimp Dip

3	(4-ounce) jars pimiento, chopped	1	scant teaspoon sugar
3	cups mayonnaise (approximately)	3	tablespoons grated onion
2	pounds sharp Cheddar cheese, grated		Dash of salt and pepper
1	full small jar horseradish, drained	5	pounds shrimp, cooked and chopped

Drain the pimientos well and save the juice. Add a scant teaspoon of sugar to 2 cups mayonnaise, with the pimiento juice added to make a fairly thin mixture. Mix the cheese, pimientos, mayonnaise mixture, horseradish and onion together and add 5 pounds of chopped, cooked shrimp. Serve with crackers. This will serve 30-40 people.

DeBordieu Clam Dip

1	(3-ounce) package cream cheese, softened	3	drops Tabasco sauce
1	tablespoon mayonnaise	1	(8-ounce) can minced clams, drained
1½	teaspoons lemon juice	2	tablespoons grated onion
¼	teaspoon salt	2	teaspoons chopped parsley
¼	teaspoon Worcestershire sauce		

Combine cream cheese, mayonnaise, lemon juice, salt, Worcestershire sauce and Tabasco sauce. Add clams, onion and parsley. Mix well. Chill and serve with crackers.

Sea Captain's House Crab Dip

1	cup crabmeat	1	tablespoon French dressing
1½	cups grated sharp Cheddar cheese	1	teaspoon horseradish
½	cup mayonnaise		Juice of ½ lemon

Mix and chill. Serve with saltine crackers. Yum.

Hot Crabmeat Dip

2	tablespoons lemon juice	1	teaspoon garlic salt
1	cup crabmeat	¼	cup mayonnaise
1	cup sour cream	½	teaspoon minced chives
2-3	drops Tabasco sauce	⅛	teaspoon salt
1	teaspoon minced onion	¼	teaspoon Worcestershire sauce

Pour lemon juice over crabmeat. Combine remaining ingredients and add to crabmeat and lemon juice. Put in saucepan and heat at low temperature. Place in serving bowl or chafing dish and serve with crackers.

My friend Melanie Ketner, passed this recipe from her mother-in-law, Ruth Hope of Debordieu, South Carolina, on to me. Ruth is known for her clam dip.

✳

If you're from North or South Carolina, many of you grew up vacationing near Myrtle Beach. The Sea Captain's House restaurant has been there since before I was a child. Lines formed out the door and the wait was long. A Myrtle Beach institution, this restaurant sits right at the ocean's feet. You can feel the surf pounding near the fabulous window view. This crab dip is served with saltine crackers while you wait for your food or most often, your She Crab Soup, which is listed in the soup section.

Horseradish Artichoke Dip

2 (14-ounce) cans artichoke hearts

1 cup mayonnaise

¾ cup Parmesan cheese

2 garlic cloves

1 tablespoon horseradish

Combine all ingredients in a food processor and blend until smooth. Pour mixture into a small casserole dish and bake in a preheated 350° oven for 20-30 minutes.

Serve with crackers or French bread slices.

Crabmeat Canapés

12	slices white bread	1	cup grated Cheddar cheese
½	pound lump crabmeat		
1	cup mayonnaise	1	small onion, grated fine
½	teaspoon salt	½	teaspoon curry powder

Remove crusts from bread and cut into squares, strips or triangles. Set aside. Mix other ingredients thoroughly and spread on bread. Place on cookie sheets and broil until brown and bubbly. Makes 36 canapés, depending on shape.

Variation: You can add artichoke hearts and Parmesan cheese if you like. This can be made into a dip and poured into a casserole dish and baked at 350° for 20 minutes. Serve with chips or crackers if using as a dip.

Crabmeat Crescents

An elegant presentation, but so easy!

½	pound lump crabmeat	¼	cup chopped spinach
1	(8-ounce) package cream cheese	3	green onions, minced
		2-3	drops Tabasco sauce
1	egg	2	rolls crescent roll dough

Combine all ingredients except for the roll dough. (This can be made ahead and kept in the refrigerator for 1-2 days.) Unroll dough and divide into triangles. Cut each triangle in half, longwise. Spread crabmeat mixture onto dough and then roll up as you would for a crescent roll. Place on cookie sheet and bake for 10-13 minutes in a preheated 375° oven.

Chipped Beef Cream Cheese Dip

1   small jar chipped beef
1   (8-ounce) package
    cream cheese
1   cup sour cream
2   tablespoons milk
¼   cup green pepper,
    chopped
2   tablespoons onion
    flakes
½   teaspoon garlic salt
1   cup chopped pecans

Remove the chipped beef from the jar and chop finely. Mix all ingredients and pour into casserole dish. Bake 350° for 20 minutes. Serve with toast points.

Curry Dip

1   cup mayonnaise
½   teaspoon minced onion
½   teaspoon
    Worcestershire sauce
    Dash of Tabasco sauce
½   teaspoon salt
    Dash of pepper
1   teaspoon curry powder
1   teaspoon lemon juice
¼   cup chili sauce or
    ketchup

Mix all ingredients until smooth and blended. Refrigerate to chill. Serve with vegetables.

Betty Beam's Roquefort Dip

2   cloves crushed fresh
    garlic
3   tablespoons chives,
    minced
2   tablespoons lemon juice
1   cup sour cream
2   cups mayonnaise
1   cup crumbled Roquefort
    cheese (may use blue
    cheese)
    Salt and pepper to taste

Mix all ingredients well and chill. You can hand mix or use electric beater on low speed for 2 minutes. This is wonderful to use as a dip for veggies or crackers.

As a child, we always had a few jars of chipped beef on the pantry shelves – to use in this dip or creamed, over toast for Sunday supper.

Easy Vegetable Dip

Use this great old standby when you're in a time bind.

1 pint sour cream

1 package Knorr's
vegetable soup mix

Lemon juice

Onion salt

Mix together and add a little lemon juice, onion salt for added taste. Chill.

Variation: Add some chopped spinach, chopped onion or any other fresh vegetables you like to this mixture – it'll just make it better.

Dill Dip

⅔ cup mayonnaise

⅔ cup sour cream

1 (3-ounce) package
cream cheese

4 teaspoons
fresh dill weed, chopped

1 tablespoon parsley, chopped

1 teaspoon seasoned salt

1 teaspoon finely
chopped onion

Mix and chill. Serve with
carrot sticks, celery, cherry
tomatoes, cauliflower and
red pepper strips.

BLT Dip

*Taken from the classic bacon, lettuce and
tomato sandwich, this BLT dip is especially good in
the summer when the tomatoes are fresh and ripe.*

8	slices crisp cooked bacon	¼	cup mayonnaise
1	large tomato, peeled, chopped and drained	¼	teaspoon salt, pepper and basil
1	(8-ounce) package cream cheese, softened		Chopped lettuce

Combine everything but the lettuce. Blend in a food processor.
Cover and chill. Place dip on top of chopped lettuce and serve
with crackers. For an interesting presentation, hollow out a head
of iceberg lettuce and mound dip in the hollowed lettuce head.
Serves 4.

This recipe can easily be doubled or tripled.

Tex-Mex Black Bean Dip

*A killer recipe your friends
will be begging you for, and it's low fat!*

1	(15-ounce) can black beans, drained	½	teaspoon chili powder
1	teaspoon vegetable oil	½	cup shredded Monterey Jack cheese
½	chopped onion	¼	cup chopped fresh cilantro
2	garlic cloves, minced		
½	cup diced tomato	1	tablespoon fresh lime juice
⅓	cup mild picante sauce		
½	teaspoon ground cumin		

Place drained beans in a bowl; partially mash until chunky. Set
aside. Heat oil in a medium nonstick skillet over medium heat.
Add onion and garlic; sauté 5 minutes or until tender. Add beans,
tomato and next 3 ingredients. Cook 5 minutes or until thickened,
stirring constantly. Remove from heat; add cheese and remaining
ingredients, stirring until cheese melts. Serve warm or at room
temperature with corn or tortilla chips.

Mount St. Helen

4	ripe California avocados	½	package taco seasoning
	Juice of ½ lemon	1	large can refried beans or 2 small cans
	Dash of Tabasco sauce		
½	teaspoon garlic salt	2	medium tomatoes, chopped
1½	cups Monterey Jack cheese, grated		
1½	cups sharp Cheddar cheese, grated	2	bunches green onions, chopped fine
1	cup sour cream		

Mash and mix the avocados, lemon juice, Tabasco and garlic salt. Set aside. Combine both Monterey Jack and Cheddar cheese and set aside. Mix the sour cream with the ½ package taco seasoning mix and set aside. Layer the following on a large platter: Refried beans. Avocado mixture. Sour cream mixture. Grated cheeses. Tomatoes. Green onions. Serve with Fritos or tortilla chips.

This layered avocado Mexican dip is always a favorite for young people, and especially for men. It can be doubled or tripled if having a large party.

Homemade Hummus

Serve with Toasted Pita Chips.

7	large cloves garlic	1½	cups freshly squeezed lemon juice (about 10 lemons)
3	teaspoons sea salt, divided		
4	cups cooked chickpeas	1	tablespoon extra-virgin olive oil
2	cups tahini		
		¼	cup water

In a food processor, blend garlic with 1 teaspoon sea salt. Add chickpeas and 2 teaspoons salt and process for about 30 seconds. Add tahini and continue to blend, pausing to scrape down sides. Repeat with lemon juice, olive oil and water. Consistency should be smooth. Serve as a dip with toasted pita bread or vegetables.

Creamy Black Bean Dip

2 cans drained black beans

1 can Rotel tomatoes or salsa, drained

1½-2 cups grated Muenster (or other) cheese

2 cloves garlic, chopped

5-6 minced green onions

1 cup sour cream

Mix and bake in casserole dish for 30 minutes at 375°. Serve with tortilla chips.

Toasted Pita Chips

2 pieces Pita Bread

4 tablespoons melted butter or butter flavored spray

Parmesan cheese, grated

Garlic salt

Cut pita bread into small triangles and split bread. Spread melted butter or use butter spray and coat the inside of the pita triangles. Sprinkle with garlic salt or garlic powder. Sprinkle with grated Parmesan cheese and broil triangles until toasted. Turn and broil the back side if desired. Serve warm or at room temperature. Store in an airtight bag or container.

This vegetable spread is an old Southern favorite at bridal showers, Junior League teas, morning coffees, or anytime you want a light finger sandwich. This can also be spread into a mold and served with crackers.

Vegetable Sandwich Spread and Mold

1	peeled cucumber, finely grated	1	green pepper
1	ripe tomato, finely chopped	1	envelope unflavored gelatin
1	small onion, finely grated	3	tablespoons cold water (or vegetable juice)
1	cup celery, finely chopped	2	cups mayonnaise

Put chopped vegetables in a colander and sprinkle with ½ teaspoon salt and drain. Soak 1 envelope plain gelatin in 3 tablespoons cold water or vegetable juice. Dissolve over hot water. Cool and add to 1 pint mayonnaise. Pour off liquid from vegetables and add to mayonnaise. Mix well. Put in jar and cover tightly. Can be molded as well. Spread on white or wheat bread and cut crusts or serve with crackers. If making sandwiches, layer between wax paper and place damp paper towel on top to keep fresh. Store in airtight container.

Variation: Add 1 jar drained, chopped pimientos to vegetable mixture.

Guacamole

This is wonderful with chips or served on a taco salad.

2	large very ripe California avocados	3	cloves garlic, minced
	Juice of ½ lemon	1-2	tomatoes, chopped and drained
⅓-½	cup chopped Vidalia onion or 1 bunch green onions	⅓	cup chopped cilantro, optional
			Salt and pepper to taste

Mash ripe avocados with fork until smooth. Mix with lemon juice for a smooth consistency, or if desired, slightly chunky. Stir in onions, garlic, tomatoes and cilantro. Season liberally with salt and pepper. Serve with tortilla chips or serve on salad.

Baked Tomato Fondue with Goat Cheese

*Use fresh goat cheese and
serve with toasted French bread slices.*

2	tablespoons olive oil	1½	teaspoons Tabasco Jalapeño sauce
1	onion, minced		
3	garlic cloves, peeled and minced	1	teaspoon Tabasco red hot sauce
1	(28-ounce) can crushed tomatoes in purée		Salt to taste
1	celery stalk	8-12	ounces goat cheese – plain or flavored with herbs
4	sprigs fresh parsley, thyme, oregano		
2	bay leaves	1	tablespoon chopped fresh parsley

In a large saucepan, combine oil, onion and garlic. Sauté over medium heat until translucent. Do not brown. Add the tomatoes directly from the can. Stir. Tie the celery, parsley, thyme, oregano and bay leaves into a bundle and add the bouquet to the tomato mixture. Continue cooking over medium heat, uncovered, until the sauce begins to thicken, 10-20 minutes. Remove from heat and discard the herb bouquet. Add both Tabasco sauces. Taste for seasoning and add salt. The sauce will be spicy.

Preheat oven to 450°. Pour tomato mixture into casserole dish. Crumble or slice goat cheese over top of tomato mixture. It will not cover entire dish. Bake until sauce is bubbly and cheese is melted, about 10-15 minutes. Sprinkle chopped parsley on top. Serve with toasted French bread slices or water crackers.

Use the best quality crushed tomatoes you can find. It will make a difference.

Baked Artichoke Spread

A favorite at Southern cocktail parties for years!

1 (14-ounce) can artichoke hearts

½ cup mayonnaise

½ cup sour cream

⅓ cup grated Parmesan cheese

⅛ teaspoon Tabasco sauce

Drain and chop artichokes. If desired, you can use the marinated artichokes in a jar instead of the canned. Stir all ingredients until well mixed. Spoon into small ovenproof dish. Bake at 350° for 30 minutes or until bubbly. Makes 2 cups. Recipe can easily be doubled or tripled to accommodate a large crowd.

Grandmother Genie's Pimiento Cheese

My cousins say that the only thing they're ever asked to bring to parties is our grandmother's pimiento cheese.

1 pound extra-sharp Cheddar cheese

½ cup mayonnaise

Several dashes of Worcestershire sauce

Several dashes of onion powder

Optional-garlic powder

½ green pepper, finely minced, about ¼ cup

1 small jar pimientos, thoroughly drained

In a large bowl, grate the Cheddar cheese. Add mayonnaise until desired consistency is reached. Add Worcestershire sauce, onion powder, garlic powder, green pepper and pimientos and blend. Store in covered jar and serve on sandwiches or with crackers as a dip.

Variation: Add 1 tablespoon dehydrated onions, dash of cayenne pepper and ½ cup chopped pecans.

Cucumber/Cream Cheese Sandwiches

1	(8-ounce) package cream cheese, very soft	1	teaspoon finely grated onion
2	tablespoons mayonnaise	2	teaspoons finely grated cucumber
	Sugar and salt to taste	1	cucumber, peeled and thinly sliced
			Paprika

Mix all of the above except the cucumber slices and paprika. Cut rounds of bread with biscuit cutter and spread with softened butter or mayonnaise before spreading with cucumber mixture. Top with slices of cucumber and sprinkle with paprika. Serve open face.

Pimiento Cream Cheese

Cream cheese makes it different.

4	large garlic cloves	¼	cup or more mayonnaise to taste
1	(4-ounce) jar chopped pimientos	½	cup finely chopped Italian parsley
1	tablespoon olive oil		Tabasco to taste
1	cup pecans, chopped		
6	ounces cream cheese, softened		

Crush 2 garlic cloves with the flat side of a knife and mince remaining 2 garlic cloves. Reserve minced garlic. Drain pimientos well. Preheat oven 350°.

In an ovenproof heavy skillet cook crushed garlic in oil over moderately low heat, stirring, until golden. Discard garlic with spoon and stir pecans into oil. Cook pecans over moderate heat, stirring, 1 minute and transfer skillet to oven. Toast pecans in oven, stirring occasionally, until golden, about 5 minutes and cool.

In a bowl stir together cream cheese, mayonnaise, and minced garlic clove. Stir in remaining ingredients and salt and pepper to taste until combined well. At this point, you can pack cheese spread into a crock and chill, covered with plastic wrap for 1 to 4 days. Let pimiento spread stand at room temperature 30 minutes and serve with crackers. Makes about 3 or more cups.

Variation: You can add 2 cups shredded extra sharp Cheddar cheese.

Cheese Ball

2	(8-ounce) packages cream cheese, softened	½	teaspoon paprika
½	pound sharp Cheddar cheese, shredded	½	teaspoon seasoned salt
2	teaspoons grated onion	¼	teaspoon salt
2	teaspoons Worcestershire sauce	1	(2¼-ounce) can deviled ham
1	teaspoon lemon juice	2	tablespoons chopped parsley
1	teaspoon dry mustard	2	tablespoons chopped pimiento, thoroughly drained
			Finely chopped pecans (about ½-¾ cup)

Soften the cream cheese in a small bowl and beat with electric beater until smooth or process in a food processor. Add the Cheddar cheese, onion, Worcestershire sauce, lemon juice, dry mustard, paprika, seasoned salt, salt and deviled ham until all is smooth and creamy. Stir in the parsley and pimientos. Cover and refrigerate overnight or for several hours until cheese is firm.

Remove and shape cheese into a ball and coat with the chopped nuts. Wrap with Saran Wrap and refrigerate until ready to serve. Garnish top of cheese ball with paprika and chopped parsley if desired.

Islander Cheese Ball

2	(8-ounce) packages cream cheese	¼-½	green bell pepper, chopped
1	(8-ounce) can crushed pineapple, drained	2	teaspoons seasoning salt
2	tablespoons green onions, chopped, including tops	2	cups chopped pecans

Mix cheese and pineapple with mixer. Stir in onion, green pepper, salt and ½ cup pecans. Roll into large ball, 2 logs or fill a scooped out fresh pineapple half. Roll or top with remaining pecans.

Drain green pepper on paper towels to dry before mixing. Serve with bacon flavored crackers.

A staple of cocktail parties in the fifties, sixties, seventies and eighties, this recipe was first printed in 1964. Although we don't see cheese balls used as often as we used to, it would be just as good today as it was forty years ago.

Christmas Cheese Ball

This cheese ball was traditionally served near Christmas, because of its resemblance to a Christmas wreath.

1 pound grated
sharp Cheddar cheese

¾ cup mayonnaise

1 medium onion, grated

1 garlic clove pressed
or minced

½ teaspoon Tabasco sauce

1 cup chopped pecans

1 jar strawberry preserves

Mix all of the above except strawberry preserves and form into a ball with a hollow center, like a small ring. Place strawberry preserves in the middle of the cheese ring. Serve with crackers.

This delicious layered cheese torta was originally prepared by my good friend and great cook Elizabeth Pitts of Charlotte, NC. She served it at my "going away" party when we moved to Greensboro from Charlotte in the early 1990's.

Do not tell your guests it's made of half butter as they may be afraid to eat it! Let them guess what makes it taste so good!

Pesto Torta

This gets better as it softens.

2	(8-ounce) packages cream cheese, room temperature	1	pound unsalted butter, room temperature

Pesto Sauce:

¼	cup pine nuts or walnuts	½	teaspoon salt
2	cloves garlic	½	cup olive oil
1	cup fresh spinach, tightly packed	¾	cup Parmesan cheese
1	cup fresh basil, tightly packed	3	tablespoons butter, room temperature
½	cup fresh parsley	1	jar sun-dried tomatoes

Beat the cream cheese and butter until smooth with an electric beater. Put to the side.

To make pesto sauce, roast pine nuts or walnuts for 10 minutes at 325°. Do not burn. In a food processor with steel blade, purée nuts, garlic, spinach, basil, parsley and salt. Add olive oil and blend. Add Parmesan cheese and 3 tablespoons butter and pulse Briefly. Do not overblend.

Cut an 18-inch square of cheesecloth and moisten with water, wring dry and smoothly line a 6-cup plain or Charlotte mold with the cheesecloth. (A small bowl will work also.) Drape excess cloth over rim of mold or bowl. With a rubber spatula, make an even layer with ⅙ of the cheese in the bottom of mold. Cover with ⅓ of the pesto, extending it evenly to the edge of the mold. Continue with cheese and pesto. Refrigerate overnight.

To unmold, turn mold upside down on platter and carefully lift off mold or bowl. Pull cheesecloth away from cheese. Top with sun-dried tomatoes if desired, or add a layer of sun-dried tomatoes as the last layer of the torta. Let soften for an hour or so and serve with crackers.

Four Cheese Pâté

1	(8-ounce) package cream cheese, softened	1	small round Camembert cheese, softened
2	tablespoons milk	1	cup Maytag blue cheese, crumbled
3	tablespoons sour cream	1	cup shredded blue cheese, softened
¾	cup toasted pecans, chopped or toasted pine nuts	1	cup shredded Swiss cheese, softened
2	(8-ounce) packages cream cheese, softened		

Line a small bowl or small casserole dish with plastic wrap. In a separate mixing bowl, combine 1 package cream cheese, milk and sour cream. Beat with electric mixer until smooth. Spread this into the casserole dish or bowl. Sprinkle with toasted chopped pecans or pine nuts.

Combine remaining cream cheese, Camembert cheese (including rind), blue cheese and Swiss cheese in a mixing bowl and beat with electric mixer until smooth. Spoon this mixture into the casserole or bowl on top of the toasted nuts, and spread to the edge. Cover with Saran Wrap and chill at least overnight. To serve, invert bowl onto platter and carefully peel away the Saran Wrap. Garnish with nuts on top or with chopped parsley and paprika. Serve with apple or pear wedges.

Baked Brie with Almonds

1	(2 pound) wheel Brie cheese	1	cup ground almonds
1	stick butter, room temperature	½	cup brown sugar
			Amaretto or bourbon to moisten

Place Brie cheese in lightly buttered round dish. Combine butter, almonds, brown sugar and liquor. Mix well. Mound on top of Brie. Bake at 325° for about 15-20 minutes until cheese is soft to touch. Let Brie cool for several minutes before serving. Serve with French bread.

3 Cheese Spread

1 (8-ounce) package cream cheese, softened

1 (5-ounce) jar Kraft Old English sharp cheese

1 (5-ounce) jar Kraft Roka Blue cheese

½ cup chopped pecans

⅛ teaspoon garlic powder

Soften cheese to room temperature. Blend well in bowl. Add nuts and garlic powder. Blend. This may be frozen in plastic container and defrosted in refrigerator overnight before serving. You may use 5 ounces of blue cheese instead of Roka which gives a thicker consistency. Serve with crackers.

In the old days, no Southern party would have ever been without ham delights. Growing up, I thought these were so good and loved it whenever we had them. I always wanted extras for breakfast. My research of family recipes found this recipe six times, with slight variations. They are easy to fix ahead of time, wrap back in the roll foil tray and refrigerate or freeze until they need heating. Enjoy!

Ham Delights

½	cup butter, softened		3	cups finely ground country ham or thinly sliced baked ham
2	tablespoons poppy seeds		2	packages party rolls, split (Pepperidge Farms small square rolls)
2	teaspoons prepared mustard			
¼	cup finely grated onion		1	cup grated Swiss cheese
½	teaspoon Worcestershire sauce		1	cup grated Cheddar cheese, optional

Mix butter, poppy seeds, mustard, onion, Worcestershire sauce and ham if it's grated. If not omit for now. Using tiny party rolls, split open and spread mixture on both sides of rolls. If using sliced ham, place small piece of ham on top of butter mixture. Sprinkle grated cheese between halves before closing. Heat covered in 350° oven until cheese is melted. This may only be enough to spread one package of rolls. Recipe can easily be doubled if serving a large crowd.

Baked Brie in Phyllo Pastry

*This makes for an elegant dish
that impresses guests but is easy to prepare.*

10-12	sheets phyllo pastry		Currant or apricot jam
2	sticks melted butter	½	cup brown sugar
1	(2-pound) wheel of Brie cheese		

Butter each sheet of phyllo one at a time, layering them carefully. Brush top of Brie with jam. Crumble brown sugar on the jam, press in gently and flip Brie face down onto the buttered phyllo sheets. Brush the exposed pastry with rest of melted butter and fold over Brie. Carefully pick up Brie and flip back over.

Bake at 350° for 20-25 minutes until pastry has browned. Let cool slightly and pour off excess butter. Serve with crackers or French bread.

Mini Corn Muffins with Smoked Turkey and Chutney

1½	cups self-rising cornmeal	¼	cup butter, melted
1	cup all-purpose flour	2	eggs
⅓	cup sugar	½	pound smoked turkey, sliced thin
	Pinch of salt	½	cup orange chutney (or cranberry chutney)
1½	cups whole milk		

Preheat oven to 400°. Mix cornmeal, flour, sugar and salt in large bowl. In small bowl, combine milk, butter and eggs. Add to dry ingredients. Spoon batter into greased mini-muffin tins. Bake 14-16 minutes. Cool 5 minutes and remove from tins. Cut muffins in half. Place turkey and a dab of chutney on each muffin bottom half. Replace muffin tops. Serve warm or at room temperature. If desired, spread mayonnaise or Dijonnaise to the bottom half before adding the turkey.

 B.J.'s Cheese Straws

No Southern home would ever be without cheese straws during the holidays, special occasions or at weddings. My friend B.J. Williams makes the best.

1	pound grated extra-sharp Cheddar cheese (Kraft)		Dash of salt (optional)
		¾	teaspoon cayenne pepper
1	pound margarine		
6	cups all-purpose flour (Red Band)	6-8	drops Texas Pete hot sauce

Grate cheese and set aside. Cream margarine. Mix cheese into margarine and add in flour and spices. You can either mix the flour in by hand or use the processor. Be sure not to over-process. You want it firm enough to put in a cookie press. Using the small star shape disk, press mixture through cookie press, making straws about 1½-2 inches long. Bake in preheated 400° oven for approximately 9 minutes. Cool on wire racks and keep in airtight containers. These will freeze well and make great gifts. Makes 10 dozen.

Variation: For spicier cheese straws, increase the amount of cayenne pepper to 1 teaspoon and use about 15 drops or splashes of the Texas Pete. Add 2 teaspoons dry mustard to the mixture as well. The mustard gives it a distinctive taste.

Cheese-Pecan Biscuits

½ pound butter, softened

½ pound sharp Cheddar cheese, grated

2 cups all-purpose flour

8-12 dashes cayenne pepper

1 egg, beaten

75 pecan halves

Cream together thoroughly the softened butter, Cheddar cheese and flour, along with some dashes of cayenne pepper. Chill in refrigerator for an hour or more. Roll dough between wax paper to ⅛-inch thickness.

Cut biscuits with a 1-inch biscuit cutter and place on cookie sheet which has been lined with parchment paper or press through cookie press. Brush tops of biscuits with well beaten egg. Place pecan half on top of biscuit and bake in a 350° oven for 15 minutes.

Remove and sprinkle with salt. Let stand until about cold, when biscuits will slide off cookie sheet. Makes about 75 small biscuits.

Variation: Shape into cheese straws and omit the pecans.

Scrabbles

A full recipe makes enough for an Army!! Recipe may be halved if you wish.

½ pound butter

½ pound margarine

2 cloves garlic

1 tablespoon onion salt

1 tablespoon celery salt

1 tablespoon garlic salt

2 tablespoons Worcestershire sauce

1 box Rice Chex cereal

1 box Wheat Chex cereal

1 box plain Cheerios cereal

1 bag thin pretzel sticks, broken

Nuts, optional

Melt butter and margarine in saucepan slowly with crushed garlic. Add the onion salt, celery salt, garlic salt and Worcestershire sauce until salts are dissolved. In a large bowl empty cereals and pretzels and mix together. Pour butter mixture over and toss good to coat cereals. Spread out on large jelly-roll pans and cover with foil. Bake at 300° for 1 hour, stirring every 15 minutes. Uncover and bake at 250° for 1 hour.

Eggplant Bruschetta

2	medium-sized eggplants	¼	cup roasted red peppers, drained and chopped
4	garlic cloves, minced		Ground black pepper
1	cup fresh spinach, chopped		Olive oil
			Parmesan cheese
4	small ripe tomatoes, chopped		French bread slices

Slice eggplant into thick slices and salt both sides well. Let drain on a wire rack for about 30 minutes. After draining, pat dry. Meanwhile, combine the minced garlic, chopped spinach, tomatoes and chopped roasted red peppers. Brush the salted and drained eggplant slices with good quality olive oil. Grill slices until they are browned, about 3 minutes per side. While still on the grill, season the eggplant with ground black pepper. Top the eggplant with the tomato mixture. Sprinkle with Parmesan cheese and continue grilling until the cheese is melted. Transfer eggplant to sliced French bread and serve immediately.

Sausage Cheese Cocktail Bites

| 1 | pound hot sausage | 2 | small bags biscuit mix (cheese if possible) |
| ½ | pound aged Cheddar cheese, grated | | |

Combine all ingredients, mixing thoroughly. Using a teaspoon, dip up just that amount of mixture and roll into a ball and place on a cookie sheet. Bake at 400° for 10-12 minutes or until brown. Serve hot.

This recipe is so old it called for 2 packages 10 cents biscuit mix. It must be the small bagged kind that you find in the flour and baking section of the grocery store, not the big package of Bisquick.

Spicy Sugared Pecans

½	cup sugar	½	teaspoon cayenne
3	tablespoons water		pepper
1	teaspoon salt	2	cups pecan halves

Preheat oven to 350°. Butter heavy large baking sheet or cover baking sheet with parchment paper. Combine sugar, water, salt and cayenne pepper in heavy small saucepan. Stir over medium heat until sugar dissolves. Boil 2 minutes. Add pecans and stir until pecans are coated with mixture, about 1 minute.

Transfer pecans to prepared sheet, spreading evenly. Bake until pecans are just beginning to brown, about 13 minutes or more. Transfer to cookie sheet lined with waxed paper and separate pecans with fork. Do this quickly because pecans will adhere to sheet very fast! Cool completely. Store in airtight container for up to one week. Makes 2 cups.

Baked Buttered Pecans

These pecans are favorites at Christmas and make great gifts.

2½	pounds pecan halves
1	stick butter
	Salt

Layer pecans in large jelly-roll pan. They will be about an inch thick. Melt butter and pour over pecans, stirring to coat throughout. Salt heavily (you'll think it's an obscene amount of salt, but it's needed). Heat in 250° oven for 30 minutes to 1 hour, checking throughout and stirring occasionally. Cool and store in airtight containers. They will keep for a week or more in the refrigerator or freeze in airtight container for later use.

Variation: Mix 1 teaspoon chili powder and ½ teaspoon black pepper to the melted butter for a spicier version.

Oyster Crackers

An addicting snack!

¾ cup vegetable oil

1 package Hidden Valley ranch dressing mix

1 teaspoon dill weed, dried

¼ teaspoon garlic powder

¼ teaspoon lemon-pepper, optional

5 cups plain oyster crackers

Mix all the ingredients together, except crackers. Put oyster crackers in large Tupperware container and pour mixture over the crackers. Cover with lid and shake off and on periodically until crackers are covered and oil is absorbed. Place in preheated 250° oven for 15-20 minutes. Stir gently halfway through baking. Store in air tight container.

While going through all of my Aunt Pal's recipes I found the following page from *Southern Living* magazine, March 1972, over thirty years old. It was a Xerox copy with notes in all the margins. It took me a few minutes to figure out why the page had been saved – my Aunt Pal's byline, Catherine Faulconer, was at the bottom of the page. I've reprinted the recipes as they appeared over 30 years ago.

Avoiding Cliché Hors d'Oeuvres by Catherine Faulconer

Planning hors d'oeuvres for a cocktail party stumps a hostess who has no trouble at all concocting a meat-vegetable-salad-and-dessert menu. To rely on cheese and crackers and the usual dips – those cocktail party cliches – is openly unimaginative. So try some interesting departures from the usual that will not be too filling, but that will keep hunger in abeyance through the cocktail hour.

The following offer variations of texture, taste, and color. All can be prepared well ahead of time. However, the Crabmeat Rolls require a few minutes in the broiler before serving.

First printed in *Southern Living* magazine – March 1972

Spiced Shrimp

Cook 2 pounds of shrimp in pickling spice. Make a French dressing (see recipe below). Place a layer of bay leaves, a layer of thin lemon slices, a layer of thin onion slices, and a layer of cooked shrimp in a casserole. Repeat the layers, and cover with French dressing. Cover. Let stand in the refrigerator for three or four days before serving.

French Dressing for Shrimp:

1	cup olive oil or salad oil	3	tablespoons Worcestershire sauce
1	cup vinegar		
1	(10¾-ounce) can condensed tomato soup	½	teaspoon salt
		½	teaspoon black pepper
¼	cup sugar	1	medium onion, grated

Combine all ingredients and mix well. Makes 2 cups.

Cheese-and-Beef Log

1 (8-ounce) package cream cheese
1 (10-ounce) can deviled ham
2 tablespoons horseradish
½ stick butter
1 tablespoon prepared mustard
1 (3-ounce) package chipped beef, cut up with scissors

Mix cream cheese, deviled ham, horseradish, butter and mustard. Spread chipped beef on a large piece of waxed paper. Spread cheese mixture over beef. Roll up paper the long way. Store in refrigerator overnight. Serve with crackers or rounds of rye bread. Makes 10-12 servings.

Guacamole Cocktail Spread

1 large avocado, ripe
1 tablespoon grated onion
1 tablespoon chili sauce
   Dash of cayenne pepper
1 clove garlic, grated
½ teaspoon or more salt

Cut avocado in half lengthwise and remove pit. Scoop out inside of avocado and mix with other ingredients, mixing well. Adjust seasonings and stuff the avocado shells with this mixture. Chill and serve with whole wheat bread or tortilla chips.

Beef Teriyaki

1 pound top round
½ cup soy sauce
¼ cup dry white wine
1 tablespoon cider vinegar
1 tablespoon sugar
1 clove garlic, crushed
½ teaspoon ground ginger
   Crackers

Cut top round into thin slices about 2 inches long. Combine soy sauce, white wine, vinegar, sugar, garlic, and ginger. Pour over sliced meat. Cover and marinate several hours at room temperature or in the refrigerator overnight. Broil about 5-7 minutes, turning once. Place in a chafing dish and serve with crackers. Makes about 18 servings.

Crabmeat Rolls

½ cup light cream

1 egg

2 sprigs parsley, stemmed

2 celery tops

Salt

½ teaspoon pepper

Dash of cayenne pepper

3 slices bread, broken

6 ounces fresh crabmeat

10 strips bacon

In a blender, put the cream, egg, parsley, celery leaves, salt, pepper, cayenne and half the bread. Cover and blend about 1 minute, until smooth. Empty into a bowl. Flake crabmeat and combine with the rest of the bread crumbs. Shape into 10 small cakes, wrap each in a strip of bacon. Broil on all sides until bacon is crisp.

Tangy Meatballs

1	pound ground beef	1	teaspoon salt
1	egg, slightly beaten	¼	teaspoon ground black pepper
¼	cup chili sauce		
¾	cup finely chopped onion	1½	cups cheese cracker crumbs, divided

Combine ground beef, egg, chili sauce, chopped onion, salt, and pepper with 1 cup cheese cracker crumbs. Mix thoroughly. Shape into tiny meatballs and roll in remaining ½ cup cracker crumbs. Sauté 5 minutes in ½-inch of hot oil, turning to brown on all sides. Remove to a chafing dish and serve with toothpicks. Makes about 30 meatballs.

Ripe Olive Mini Pizzas

⅓	cup tomato sauce	1	cup pitted ripe olives
½	teaspoon oregano	1	(8-ounce) package refrigerated biscuits
	Freshly ground black pepper		
2	cups shredded American cheese, divided		

Blend tomato sauce, oregano, pepper, 1½ cups cheese, and ripe olives cut into thin wedges. Cut each biscuit into quarters; roll quarters into balls. Press on floured board with metal end of biscuit package to make circles of equal size. Place on greased baking pan. Top with ripe olive mixture and sprinkle with remaining ½ cup cheese. Bake in preheated 450° oven for 6-8 minutes. Makes 40 (1½-inch) pizzas.

Variation: For a more current version of this, omit the American Cheese, mozzarella and Parmesan cheese instead. Also, Boboli pizza bread can be substituted for the biscuits.

Strawberry Lemonade

This would especially be good in the late Spring and early Summer when the strawberries are at their peak. To get the most juice out of lemons, make sure they're at room temperature before squeezing.

½	pound strawberries (1½ cups), trimmed and halved	1½	cups fresh lemon juice (from about 5 lemons)	
		1-1½	cups sugar	
		3	cups cold water	

Purée strawberries with 2 tablespoons lemon juice in a blender until smooth, then force through a fine sieve into a bowl to remove seeds. Stir together strawberry purée, remaining lemon juice, 1 cup sugar, and water in a large pitcher until sugar is dissolved. Taste, then add more sugar if needed. Serve over ice. Makes about 6 cups.

 # Mel's Breakfast Smoothie

This is one of my favorite breakfast drinks – or anytime you need a healthy pick me up.

8	ice cubes	½	cup pineapple juice	
1	small container berry yogurt	⅓	banana	
		5	large strawberries or 7-8 smaller ones	

Place all of the ingredients in a blender and purée until smooth. I freeze my summer strawberries in small sandwich bags so that I can have fresh strawberries in the smoothie after strawberry season is over. I also freeze the peeled cut bananas. They do turn brown in the freezer, but the frozen banana makes the smoothie thicker and smoother. Add some fresh pineapple, peaches or blueberries if you have them. I like blueberry or strawberry/banana yogurt the best, but any fruit yogurt will do.

In the South, many beverages are known as staples and were especially so twenty-thirty years ago. Homemade sweet iced tea, fresh squeezed lemonade, punch served at ladies teas and prepared adult drinks are just a few. Take the time when you entertain to prepare a homemade drink and notice the comments you'll receive from your guests. Everyone loves a house drink!

Instant Russian Tea Mix

Russian tea mix used to be given as gifts at Christmas, but you rarely see it anymore. Place the mixture in small decorative jars.

1 container Tang

½ cup instant Lipton tea (powdered kind)

1½ cups sugar

1 teaspoon ground cinnamon

1 teaspoon ground cloves

Mix all ingredients together and pour into jars. To serve, mix 2 rounded teaspoons with 1 cup hot water and stir.

Southern Style Iced Tea

You really know you're in the South when people only serve sweetened tea.

3	family-size Lipton tea bags	1	cup sugar
1	quart boiling water		Juice of 2 lemons, optional
1	quart cold water		

Place the 3 family-size tea bags in a large pitcher with a cover. Pour 1 quart of boiling water over the tea bags. Cover and steep for 5-10 minutes. Add another quart of cold tap water. While tea is still warm, add about a cup of sugar, depending on your taste. Stir until sugar is dissolved. Add juice of 2 lemons, if desired. Enjoy. To cut down on sugar, try using ½ cup and add artificial sweetener.

Russian Tea

18	cups cold water	2-3	cups sugar
1	stick cinnamon	1	(12-ounce) can frozen orange juice
12	whole cloves		
6	family-size tea bags	4-6	tablespoons lemon juice

Boil water, cinnamon and cloves. Add tea bags and steep 10 minutes. Strain. Add sugar, orange juice and lemon juice. Adjust sugar to your likening. Can make ahead and put in fridge. This is nice during the holidays. Makes 5 quarts.

Piña Coladas

2	ounces coconut cream	3	ounces Rum
4	ounces unsweetened pineapple juice	1	large cup ice cubes

Blend all ingredients in a blender and serve over ice. Substitute Vodka for Rum if desired. Makes 2 drinks.

beverages

Bloody Mary

3	quarts tomato juice	2½	tablespoons salt
3	cups Vodka	3	teaspoons sugar
⅓	cup steak sauce, such as Heinz 57	¼	teaspoon hot sauce
¼	cup Worcestershire sauce		Juice of 12 limes
			Celery sticks
			Lime slices

Combine all ingredients but celery sticks and lime slices, stirring well. Pour into pitchers and float lime slices on top. Serve drinks with a celery stick. Makes 4 quarts.

Screw Drivers

3	quarts orange juice	½	cup lime juice (this really helps)
3	cups Vodka		Lime slices, optional

Combine orange juice, Vodka and lime juice. Mix well and pour into punch bowl or pitchers. Serve over ice. Makes 4 quarts.

 Peach Fuzz

6	peaches, washed and cut	1	small can frozen lemonade
½	heaping cup sugar	1½	cups light Rum

Blend ingredients in a blender and remove ½ of the liquid from the blender. Fill blender (½ full with peach liquid) with ice and blend. Makes 1 blender full. Pour into a pitcher, then blend the second half with ice again.

My mother's friend, Betsy Flowers, had given my mother most of the following drink recipes. They're great if you're having a party. There's nothing better than serving a "house drink" – whether it's my Christmas Bourbon Punch or a Bloody Mary. Keep them in a pitcher and let your guests serve themselves.

Pink Cloud Punch

2 (3-ounce) packages
cherry gelatin

1-2 cups sugar

10 cups hot water

3 small cans frozen lemonade

2 (20-ounce) cans
pineapple juice

1 large bottle ginger ale

½ gallon vanilla ice cream

Dissolve gelatin and sugar
in hot water. Add juices and
chill. Add ginger ale and ice
cream just before serving. Serve
in large punch bowl. Serves
50 small punch glasses.

This bourbon punch
originated at our Christmas
neighborhood progressive
dinner parties in Charlotte,
North Carolina and has
been served annually for
the past twenty years! After
moving to Greensboro, we
kept up the tradition. Even
friends who don't like
bourbon guzzle this drink
down. We've had to
call taxis to take some
people home. I think
you'll enjoy this one!

Vodka Margarita

1½	ounces Vodka	Lime peel
½	ounce Triple Sec	Salt
	Juice of ½ lime	

Rub rim of glass with lime peel and dip in salt. Stir Vodka, Triple Sec and lime juice with crushed ice. Makes 1 drink. You can add more lime juice if desired. Can be doubled or tripled for more drinks.

Frozen Daiquiris

1	(12-ounce) can limeade, softened	12	ounces dark Rum (Myers)
12	ounces light Rum		Fresh bananas
			Fresh ripe fruit of choice

Mix limeade and both rums together and pour 1 cup of the rum mixture into a blender. Add 1 banana and fresh ripe fruit of choice – peaches, strawberries, cherries, etc. Add ice and blend. Continue to add ice and rum mixture as needed to fill blender to desired consistency.

Holiday Bourbon Punch

1	large can frozen lemonade	1	(32-ounce) bottle Club Soda
1	small can frozen lemonade	1	fifth of Bourbon (almost a quart)
		2	cups orange juice

Mix an hour before the party begins and freeze in the freezer. It will be slushy. This recipe makes 16 large glasses or 32 small cups.

Mocha Punch

2	cups cold water	1	quart milk
½	cup instant coffee granules	½	gallon vanilla ice cream, softened
1	cup chocolate syrup	1	large bottle soda water

Mix together cold water and coffee granules. Stir to dissolve. Blend syrup, milk and ice cream together in a large bowl. Add the coffee water and mix well. Before serving, add soda water. Add floats of ice cream on top – vanilla or chocolate. Makes 24 cups.

Holiday Cranberry Punch

64	ounces chilled cranberry juice	6	tablespoons lemon juice
		½-¾	cup sugar
2	(46-ounce) cans chilled pineapple juice	28	ounces chilled ginger ale
			Vodka to taste

Combine chilled cranberry juice, chilled pineapple juice and lemon juice. Stir in cup sugar until dissolved. Add ice and chilled bottle of ginger ale. Add Vodka to taste. Makes 50 (½ cup) punch glasses.

Homemade Apple Cider

1	jug apple cider	1	tablespoon whole cloves
1	(48-ounce) bottle cranberry juice		Peel of 1 orange
4-5	cinnamon sticks		Peel of 1 lemon

Boil all of the above together, strain, and pour back into containers to give as gifts.

No bridal party in my hometown would be complete without this Mocha Punch. Its sweetness varies, but it's always the same. Since my generation rarely serves punch from a punch bowl anymore, you could make this up in a large bowl and pour it into silver pitchers.

Percolator Punch

1 (64-ounce) bottle apple juice

1 (64-ounce) bottle cranberry juice

1 cup brown sugar

4 cinnamon sticks

2 tablespoons whole cloves

Pour apple juice and cranberry juice into large coffee pot. Add the brown sugar, cinnamon and cloves to the strainer basket. Plug in percolator and perk.

Whiskey Sour

1 pint water

Scant cup of sugar

1 pint Whiskey

Juice of 5 lemons

Combine water and sugar in saucepan and let come to a boil. Remove from heat and cool. Mix with 1 pint whiskey and juice of 5 lemons. Serve chilled over ice. Makes 1½ quarts.

Egg Nog

This recipe is over seventy years old and was written as "Egg Nog Receipt".

1	dozen eggs	1	quart milk
1	pound sugar (about 2 cups)	1	pint whipping cream
1	quart liquor	1	pint half-and-half

Separate eggs, beat yolks thoroughly and add sugar. Pour liquor over this very slowly, beat constantly and add 1 quart of milk and pint of half-and-half. Add egg whites, which have been beaten stiff. Stir thoroughly. Lastly, add the whipping cream which has been whipped stiff. Pour into glasses and sprinkle with ground nutmeg. Makes about 4 quarts.

Homemade Vanilla Flavoring

2	vanilla beans	1	pint Vodka

Split vanilla beans in half lengthwise. Put 4 pieces of vanilla beans in pint of vodka and let sit several weeks. Shake up every couple of days. Serve as after dinner drink or over ice cream.

soups, salads and
dressings

Martha Long
Women's Editor
Greensboro Daily News
Greensboro, North Carolina

BRUNSWICK STEW

(Family quantity, for "doin's" on a small scale.)

For gatherings, large or small, Brunswick Stew is traditional in
Greensboro, as it is over much of the South. Numerous civic groups
sell this specialty to benefit worthwhile causes. One women's group
works in shifts throughout the night, cooking Brunswick Stew to raise
money for a favorite charity. There are many recipes for this favorite --
this particular one comes from eastern North Carolina, by way of my
mother's kitchen.

1 stewing chicken (about 5 pounds)
2 cans (20 oz. each) Lima beans
2 cans (20 oz. each) tomatoes
3 cups chopped cabbage
3 large onions, chopped
5 slices salt pork or slab bacon, cooked
    and crumbled (reserve drippings)
4 large potatoes, cooked and mashed
2 cans (20 oz. each) cream style corn
2 teaspoons salt
1-1/2 teaspoon sugar
1 teaspoon <u>each</u> pepper and paprika
1/4 teaspoon cayenne pepper
Pinch

Simmer chicken in water to cover until tender. Remove from broth and
set aside to cool. To broth, add Lima beans, tomatoes, cabbage, and
onions. Cook 3 hours, stirring frequently, and occasionally pressing
vegetables against sides of pot to mash.

Meanwhile, remove bones from chicken and finely dice the meat and skin.
Add chicken, crumbled salt pork, and reserved drippings to the vegetable
broth mixture; continue cooking for 1 hour longer, stirring frequently. Add
mashed potatoes and corn, continue cooking for 20 minutes, stirring constantly. Remove from heat and stir in seasonings. Makes 3 to 4 quarts.

soups, salads and dressings

YUM YUM - Pineapple Salad

2 Pks. Lime Jello
1 No. 2 can crushed pineapple
1 Pt. xx cream
1 Cup grated cheese

Dissolve Jello in 2 cups boiling water. Add
juice from pineapple with enough cold water
to make 2 more cups of liquid. When mixture
begins to cool and set add cheese, pineapple,
pinch of salt and cream whipped stiff.

Dressing for Salad

1 Cup mazonnaise
2 Tablespoons chopped celery
2   "   "   Green pepper
2   "   "   Red pepper
Few drops onion juice

HERE'S WHAT'S COOKIN'

Bing Cherry Salad

1 can dark sweet Bing
                    Cherries
Pecans
small cream cheese
Cherry Jello + 1/2 pk. natural jello—
1 cup juice from cherries [pineapple juice to fill out]
1 cup sherry (Richard's wild
                    Irish Rose)
Put cherries on bottom
  " cheese in chunks spread
                    around
Nuts —

Recipe from Mary Bess Wilson Serves 7 or 8
mrs. Banks Wilson

FROZEN FRUIT SALAD

1 cup orange sections
1 cup diced pineapple
1 cup mayonnaise dressing
1 cup whipped cream
1/2 cup seeded and halved white grapes
1/2 cup chopped maraschino cherries
fruit salad dressing
1/4 cup cold water
1 tablespoon gelatin

Soften gelatin in cold water. Dissolve
over hot water. Add mayonnaise. Mix
thoroughly. Fold in cream. Fold in
fruits. Pour into mold. Cover tightly.
Pack in ice and salt. Let stand 4 hours.
Unmold. Slice. Serve on crisp lettuce.
Serve with fruit salad dressing. 6 servings.

Chicken Noodle Soup

*This is especially nice for anyone who has
been sick. It's very comforting and low calorie.*

1	cup finely chopped celery	1	tablespoon olive oil	

1 cup finely chopped
   celery

1 cup chopped or sliced
   carrots

1 cup finely chopped
   onions

2 cloves garlic

8 ounces sliced
   mushrooms

1 tablespoon olive oil

8 cups chicken broth
   Additional chicken
   broth if desired

4-5 split chicken breasts
     on the bone

2 cups thin egg noodles

Chop the celery, carrots, onions, garlic and mushrooms. In a Dutch
oven, sauté all the vegetables in olive oil for about 10 minutes,
until soft, and set aside. In the same pot, add approximately
8 cups of chicken broth. Simmer the chicken breasts in the chicken
broth for 45 minutes or until cooked and tender. Let chicken set
for another 30 minutes or so with the lid on. Strain the broth and
get rid of any debris.

Take the chicken out and pull meat off the bone. Cut or shred
chicken in small pieces. Put the chicken back in the chicken broth
with the sautéed vegetables. Add the egg noodles and continue
simmering until the noodles are cooked, another 20-30 minutes.
You may need to add more broth at this point, depending on how
"meaty" you like your soup. Make 1 gallon.

*Variation: Instead of stewing the chicken breasts in the broth, add
4 cups of already cooked chicken meat (from grocery store rotisserie
chicken) and let simmer in the chicken broth for 10-15 minutes before
adding the noodles.*

*There's nothing better
on a Sunday night
than homemade soup
and a loaf of hot,
homemade bread or
grilled cheese
sandwiches. All of the
soups included here are
old-fashioned and
homemade – just the
kind my mother
always makes.*

Potato Soup

2-3 slices bacon

3 medium potatoes

2 stalks celery, chopped

2 medium carrots, chopped

1 small onion, chopped

1 cup chicken broth

Salt and pepper to taste

2 tablespoons flour

2 cups milk

In a saucepan, cook bacon until crisp, remove and set aside. To drippings, add potatoes, celery, carrots, onions, chicken broth, salt and pepper. Cook, covered, about 15 minutes or until tender.

Combine flour with small amount of milk until dissolved. Add to the potato mixture along with the rest of the milk. Cook over medium heat until mixture starts to boil. Serve hot. If desired, sprinkle chopped cooked bacon bits on top or grated Cheddar cheese.

Emily's Brunswick Stew

1	(3-pound) chicken	1	cup chopped onion
2	stalks celery, cut in large pieces	3	(15-ounce) cans whole tomatoes, undrained and chopped
1	small onion, quartered		
7	cups water, divided	1-1½	teaspoons black pepper
2	(10-ounce) packages frozen lima beans or 1 (16-ounce) bag	1	teaspoon crushed red pepper
2	(10-ounce) packages frozen corn or 1 (16-ounce) bag	½	cup Worcestershire sauce
		2	teaspoons garlic salt

Combine the chicken, celery, onion quarters and 5 cups of water in a large Dutch oven or stock pot; bring to a boil. Cover and reduce heat. Simmer for approximately 1 hour. Remove chicken, celery and onion. Cool chicken; pull meat off the bone and coarsely chop meat. (If you prefer all white meat, substitute whole chicken with 4 chicken breasts on the bone.)

Add the chopped chicken to the stock, along with the frozen lima beans and remaining ingredients. Bring to boil and reduce heat and simmer, uncovered, for about 4½ hours or until desired consistency, stirring often. Add remaining water as needed.

Brunswick stew is good for days after it's cooked. It just keeps getting better and better. Serve with Saltine crackers.

Variation: For a different variation of Brunswick Stew, try Martha Long's version which is printed on the divider page. She says it is an eastern North Carolina recipe that belonged to her mother.

Aunt Pal's Cassoulet

1½	pounds dried white beans	1½-2	pounds Italian sausage	
1	quart water	⅔	cup celery, sliced thin	
10	ounces chicken broth	⅔	cup green pepper, chopped	
1½	cloves garlic, minced	1	(8-ounce) can tomato sauce	
1	onion, chopped fine	⅔	cup dry white wine	
2	carrots, quartered		Oil for sautéing	
	Bouquet garni (parsley, celery leaves, bay leaf, thyme)			

Soak beans overnight in 2 quarts cold water. Drain and rinse. Put beans in large kettle with 1 quart water, chicken broth, minced garlic, chopped onion, quartered carrots and bouquet garni. Bring to a boil and reduce heat. Cook gently 1 hour, skimming foam when necessary. Heat oil in skillet and sauté sliced sausage until browned. Remove sausage and reserve.

In skillet with drippings, sauté thinly sliced celery and chopped green pepper. Add tomato sauce and white wine. Simmer 5 minutes. Add this mixture to the beans. Add sausage to the beans as well. Cover and simmer until beans and meat are tender, about 1 hour, adding water if necessary to cover beans. Skim off excess fat. Discard bouquet garni and serve.

Vichyssoise

4 cups chicken broth

1 pound potatoes, peeled and diced

2 cups onions, chopped

½ teaspoon salt

¼ teaspoon white pepper

½ cup Hellmann's mayonnaise

Place chicken broth, potatoes, onions, salt and pepper in saucepan. Bring to a boil over high heat. Reduce heat to low and simmer 15 minutes or until potatoes are tender. Cool and place mixture into blender. Blend until smooth and pour into a large bowl. Stir in the mayonnaise until well blended. Cover, chill overnight. Makes 4 cups.

Variation: Substitute ½ cup sour cream for the mayonnaise.

Lima Chowder

2 slices fat salt pork

1 small onion, sliced

2 cups potatoes, diced

1 cup boiling water

2 cups lima beans, cooked

3 hard-cooked eggs, sliced

3 cups hot milk

1 teaspoon salt

⅛ teaspoon pepper

4 tablespoons butter

4 tablespoons flour

Dice 2 slices fat salt pork. Place in saucepan and cook 5 minutes. Add sliced onion and cook until just turning yellow, then add diced potatoes and boiling water. Cook until potatoes are tender; then add cooked lima beans. In a separate saucepan, melt butter and add flour, and stir until smooth. Add milk and cook, stirring constantly until slightly thickened.

Add lima mixture to the milk and season with salt and pepper. Continue simmering until thickened a little more. Serve with crusty French bread or saltine crackers.

Black-Eyed Pea Soup

½	pound bacon, cut into pieces	2	(14-ounce) cans whole tomatoes, undrained and chopped
2	cups celery, finely chopped	2	(15-ounce) cans black-eyed peas, rinsed and drained
2	cups green pepper, finely chopped	1	can beef broth
2	cups onion, finely chopped		Salt and pepper to taste

Sauté bacon with celery, green pepper and onion until vegetables are tender. Add chopped tomatoes with the black-eyed peas to the vegetables. Pour in the beef broth and add salt and pepper to taste. Simmer for 30-45 minutes. Serve hot with homemade bread, or cornbread.

Variation: You may use chicken broth instead of the beef broth, if desired.

Bean and Ham Soup

2	cups dry navy beans	6	peppercorns
2	pound ham shank	2	quarts water
1	small onion, chopped	2	stalks celery, sliced
½	teaspoon salt	1	carrot, diced
½	teaspoon dried basil		

In large saucepan, combine all ingredients. Simmer covered for 1½-2 hours or until beans are tender and soup thickens. Remove peppercorns and ham shank. Cut meat from bone and return to soup. Heat thoroughly.

Variation: For split pea soup, add 2 cups split peas to recipe.

Michie Tavern's Vegetable Soup

3	quarts water	2	cups corn
5	strips bacon	2	cups cauliflower, chopped
1	bay leaf	2	cups broccoli, chopped
2	teaspoons garlic salt	2	cups carrots, thinly sliced
2	teaspoons ground pepper	8	medium potatoes, diced
2	tablespoons parsley, chopped	32	ounces V-8 or tomato juice
1	cup celery, diced	2	cups green peas
1	cup onion, diced	1	medium cabbage, coarsely chopped
½	cup green pepper, diced	3	tablespoons butter
3	cups green beans	1	tablespoon Parmesan cheese, grated
2	cups tomatoes, chopped		
½-1	pound spinach, shredded coarsely		

Bring water to a boil. Add bacon, bay leaf, salt, pepper and parsley. Boil for 25 minutes and remove bacon. Add the celery, onions, green pepper, green beans, tomatoes, spinach, corn, cauliflower, broccoli, carrots, potatoes and tomato juice. Simmer over low heat for 1 hour. Add green peas, cabbage, butter and Parmesan cheese. Simmer another 15 minutes and serve. Makes 24 servings.

The Michie Tavern, an old Stagecoach stop, is a 220-year old restaurant and tavern in Charlottesville, Virginia and was founded by and named after a distant relative of mine, William Michie. My great-grandmother was a Michie. My mother's brother (Bubba's son) was named Michie, as was his son, after this side of the family.

This recipe makes a huge amount, so please feel free to reduce portions in half. Although the recipe says to use fresh vegetables, it is perfectly acceptable to use frozen peas, beans, corn, etc. if you cannot get them fresh.

Mel's Tenderloin Beef Stew

1½	pounds tenderloin beef, cut into cubes	2	bay leaves
			Salt and pepper
1	cup flour seasoned with salt and pepper	1	(28-ounce) can ground tomatoes (don't use entire can)
2	tablespoons oil		
1	can beef broth	1	(15-ounce) can whole tomatoes, chopped and drained
½	can chicken broth		
½	cup red wine	1	teaspoon Worcestershire sauce
2	carrots, chopped		
4	celery stalks, chopped	2	large potatoes, cubed
1	onion, chopped	2	carrots, sliced
4	garlic cloves, chopped	1	ripe tomato, chopped
½	teaspoon paprika		

In skillet, dredge beef cubes in seasoned flour and brown in hot oil on all sides. Remove and put in large Dutch oven. Add beef broth, chicken broth, red wine (you can add more than ½ cup if desired), sliced carrots, chopped celery and onions, chopped garlic, bay leaves, paprika, salt and pepper, ground tomatoes, chopped canned tomatoes, Worcestershire sauce and heat covered for about 1 hour. Add 2 large potatoes, peeled and cubed, 2 more sliced carrots and 1 chopped vine ripe tomato and simmer, uncovered, for another 60 minutes.

To thicken stew, pour ½ cup cold water and ¼ cup flour into a shaker and shake to blend. Remove stew from heat and push meat and vegetables to the side. Stir in flour mixture as needed and stir over medium heat until gravy thickens. Serve with crusty French bread or over hot rice.

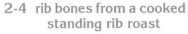 # Christmas Day
Vegetable Beef Soup

2-4	rib bones from a cooked standing rib roast		1	(8-ounce) can tomato sauce
4	cups water or more			Leftover vegetables from Christmas dinner – green beans, corn, lima beans, carrots
1	tablespoon sugar			
1	tablespoon salt			
½	tablespoon pepper			
1-2	stalks celery, chopped		2	chopped potatoes, peeled
½	onion, chopped			
1	can stewed or diced tomatoes			

Take the leftover rib bones and place in large Dutch oven. Cover with water and boil for several hours, replacing water as it evaporates. When meat falls off the bone, strain broth and remove fatty pieces and bones. Return broth to Dutch oven and add sugar, salt, pepper, celery, onion, tomatoes, tomato juice and simmer for another 30 minutes – 1 hour.

If you have roast beef leftover from your rib roast, cut up the meat and add to the soup. Then add all leftover vegetables – corn, green beans, lima beans, chopped carrots, potatoes (you can substitute with frozen vegetables) and simmer for another half hour. Season with more salt and pepper.

Cool slightly and refrigerate. Scoop off fat after soup has cooled. This is better the next day. Enjoy. Omit potatoes if you're going to freeze the soup.

My mother and I always make this vegetable beef soup after having a standing rib roast the night before. My mother says that the prime rib bones make the best soup broth ever.

Mel's Beef Chili

This is my favorite dish during football season, especially during the NFL playoffs and Super Bowl games. This is great for adults and because I don't make it too spicy, kid's love it as well. Serve bowls of shredded cheese, sour cream and chopped green onions on the side so guests can top their chili as they desire.

During one recent Super Bowl party, I made "Bread Bowls" to serve the chili in. Purchase small round white bread loaves from the bread store or grocery store. Hollow out the center of the bread with a sharp knife.

Heat the bread bowls for 5-10 minutes in a 350° oven. Just before serving, ladle the chili in the center of the bread and serve immediately. It's always a big hit!

2	pounds ground chuck
1	cup onion, chopped
1	cup green pepper, chopped
3	(16-ounce) cans dark red kidney beans, drained
1	(29-ounce) can diced tomatoes
1	(12-ounce) can tomato paste
2	(11-ounce) cans whole kernel corn, drained
1	(15-ounce) can Hunt's seasoned tomato sauce
1	cup water
3-4	teaspoons chili powder (or more)
2-3	teaspoons salt
1	teaspoon black pepper
1	additional (15-ounce) can tomato sauce if needed to prevent drying out at end

Brown meat, onion and green pepper in stock pot or large saucepan until beef is browned and crumbled. Add all remaining ingredients and bring to a boil. Reduce heat and cover. Heat on low for 30 minutes-1 hour. Uncover and simmer for another 30 minutes or so, adding up to one more can of tomato sauce to keep chili from drying out.

This will freeze nicely. Serve with cheese, sour cream and chopped green onions on the side. Serve Biddy's cornbread with this, as well. Makes 12-16 servings.

You can use Mexican-style canned corn instead of regular corn.

Hearty Vegetarian Chili

Low-fat and delicious!

	Vegetable cooking spray	1	cup tomato sauce
1	large carrot, peeled and chopped	3	tablespoons chili powder
1	large green pepper, chopped	1	jalapeño pepper, chopped
⅔	cup onion, chopped	¾	teaspoon ground cumin
3	cloves garlic, minced	¾	teaspoon dried whole oregano
1	(15-ounce) can kidney beans, rinsed and drained	½	teaspoon ground cinnamon
1	(15-ounce) can pinto beans, rinsed and drained	1	bay leaf
		⅛	teaspoon Tabasco sauce
1	(15-ounce) can black beans	1¼	cups shredded Cheddar cheese
2½	cups vegetable broth	¼	cup plus 2 tablespoons sour cream

Coat a non-stick skillet with cooking spray; place over medium-high heat until hot. Add carrot, pepper, onion, and garlic and sauté until crisp tender. Set aside.

Place beans in a large Dutch oven; add vegetable broth to cover beans and add reserved vegetable mixture. Next, add tomato sauce, chili powder, jalapeño pepper, cumin, oregano, cinnamon, bay leaf and Tabasco sauce to pot. Bring mixture to a boil, reduce heat and simmer, uncovered for 45 minutes.

Remove and discard bay leaf. Ladle hot chili into serving bowls; top each serving with 3 tablespoons shredded cheese and 1 tablespoon sour cream. Makes 6-9 servings.

This was an original recipe of my aunt, Catherine Farriss. I'm not sure I want to know why, but she called it "Naked Lunch."

Gussied-Up Gazpacho (with Shrimp)

½ pound or more fresh shrimp, cooked
6 tablespoons lemon juice
2 cloves garlic, peeled and whole
3 cups finely chopped tomatoes (about 6 large tomatoes), peeled and seeded
2 cups tomato juice
2 cups finely chopped cucumber, peeled and seeded
½ cup finely chopped onion
½ cup finely diced green pepper
¼ cup minced parsley
2 tablespoons chopped chives
4 teaspoons salt
1 teaspoon Tabasco sauce
⅓ cup olive oil
3 tablespoons red wine vinegar
½ cup ice water

Pour the lemon juice over the cooked shrimp and put in the refrigerator; let chill while you prepare remainder of ingredients. Combine everything but the garlic. Rub the garlic around the sides of a large glass bowl. Add the shrimp and lemon juice to the bowl; then add the vegetables and seasonings to the shrimp and mix thoroughly. Correct the seasonings. Chill until serving time. May be served over ice. Makes about 10 cups of soup.

Asparagus Bisque

2 pounds fresh asparagus
2 tablespoons butter
4 green onions, diced, including some tops
1 small potato, peeled and diced
3 cans chicken broth
Salt and pepper to taste
½ teaspoon Worcestershire sauce
½ teaspoon dill weed
½ cup cream
Dry sherry, optional

Break off tough ends of asparagus and throw away. Wash asparagus and cut into 1-inch pieces. In large pot, melt butter and add green onions. Cook until soft, about 3-4 minutes. Add asparagus, potato, chicken broth and seasonings. Cover and simmer until asparagus and potato are soft, about 25 minutes. Remove from heat and place in blender, a little at a time. Return to pan and add cream. Heat to just boiling and simmer for a few minutes. Add 1-2 tablespoons dry sherry, if desired. Serve hot. Makes about 6 servings.

soups

Cream of Cauliflower Soup

2	small onions, chopped		Salt and pepper to taste
1	clove garlic, minced	1	cup shredded fresh spinach
2	tablespoons butter		
4	cups chicken broth	1	tablespoon dill weed
1½	head cauliflower florets		
1	cup half-and-half		

In a large stock pot, sauté onions and garlic in butter until onion is soft. Add the chicken broth and cauliflower. Bring to a boil. Reduce heat, simmer 20-25 minutes or until cauliflower is very tender. Remove vegetables to a food processor. Purée until smooth. Return purée to broth. Stir well and add cream. Season to taste with salt and pepper and heat for 5-10 more minutes. Do not boil. Ladle into soup bowls and add shredded spinach and dill weed on each serving. Makes 8 servings.

Variation: You can substitute potatoes (1½ pounds), broccoli (1½ bunches) or mushrooms (1½ pounds), if desired, for the cauliflower. If using mushrooms, only simmer for 5 minutes.

This version of Cauliflower Soup was prepared by a friend at a supper club we belonged to in Charlotte, NC in the 1980's. It was so good, I requested the recipe and kept it for almost 20 years.

The beauty of this recipe is that it works for almost any vegetable!

Cream of Tomato-Basil Soup

4	shallots, diced	3	tablespoons fresh basil, chopped
½	pound leeks, chopped		
1	celery stalk, chopped	2	cans chicken broth
2	garlic cloves, minced	¼	teaspoon salt
2	tablespoons olive oil	1	cup whipping cream
1	(28-ounce) can Italian style tomatoes, undrained and chopped		

Cook shallots, leeks, celery and garlic in hot oil in a Dutch oven or stock pot over low heat for about 10 minutes or until tender. Do not burn garlic. Add tomatoes and basil and cook over medium heat for about 10 minutes. Add chicken broth and salt, bring to a boil. Reduce heat and simmer, stirring occasionally for about an hour. Cool slightly.

Purée half of the soup in a food processor or blender until smooth. Transfer back into saucepan with rest of soup and add whipping cream. Cook on medium heat until thoroughly heated. Do not boil. Garnish with fresh basil strips if desired.

Cream of Brie Soup

½ cup onion, chopped

½ cup celery, chopped

4 tablespoons butter

½ cup flour

2 cups milk

2 cups chicken broth

¾ pound Brie cheese
(do not peel), cubed

Salt and pepper to taste

Chopped chives as garnish

In a large saucepan, melt
butter and sauté onion and
celery until soft. Stir in the flour
and cook 2-3 minutes. Take off
the heat and add milk and
broth. Return to heat and stir
until thickens. Add cheese and
stir until cheese is melted. Purée
mixture in food processor
and strain. Serve hot.

Cream of Mushroom Soup

1	pound mushrooms, sliced		1½	cups cream or half-and-half
1½	cups chopped green onions with tops		1	teaspoon Worcestershire sauce
3	cloves garlic, minced			Fresh ground white pepper and salt to taste
½	cup plus 1 tablespoon butter			
3	cans chicken broth			

Cut mushroom slices for garnish and set aside. (You'll need about 16-20 slices.)

Sauté green onion and minced garlic in ½ cup butter for about 5 minutes. Add mushrooms with a grind of pepper and salt. Cook until mushrooms are soft. Remove from heat and purée mushroom mixture with 1 can of chicken broth. Add this to the remaining 2 cans of broth and bring to simmer on medium heat for about 15 minutes. Stir in cream or half-and-half and Worcestershire sauce and simmer 5 minutes. Add 1 tablespoon butter; remove from heat. Garnish with mushroom slices. Serves 8-10.

Old English Cheese Soup

¾	cup butter, divided		½	cup green pepper, finely chopped
½	cup celery, finely chopped		6	tablespoons flour
½	cup carrots, finely chopped		4	cups milk
½	cup onion, finely chopped		1	teaspoon salt
			2	cups shredded Velveeta cheese
			2	cups chicken broth

Melt ¼ cup butter in skillet and add vegetables. Sauté until crisp tender. Set aside. Melt ½ cup butter in Dutch oven over low heat. Gradually stir in flour. Cook, stirring constantly, until bubbly. Gradually stir in milk, stirring constantly, until mixture is smooth and thick. Add vegetables, salt, cheese and broth. Keep stirring frequently until cheese melts and mixture is well blended.

Crab and Corn Bisque

3	tablespoons carrots, finely chopped	¼	cup brandy, warmed
3	tablespoons onion, finely chopped	4	cups chicken stock
		2	tablespoons flour
2	tablespoons celery, finely chopped	2	tablespoons butter
		3	cups heavy cream
2	tablespoons tomato paste	½	pound crabmeat
		½	cup fresh or frozen corn kernels
4	sprigs fresh tarragon (or 1 teaspoon dried)	1	small tomato, peeled, seeded and diced
¼	cup olive oil		

Sauté carrots, onion, celery, tomato paste and tarragon in olive oil over medium high heat, stirring constantly. Cook for 4-5 minutes. Pour in brandy and ignite. When flames die down, pour in chicken broth and lower heat to medium/medium low. Simmer soup base until it reduces in half, for about 30 minutes.

While soup base simmers, prepare a roux to thicken the soup. Melt 2 tablespoons butter in a small heavy saucepan and add flour. Cook, stirring constantly, for 5 minutes or so. Do not let roux brown.

Whisk the roux into the soup base. Slowly boil for about 5 minutes. In another pot, strain the soup through a colander lined with damp cheesecloth. Discard the vegetables. The soup base may be cooled and kept refrigerated for a day if necessary.

To serve, heat up soup base, stir in heavy cream, crabmeat, corn and diced tomatoes. Salt and pepper to taste and serve immediately. Makes 6-8 servings.

Variation: If desired, replace the crabmeat with 1 pound cooked, chopped shrimp.

Low Country She Crab Soup

2 large onions, finely diced

1 cup clarified butter

2 cups flour

2½ quarts half-and-half

1 quart heavy cream

1½ teaspoons mace

1 cup good quality sherry

Salt and pepper to taste

1 pound jumbo lump crabmeat, picked clean

In a large stockpot, cook onions in butter until soft. Add flour, reduce heat to low, and cook, stirring constantly for about 15 minutes. Add half-and-half and cream, and continue stirring. Add remaining ingredients and simmer 30 minutes, stirring frequently. Serve hot, topped with an additional dash of sherry.

Note: This recipe makes 1 gallon. It could easily be reduced in half. I wouldn't necessarily reduce the crabmeat.

Fresh Vegetable Stock

10 cups water

1 medium onion, unpeeled and studded with 4 whole cloves

2 cloves garlic, unpeeled and bruised

2 celery ribs with leaves, cut into large chunks

8 button mushrooms, halved

2 carrots, unpeeled and cut into large chunks

2 leeks, trimmed and cut into large chunks

2 medium tomatoes, quartered

4 medium potatoes, halved

8 sprigs fresh parsley

2 fresh dill sprigs

1 bay leaf

8 black peppercorns

1 teaspoon course salt

Rinse all vegetables well. Add to pot of water. Bring to boil, reduce heat and simmer, uncovered for 1 hour. Adjust seasonings to taste and simmer 30 minutes longer. Strain broth, discard bay leaf. Let broth cool to room temperature and then refrigerate. It will keep for 4 days. This can easily be doubled and frozen.

Summer Corn Chowder

2	tablespoons olive oil	½	cup red bell pepper, diced
2	tablespoons butter	½	green pepper, diced
1	large onion, diced		Salt and pepper to taste
3	tablespoons flour	1	cup half-and-half
5	cups fresh vegetable broth	2	ripe plum tomatoes, diced for garnish
2	russet potatoes, peeled and diced	½	cup finely slivered basil leaves for garnish
4	cups fresh corn kernels		

Place oil and butter in pot over low heat. Add diced onion and wilt for 10 minutes. Sprinkle the flour over the onion and cook, stirring for an additional 5 minutes. Add the vegetable broth and potatoes. Bring to a boil. Reduce heat to medium and cook, partially covered, for 10 minutes or until diced potatoes are tender.

Add corn, red and green pepper, salt, pepper, and half-and-half. Cook over low heat for 8 minutes, stirring occasionally. Ladle 2 cups of soup in each bowl. Before serving, place 1 tablespoon tomatoes in center and top with slivered fresh basil.

You can substitute canned chicken or vegetable broth for the homemade vegetable broth if you have to. It'll just be a little better with the homemade broth.

# Mel's Famous Salad

Bibb or butter lettuce	Crumbled blue cheese
Radicchio	Roasted pine nuts
Sliced red onion	Mandarin oranges

Make salad with lettuces. You can substitute mesclun greens instead if you want. Add onions, pine nuts, blue cheese and Mandarin oranges. Toss together with raspberry dressing. Add a little extra blue cheese on top if you like.

Best Ever Raspberry Vinaigrette:

½	cup good quality raspberry vinegar	1	teaspoon Dijon mustard
½	cup olive oil	1	teaspoon fresh chopped tarragon
½	cup vegetable oil	1	teaspoon salt
½	cup maple syrup		Fresh ground pepper

In a bowl or jar, whisk or shake all ingredients together for raspberry dressing. Before serving, shake or whisk well. Refrigerate and let dressing sit out before serving.

Gourmet Cobb Salad

½	head romaine lettuce, chopped fine	3	ripe avocados
½	head Boston lettuce, chopped fine	2	whole skinless boneless chicken breasts, cooked and diced
1	small bunch curly endive, chopped fine	1	tomato, seeded and chopped fine
½	bunch watercress, chopped fine	½	hard-boiled egg, grated
6	slices lean bacon, chopped fine	2	tablespoons chopped chives

Chop romaine lettuce, Boston lettuce and curly endive to total about 4 cups each. Chop watercress, discarding stems, to total about 2 cups. Toss greens together. Cook bacon until crisp and drain. Cut avocado in ½-inch pieces. Arrange chicken, bacon, tomato, avocado over greens. Garnish with grated eggs and chopped chives. Toss with Cobb Salad Dressing.

Variation: For a simpler version, use iceberg or romaine lettuce and use rotisserie chicken from the grocery store.

I always prepare Mel's Famous Salad when someone says, "You bring the salad." It gets compliments at every meal, especially the dressing. There are many different ways to vary this salad, using Granny Smith apples or Bartlett pears instead of the Mandarin oranges. You can substitute the blue cheese crumbles for goat cheese or feta. Sometimes I make sugared pecans or walnuts instead of the toasted pine nuts. But I never vary the raspberry vinegar dressing, it's the best.

Cobb Salad Dressing

⅓ cup red wine vinegar

1 tablespoon Dijon mustard

⅔ cup olive oil

½ cup Roquefort cheese, grated

Whisk dressing until blended and stir in Roquefort cheese. Pour over salad and toss. Serves 6.

Townhouse Dressing

1 cup mayonnaise

⅓ cup sour cream

2 teaspoons fresh dill, chopped

Make dressing by combining mayonnaise, sour cream and dill; mix until well blended. Combine chicken, avocado, cucumber, tomato, eggs and dressing; mix lightly. Chill thoroughly

Townhouse Salad

	Iceberg lettuce or Romaine lettuce	3	hard-boiled eggs, chopped
3	cups cubed, cooked chicken	2	cups bread cubes, cut into ½-inch cubes
1	peeled California avocado, cubed		Vegetable oil
1	cup chopped, peeled cucumber	6	slices crumbled, cooked crisp bacon
1	cup cubed, peeled tomato	½	cup blue cheese crumbles

In large lettuce lined salad bowls, position cubed chicken, cubed avocado, chopped cucumber, chopped tomatoes and chopped eggs. Just before serving, add the bread cubes, which have been fried in a few tablespoons of oil until brown. Add the bacon and blue cheese to salad and toss lightly. Serve with Townhouse Dressing.

Farmer's Market Salad

Mesclun greens	Red pepper
Summer ripe tomatoes	Spring onions
Cucumber	Goat cheese crumbles
Avocado	Chopped herbs, such
Radishes	as tarragon, parsley
Carrots	or basil

Coarsely chop all the vegetables and avocado. Place on top of the greens. Top with goat cheese crumbles (feta or blue cheese will do as well). Pour light coating of Grimes Tarragon Vinaigrette over salad and toss.

Grimes Tarragon Vinaigrette:

2	cups good quality olive oil	½	tube anchovy paste
¾	cup tarragon vinegar	1	teaspoon Tabasco sauce
3	garlic cloves, pressed or minced	2	teaspoons Worcestershire sauce
3	teaspoons smooth Dijon mustard	1	tablespoon chopped tarragon

Combine all ingredients in a jar and shake well. When refrigerated, dressing will congeal. Before using, bring dressing to room temperature.

Layered Salad

Perfect for large crowds

1	head romaine lettuce or iceberg lettuce, chopped	1	small red onion, thinly sliced and separated into rings
6	hard-boiled eggs, sliced	1	pound bacon, cooked and crumbled
1	cup shredded Swiss cheese, divided	1	cup mayonnaise
1	pound fresh baby spinach	1	cup salad dressing (Miracle Whip)
1	(10-ounce) package frozen baby English peas, thawed and drained	1-2	teaspoons sugar
		1	cup shredded Cheddar cheese

Arrange lettuce in a 13x9x2-inch dish or a large round casserole dish. Then layer ingredients in the following order: eggs, ¼ cup Swiss cheese, spinach, ¼ cup Swiss cheese, peas, ¼ cup Swiss cheese, red onion, ¼ cup Swiss cheese, and bacon over the romaine lettuce.

Combine mayonnaise, salad dressing and sugar in a small bowl. Mix well. Spread over top of salad, sealing to edge of bowl. Sprinkle with Cheddar Cheese. Cover salad tightly and refrigerate several hours or overnight. To serve, cut salad into squares. Makes 12 servings.

Variation: Try using different vegetables and cheeses such as chopped green pepper, radishes, celery, carrots, zucchini, Parmesan, Cheddar or Jack cheeses.

Layered Spinach Salad

½-¾ pound baby spinach

½ pound fried bacon

4-6 hard-boiled eggs, sliced

Chopped lettuce

1 (10-ounce) package frozen peas, thawed

Slices of sweet onion

Mayonnaise

Layer salad in the following order and season as directed after each layer.

Spinach – sprinkle with salt

Crumbled bacon – sprinkle with pepper, salt, and sugar

Sliced hard-boiled eggs – sprinkle with salt

Chopped lettuce – sprinkle with salt and pepper

Frozen peas – sprinkle with ½ teaspoon sugar

Slices of sweet onion

Cover the top layer with mayonnaise.

Cover salad with Saran Wrap and refrigerate overnight.

Greek Dressing

⅓ cup vegetable oil

1 tablespoon vinegar

2 tablespoons sugar

½ teaspoon salt

¼ teaspoon dry mustard

¼ teaspoon celery seed

¼ teaspoon paprika

2 cloves garlic

Make dressing by combining oil, vinegar, sugar, salt, dry mustard, paprika, celery seed and garlic cloves in a jar. Shake well and refrigerate 2 hours. Remove garlic cloves from the dressing.

Tossed Greek Salad

	Chopped or torn lettuce	1	(4.5-ounce) can pitted ripe olives
5	large tomatoes, cut in wedges	1	teaspoon salt
3	medium cucumbers, peeled and diced	1	teaspoon oregano
½	green pepper, diced		Feta cheese, crumbled

Mix together in a salad bowl – lettuce, tomatoes, cucumbers, green pepper, onion and olives. Sprinkle with 1 teaspoon salt and oregano. Pour Greek Dressing on salad. Add feta cheese.

Potato, Corn and Cherry Tomato Salad with Basil Dressing

2	tablespoons white wine vinegar	2½	pounds small red potatoes
½	cup olive oil	6	ears fresh corn, kernels cut from cob
1	cup packed fresh basil leaves	½	pound cherry tomatoes, halved
	Salt and pepper to taste		

In blender or food processor, blend together the vinegar, oil, basil leaves and salt and pepper to taste until the dressing is emulsified. In a large saucepan, combine the potatoes with enough water to cover. Bring water to boil and simmer potatoes for 15 minutes. Drain and let cool. Quarter potatoes and set aside. In a large bowl combine corn, potatoes, tomatoes and dressing and salt and pepper to taste. Toss the salad gently. Serves 8.

salads

Corn Salad

A summertime favorite!

4	cans white shoepeg corn or 12 ears sweet white summer corn
1	green pepper, chopped
1	large Vidalia onion, chopped
3	ripe tomatoes, chopped
1	teaspoon yellow mustard
½	cup mayonnaise, approximately

Drain canned corn or if using fresh corn, cut kernels from cob and do not drain any liquid from the fresh corn. Add other ingredients and gently mix together. Refrigerate overnight.

Majelle's Pasta Salad

1	pound cooked small pasta shells
1	thinly sliced red onion
1	package frozen peas, thawed

Pasta Salad Dressing:

1	package frozen chopped spinach, thawed and squeezed dry
½	cup Parmesan cheese
⅔	cup regular oil
⅓	cup olive oil
⅓	cup vinegar
2	cloves crushed garlic

Put dressing ingredients in blender or food processor and blend. Pour over shells, peas and onions. Toss well to coat. Chill overnight for best flavor. Add ½ to 1 teaspoon salt if desired. Garnish with tomatoes before serving.

Broccoli Salad

2 bunches broccoli

8 strips bacon, cooked and crumbled

⅓ cup chopped onion

1 cup chopped tomato

2 hard-boiled eggs

Broccoli Salad Dressing:

1 cup mayonnaise or Miracle Whip

⅓ cup sugar

2 tablespoons vinegar

Cut broccoli into florets and blanch for 2 minutes in boiling salted water. Drain and cool with ice immediately. When completely cool, prepare dressing and pour over broccoli. Add bacon, onion, tomato and hard-boiled eggs and mix together. Serve immediately.

Variation: Omit the tomatoes and eggs and add ⅔ cup raisins and 3 tablespoons chopped peanuts.

Creamy Macaroni Salad

1 cup Hellmann's mayonnaise

2 tablespoons vinegar

1 tablespoon prepared mustard

1 teaspoon sugar

1 teaspoon salt

¼ teaspoon pepper

8 ounces elbow macaroni, cooked and drained

1 cup celery, chopped

1 cup green or red pepper, chopped

¼cup chopped onion

In large bowl, stir together first 6 ingredients until smooth. Add remaining ingredients; toss to coat well. Cover and chill. Makes 5 cups.

Variation: Add chopped, cooked chicken and shredded cheese to salad.

Chicken Pasta Salad

6	ounces fresh snow peas, remove strings	1	(14-ounce) can artichoke hearts, cut into quarters
2	medium carrots, peeled and cut into diagonal slices	1	(16-ounce) box Rainbow rotini pasta, cooked and drained
2	cups frozen green peas, thawed		Salt and pepper to taste
½	cup each of red, yellow and green pepper, cut into thin strips		Chopped lettuce

Dressing:

¾	cup mayonnaise	¼	cup Zesty Italian dressing
¼	cup milk	¼	cup Parmesan cheese

Chicken and Marinade:

8	boneless chicken breasts	¼	cup olive oil
		⅛	cup soy sauce

Blanch vegetables, except for artichokes, in the microwave for 1-2 minutes if desired. Mix cooked rotini with vegetables. Pour dressing over and toss to coat. Add salt and pepper to taste and refrigerate.

Marinate chicken all day in olive oil and soy sauce. 45 minutes before serving pasta, remove pasta and vegetables from refrigerator and let come to room temperature. Grill marinated chicken and slice into strips. Plate chopped lettuce, pasta and vegetables, with grilled chicken on top. Garnish with parsley or fruit or tomatoes. Serve with a muffin.

Spaghetti Salad

2	pounds spaghetti, cooked and drained		Garlic powder and paprika, to taste
2	cucumbers, chopped		Salt and pepper
5	fresh ripe tomatoes, chopped	1	large bottle Zesty Italian dressing (1 pint)
1	large onion, chopped	1	package dry Italian dressing
2	green peppers, chopped		
		1	cup Parmesan cheese

Combine vegetables with cooked spaghetti. Combine dry dressing mix with bottled dressing and pour over salad mixture. Add cheese last and toss lightly. Let set overnight.

Mom's Sweet Frozen Fruit Salad

Perfect for ladies lunches and brunches!

1	(8-ounce) can sliced pineapple	4	tablespoons mayonnaise
2	oranges, sliced	½	pint whipping cream
2	maraschino cherries	1	cup seedless white grapes (optional)
1	banana, sliced		
½	cup brown sugar		

Cut pineapple in cubes; mix other fruits, sugar and mayonnaise together. Whip cream until thick. Fold cream into fruit mixture. Freeze in mini muffin tins lined with foil cups or freeze in a square pan and cut into little squares once frozen. When ready to serve, leave out for 10 minutes or so before serving to soften a while.

Majelle's Frozen Fruit Salad

Keep these in the freezer and pull out whenever you need them.

1	cup pineapple juice	¾	cup sugar
1	(15-ounce) can sliced peaches	1	(10-ounce) package frozen strawberries, or 8 ounces fresh strawberries
1	regular can sliced apricots		
1	(6-ounce) can frozen lemonade, thawed	2	bananas, diced

Mix all together and put in large muffin tin papers and freeze. Keep in freezer bag after frozen and unwrap when serving. Thaw slightly before serving. Makes about 15 servings.

Waldorf Salad

Originally served at the Waldorf Astoria Hotel in New York City, this recipe has been around for years. Growing up, my mother would serve this as a little side dish in place of a tossed salad at dinner.

4 red apples, diced, but not peeled

2 tablespoons fresh lemon juice

2 cups chopped celery

½ cup chopped walnuts, optional

1 cup mayonnaise, approximately

Lettuce leaves, washed and dried

Place apple cubes in a bowl and gently toss with lemon juice. Add celery and walnuts. Add enough mayonnaise to bind ingredients. Serve on lettuce leaves. Makes 4 large servings.

Variation: Add 1 cup raisins.

Traditional Egg Salad

7 hard-boiled eggs

½ cup mayonnaise

Salt and pepper to taste

Place 7 eggs in small saucepan and cover with cold water. Place on stove and bring water to a hard boil. Boil uncovered for 5 minutes. Turn off stove but leave pot on hot stove for 20 minutes with the pot covered. Remove eggs from hot water and run under cold water until eggs are cooled to touch. Peel hard-boiled eggs and grate eggs or finely chop in a bowl. Add mayonnaise and salt and pepper to taste. Serve on crackers, as a sandwich or all alone on lettuce.

Variation: You can add 1-2 tablespoons chopped pickle relish if desired. Some people like a touch of mustard in their egg salad.

Traditional Coleslaw

1	small head cabbage	2	stalks celery, chopped fine
	Celery seed		
1	carrot, peeled and grated	3	tablespoons red pepper, chopped

Coleslaw Dressing:

1	teaspoon salt	¼	cup vegetable oil
¼	teaspoon pepper	3	heaping tablespoons sugar
1	tablespoon tarragon vinegar	½	cup mayonnaise

Finely grate or roughly shred the cabbage, depending on the consistency you desire. Sprinkle with celery seed. Add carrot, celery and red pepper, and place this mixture in the refrigerator to chill thoroughly. Cover with Saran Wrap. Mix the dressing in a small bowl – 1 teaspoon salt, ¼ teaspoon, tarragon vinegar, sugar and mayonnaise. Pour over chilled cabbage and serve. Add finely chopped green peppers to cabbage if desired.

Variation: Use Napa cabbage and do not shred. Chop fine. To the traditional recipe, increase mayonnaise to 4-5 tablespoons and add ¾ cup chopped cashews.

Coleslaw with Ramen Noodles

1	package chicken flavored Ramen noodles with oriental seasoning		Small head cabbage, shredded
		6-8	ounces toasted almonds
¼	cup vegetable oil	1	bunch green onions, chopped
¼	cup white wine vinegar		

Mix seasoning pack with ¼ cup vegetable oil and ¼ cup white wine vinegar. Break noodles and mix with cabbage, almonds and onions.

The Cutting Board's Potato Salad

The secret is baking the potatoes!

6-7	pounds baking potatoes	⅓	cup green pepper, finely diced
½	cup hot water	2	teaspoons celery seed
⅓	cup sugar	1-2	teaspoons salt
4	cups mayonnaise	½	teaspoon (or more) black pepper
1½	cups sweet pickle relish		
⅓	cup onions, finely diced	2	teaspoons prepared yellow mustard

Wash and clean baking potatoes. Lay out on a cookie sheet and bake in a 350° oven for 1-1½ hours (depending on size), until potatoes are cooked, but not too soft. Let cool. Meanwhile, dissolve sugar in hot water, making a simple syrup.

In a large mixing bowl, using an electric beater, mix together the mayonnaise, pickle relish, onions, green pepper, celery seed, salt, pepper, mustard and sugar water until well blended. Peel potatoes and chop into small cubes. Pour mayonnaise mixture over potatoes and stir together with hands or large spoon until well blended. You may not want to use all of the dressing; use sparingly at first and add more as needed.

Refrigerate overnight for the best taste — or at least for 4 hours. Makes about 10 pounds or one gallon potato salad.

Kathleen's Potato Salad

5	pounds diced, cooked potatoes	¼	cup celery tops and stem leaves
¼	cup dill pickle cubes	¼	cup parsley
¼	cup green pepper, diced	¼	cup fresh baby spinach, chopped
¼	cup green onions, chopped	1	cup mayonnaise
		1	cup French dressing (oil and vinegar)

Mix together and pat and season with salt and pepper. This will keep in the refrigerator for 5 days.

The Story Behind the Salad

This is the only new recipe in my second printing and it's here for a good reason. I tried really hard to get it included in the first printing. But I couldn't get it. So I did what I know best — I begged and begged and begged.

The Cutting Board in Burlington, NC was an institution for over 30 years. Unfortunately, it had to close in 2004 when a fire destroyed most of the building. My best friend's family owned the restaurant and I even worked as a waitress there while I was in college.

Even though the cornerstone of the restaurant centered on its chuck burgers, steaks and chicken sandwiches, their homemade potato salad was a local favorite! Everyone wanted the recipe and the owners would never give it out until now — only on the condition that any proceeds go to charity and the recipe could only be used in this book.

I agreed and received the coveted recipe from the owner's vault. Then I had to convert the recipe from 50 pounds of potatoes to 6 pounds! I hope you enjoy this as much as I do! Thanks Burney for the recipe.

Pink-Eye Pea Salad

2 cups cooked, drained pink-eye peas

1 cup fresh corn kernels

½ large red onion, finely chopped

½ red bell pepper, finely chopped

2 tablespoons chopped fresh cilantro

¼ cup olive oil

¼ cup fresh lime juice

¼ teaspoon salt

Stir together all of the above ingredients. Chill 1 hour. Serve with grilled chicken. Makes about 4 cups.

Mel's Old-Fashioned Chicken Salad

4-6	chicken breasts or 2 roasted store-bought chickens, meat pulled	⅛	cup onion
½	cup celery	½	cup Hellmann's mayonnaise
			Salt and pepper

Simmer chicken breasts in water on low temperature (after water has come to a boil) until tender or use the white meat from 2 store bought roasted chickens. Chop chicken meat finely. In small food processor or chopper, pulsate onion and celery until very fine. Drain in a colander for several minutes. Mix with chicken and salt and pepper to taste. Mix mayonnaise into chicken until liberally coated. Chicken salad will dry up slightly in refrigerator. Serve with crackers, on sandwiches or on croissants.

Variation: You can add finely chopped green pepper and ½-1 teaspoon celery seed to traditional chicken salad recipe.

Hot Chicken Salad

4	large chicken breasts, poached	1	teaspoon Accent, optional
1	carrot, cut in several pieces	4	teaspoons grated onion
1	onion, quartered	2	cups Hellmann's mayonnaise
	Salt and pepper	1½	jars artichoke hearts, quartered
1	teaspoon tarragon	1	cup Chow Mein noodles
2½	cups diced celery	2	cups grated sharp Cheddar cheese
1	cup slivered almonds		

In low simmering water, gently poach the chicken breasts in water to which carrot, onion, tarragon and salt and pepper to taste have been added – about 30 minutes for boneless breasts and about an hour for bone-in breasts. Remove from water and cool. Cut into cubes or small pieces.

Combine the cubed chicken with the diced celery, almonds, Accent, grated onion and mayonnaise. Add the artichoke hearts. Mix and place in buttered casserole dish. Top with grated cheese and Chow Mein noodles. Bake 10 minutes at 400°; then turn down oven to 300° and bake for 20 minutes. Serves 8.

Kitchen Sink Chicken Salad

1	large whole chicken or 4-5 chicken breasts, stewed, cooled and diced		1	small jar pimientos
2	cups celery, finely chopped		½	cup cashew nuts, ground
1	cup water chestnuts, finely slivered		2	teaspoons soy sauce
¼	cup green pepper, finely chopped		1	teaspoon curry powder
2	tablespoons onion, finely chopped		½	teaspoon salt
2	cups white seedless grapes, halved		½	teaspoon black pepper

1   large whole chicken or 4-5 chicken breasts, stewed, cooled and diced
2   cups celery, finely chopped
1   cup water chestnuts, finely slivered
¼   cup green pepper, finely chopped
2   tablespoons onion, finely chopped
2   cups white seedless grapes, halved

1   small jar pimientos
½   cup cashew nuts, ground
2   teaspoons soy sauce
1   teaspoon curry powder
½   teaspoon salt
½   teaspoon black pepper
½   teaspoon Tabasco sauce
½   cup cashew nuts, ground
1   cup Hellmann's mayonnaise

In a large bowl, mix together the chicken, celery, water chestnuts, green pepper, onion, grapes, pimientos and ½ cup of the ground cashews. In a separate bowl, mix together the mayonnaise with the soy sauce, curry powder, salt, pepper, Tabasco sauce and ½ cup ground cashew nuts. Mix the dressing into the chicken mixture and chill. Serve on top of lettuce with a fruit salad.

Company Chicken Salad

2   cups diced cooked chicken breasts
1   cup diced celery
1   cup seedless white or red grapes, halved
½   cup crushed pineapple, drained (optional)

⅓   cup toasted almond slices or slivers
½   teaspoon salt
¼   cup sour cream
¼   cup mayonnaise

Mix all of the above and serve on soft rolls or croissants.

Variation: Omit the pineapple and add 1 drained can of pitted dark sweet cherries and ¼ teaspoon curry powder. Decrease amount of celery to ⅓ cup. Add cherries and almonds immediately before serving.

Chicken and Rice Salad

A great ladies luncheon salad!

4 cups cooked rice or
4 cups cooked chicken
Rice-A-Roni

1 cup sliced mushrooms

½ cup chopped green pepper

2 tablespoons chopped parsley

1 teaspoon curry powder

½ cup sour cream

½ cup mayonnaise

2 cups cooked diced chicken

2 (6-ounce) jars marinated artichoke hearts, undrained and chopped

Mix all ingredients and refrigerate overnight or at least 6 hours. Serve cold or at room temperature. Serves 8.

You may eliminate the chopped chicken and serve salad as a side dish.

Lucy Lee's Shrimp Salad

2	pounds cooked shrimp	1	jar diced pimientos
2	green peppers, finely diced	1	small package elbow macaroni, washed and cooked
6-8	pieces celery, finely diced		Seasoned salt to taste
6-8	hard-boiled eggs		Mayonnaise to blend

Combine ingredients and season with seasoned salt and enough mayonnaise to blend salad near serving time. Serve cold.

Woodley's Shrimp Salad

1½	pounds shrimp	1	tablespoon chopped parsley
1	cup bottled Italian-style salad dressing	1	tablespoon grated onion
1	cup mayonnaise	1	teaspoon salt
2	teaspoons prepared mustard	⅛	teaspoon pepper
1	teaspoon lemon juice	2	cups thinly sliced celery
			Paprika

Clean and devein shrimp. Cover in cold water and cook shrimp until pink – just a couple of minutes. Rinse in cold water, drain and peel shrimp. You can chop shrimp if you like, depending on how large the shrimp are. In a medium bowl, pour Italian dressing over shrimp. Cover; refrigerate all day or overnight, stirring several times.

In another bowl, combine the mayonnaise, mustard, lemon juice, parsley, onion, salt and pepper. Drain the shrimp and add the sliced celery. Toss the shrimp and celery with the mayonnaise mixture. Serve on lettuce cups or in center of molded grapefruit salad. Dust with paprika. Makes 6 to 8 servings.

# Lobster Salad

1	pound or more cooked lobster meat
	Large Lettuce leaves

Vegetables of choice: asparagus, cauliflower, red and yellow bell pepper, cherry tomatoes

I buy pre-cooked lobster meat at the seafood market. You'll need about 1 pound for 3-4 people. Parboil your vegetables except for tomatoes, for 1 minute or so. Cool. This can be done the day before serving. On the day of serving, marinate vegetables in Tarragon Vinaigrette for several hours.

Right before serving, drain vegetables well. On a large plate lay out the large lettuce leaves. Place the cooked lobster meat in the center of the plate. Sprinkle the marinated vegetables around the outer edge of the plate.

Top the lobster with Watercress Dressing. Sprinkle entire plate with chopped parsley for garnish. Serves 3 to 4.

Tarragon Vinaigrette:

2	cups olive oil		1	teaspoon Tabasco sauce
¾	cup tarragon vinegar		2	teaspoons Worcestershire sauce
2	cloves garlic, pressed			
3	teaspoons Dijon mustard		1	teaspoon chopped tarragon, optional
½	tube anchovy paste			

Combine all ingredients and shake or whisk well. Refrigerate, but let dressing sit out before using.

Watercress Dressing

¾ cup mayonnaise

¼ cup watercress leaves

1 tablespoon fresh tarragon, chopped

1 teaspoon tarragon vinegar

Ground pepper to taste

⅛ teaspoon cayenne pepper, optional

Blend ingredients in processor and chill. Spoon dressing over lobster meat in center of plate.

I was first served this delightful Lobster Salad at the home of Joann and David Grimes. It was so good I requested the recipe and served it on Mother's Day for my entire family.

Fresh Cranberry Salad

1 pound raw cranberries, ground

1½ cups sugar

1½ cups crushed pineapple, well drained

1 cup seedless grapes

1 cup nuts

3 cups miniature marshmallows

1 cup whipping cream

Combine ground cranberries and sugar and let stand in refrigerator overnight. Add pineapple, grapes, marshmallows and nuts. Mix well. Whip cream and blend into cranberry mixture. Chill and serve.

Woodley's Tomato Aspic and Shrimp

2	envelopes unflavored gelatin	1	cup mayonnaise
½	cup cold water	1	tablespoon horseradish
1	(8-ounce) package cream cheese	1½	cups chopped celery
1	can condensed tomato soup	½	cup chopped green pepper
		½	cup finely diced onions
		1	pound cooked shrimp

Soften gelatin in cold water. Combine gelatin with cream cheese and tomato soup and simmer over low heat, stirring constantly until gelatin is dissolved. Do not boil. Cool mixture and stir in mayonnaise, horseradish, celery, green pepper and onion. Pour into 1-quart mold and chill. Unmold on crisp lettuce and circle with shrimp.

Cucumber Aspic

½	cup boiling water	1	cup mayonnaise
1	package lime Jell-O	2	tablespoons vinegar
1	cup grated cucumber (use skin and meat)	2	teaspoons wet horseradish
1	medium onion, grated		Salt to taste
1	cup cottage cheese (large curd)		

Mix boiling water with Jell-O and cool. When Jell-O thickens, add rest of ingredients and pour into mold. Unmold and serve on lettuce. Serve with mayonnaise, cream cheese or onion dressing.

Molded Nippy Salad

1 (3-ounce) package
   lime Jell-O
1¼ cups hot water
1 cup well-drained
   crushed pineapple

2 tablespoons
   horseradish
½ cup mayonnaise
1 cup cottage cheese

Dissolve gelatin in hot water. Chill until partially set. Stir in remaining ingredients. Chill until firm. Unmold on lettuces.

Sunset Salad

This is an award-winning recipe from the 70's.

1 (3-ounce) package
   orange-pineapple
   Jell-O
½ teaspoon salt
1½ cups boiling water

1 (8-ounce) can crushed
   pineapple
1 tablespoon lemon juice
1 cup coarsely grated
   carrots
⅓ cup chopped pecans

Dissolve Jell-O and salt in boiling water. Add undrained pineapple and lemon juice. Chill until very thick. Then fold in carrots and pecans. Pour into a quart mold. Chill until firm. Garnish with additional pineapple and Mandarin orange slices and parsley if desired.

Mandarin Orange Salad

1 (3-ounce) package
   orange Jell-O
1 large carton cottage
   cheese
1 large carton Cool Whip
1 (20-ounce) can
   crushed pineapple

1 (15-ounce) can
   Mandarin oranges
Miniature
   marshmallows,
   optional

Drain pineapple, Mandarin oranges and mix with cottage cheese and Cool Whip. Sprinkle Jell-O powder over and mix. Chill in bowl.

Jell-O Salads

My contemporary friends bristle with the thought of a Jell-O salad. However, between my grandmother's and mothers' recipes and that of my good, old fashioned Southern friend Katie Redhead, I probably had 30 different Jell-O salad recipes. Everyone loves a good Jell-O salad. Many of the following recipes did not indicate what size can of fruit to use. In most cases, use a 15-20 ounce can, unless it says a "small" can, and then use about 1 cup of the fruit. It will not hurt the recipe if you use a little more or a little less fruit.

A Favorite Salad

1 (3-ounce) package
lemon Jell-O

1 (3-ounce) package
lime Jell-O

2½ cups small marshmallows
or 24 large ones

3 cups boiling water

1 (8-ounce) package
cream cheese

2 teaspoons vinegar

1 (8-ounce) can
crushed pineapple

1 cup chopped pecans

Mix all of the above
and pour into bowl or
mold and chill.

Yum-Yum Pineapple Salad

2	(3-ounce) packages lime Jell-O	1	cup grated cheese
1	(20-ounce) can crushed pineapple	1	cup cream, whipped stiff or 2 cups Cool Whip

Dissolve Jell-O in 2 cups boiling water. Add juice from pineapple with enough cold water to make 2 cups of liquid. When mixture begins to cool and set, add cheese, pinch of salt and pineapple and whipped cream. Serve with dressing.

Dressing for Yum-Yum Salad:

1	cup mayonnaise	2	tablespoons red pepper, chopped
2	tablespoons chopped celery		Few drops of onion juice
2	tablespoons green pepper, chopped		

Mix dressing ingredients and chill.

Bavarian Salad

20	large marshmallows	1	small bottle cherries, drained on paper towels
2	cups hot water		
1	(3-ounce) package lime Jell-O	1	(15-ounce) can crushed pineapple, drained
1	cup chopped pecans		
1	cup grated sharp cheese	1	(10-ounce) carton Cool Whip

Melt marshmallows in hot water; add Jell-O package. Let set in refrigerator until it begins to thicken, but not set. Take out and whip mixture until all the large bubbles disappear. Add all other ingredients. Refrigerate until set. For best flavor, refrigerate overnight before serving.

Black Raspberry Jell-O Salad

1   (3-ounce) package
    black raspberry Jell-O
1   cup hot water
1   small can applesauce
1   (10-ounce) package
    frozen raspberries

1   (3-ounce) package
    lime Jell-O
1   (8-ounce) can crushed
    pineapple
1   cup sour cream

In a dish, mix together the black raspberry Jell-O and hot water, and mix with applesauce and raspberries. Cool. In a separate bowl, mix together lime Jell-O, crushed, drained pineapple and sour cream. Layer on top of raspberry Jell-O and chill.

Lemon Pineapple Banana Salad

1   (5.4-ounce) package
    lemon Jell-O
4   cups boiling water
12 large marshmallows or
    30 small

1   (32-ounce) can
    crushed pineapple,
    drained (reserve juice
    for topping)
2   diced bananas
    Chopped maraschino
    cherries (as many as
    you like)

Topping:

½   cup sugar
2   tablespoons flour
2   whole eggs beaten
1   cup reserved pineapple
    juice

2   tablespoons butter
1   cup Cool Whip
    Nuts and cherries for
    garnish

Dissolve Jell-O and marshmallows in 1 quart boiling water and let cool. Add pineapple, bananas, and cherries. Let congeal overnight.

Prepare topping: Cook sugar, flour, eggs, pineapple juice and butter in saucepan on stove for 5-10 minutes on low heat. DO NOT BOIL! Cool. Stir in 1 cup Cool Whip and spread over top of Jell-O. Garnish with nuts and cherries. This makes a large salad.

Golden Glow Salad

1½ (3-ounce) packages
    lemon Jell-O

1½ cups hot water

1½ tablespoons
    strong vinegar

1½ cups pineapple juice

¾ cup chopped pecans

1½ cups grated raw carrots

1½ cups crushed pineapple

Dissolve Jell-O in hot water. Add vinegar and pineapple juice. Cool. When mixture begins to set, add pecans, carrots and pineapple. Pour into molds and let stand in the refrigerator.

Apricot Salad

¾ cup small marshmallows

2 (3-ounce) packages
orange Jell-O

2 cups hot boiling water

1 (20-ounce) can
peeled apricots

1 (20-ounce) can
crushed pineapple,
juice reserved

Dressing:

1 egg

2 tablespoons flour

½ cup sugar

1 cup juice from either fruit

1 tablespoon butter

1 cup Cool Whip

Dissolve marshmallows
in Jell-O and hot water.
Add drained apricots and
pineapple. Chill until set.
For dressing, heat egg, flour,
sugar and juice in double
boiler like you would a
custard. Remove from heat
and add 2 tablespoons butter
and fold in 1 cup Cool Whip.
Layer on top of apricot/
pineapple Jell-O. Chill.

Strawberry Jell-O Salad

2	(3-ounce) packages strawberry Jell-O	2	(10-ounce) boxes frozen strawberries
2	cups boiling water	1	(8-ounce) carton sour cream
1	(20-ounce) can crushed pineapple	1	cup pecans, chopped

Mix Jell-O with boiling water and crushed pineapple and frozen strawberries. Divide mixture and pour ½ into dish. Let sit in refrigerator until congealed. Layer with sour cream. Add nuts to remaining Jell-O and pour over sour cream.

Pie Cherry Salad

1	(14.5-ounce) can red sour pie cherries	1	(3-ounce) package cherry Jell-O
1	(8-ounce) can crushed pineapple	1	cup hot water
		1	cup orange juice
		¼	cup chopped pecans

Drain cherries and pineapple, saving juices. Add 1 cup hot water to dissolve Jell-O and add 1 cup orange juice. Stir in fruit and nuts. Pour into dish or mold. Refrigerate. Serves 6-8.

Cherry Coke Congealed Salad

1	(16-ounce) can red sour pitted cherries, juice reserved	½	cup ground pecans
		1	tablespoon sugar
1	(32-ounce) can crushed pineapple, juice reserved	3	(3-ounce) packages Cherry Jell-O
		12	ounces Coca-Cola sodas

Heat Jell-O powder in syrup made from cherry and pineapple juice. Cool. Mix in Coca-Cola and add fruit and nuts. Chill in refrigerator.

salads

Lemon Blueberry Salad

1	(3-ounce) package lemon Jell-O	1	tablespoon lemon juice
1	(3-ounce) package black raspberry Jell-O	1	(21-ounce) can blueberry pie filling
1	cup boiling water	¼	cup sifted confectioners' sugar
½	cup cold water	1	cup sour cream

Dissolve gelatins together in boiling water; add cold water and lemon juice. Gradually stir blueberry pie filling into gelatin mixture. Pour mixture into an 8x8-inch oiled baking dish; chill until firm. Fold sugar into sour cream just until blended. Spread over gelatin mixture. Chill until serving time. Cut into squares.

Variation: Add sliced bananas and canned pineapple chunks.

Orange Salad

1	(6-ounce) package orange Jell-O	2	(6-ounce) cans frozen orange juice, thawed
1	envelope unflavored gelatin	2	(11-ounce) cans Mandarin oranges
1½	cups boiling water		

Dissolve Jell-O and mix other ingredients in bowl. Pour into 13x9x2-inch pan and refrigerate until congealed. Serves 12.

Cranberry Orange Relish Salad

1	(3-ounce) package orange Jell-O	1	(8-ounce) can crushed pineapple, do not drain
1	cup boiling water	2	cans cranberry-orange relish

Heat orange Jell-O in boiling water and remove from heat. Cool. Add pineapple and orange cranberry relish and mix. Pour into casserole dish and refrigerate until congealed.

Dream Salad

1 cup pineapple juice

1 (3-ounce) package lime Jell-O

½ cup sugar

1 cup small marshmallows

1 cup ground pecans

1 cup cottage cheese

1 (20-ounce) can crushed pineapple

1 cup whipping cream or 2 cups Cool Whip

Bring juice, Jell-O and sugar to a boil. Turn off heat. Add 1 cup small marshmallows. Stir until melted. Cool and add 1 cup ground pecans, cottage cheese and crushed pineapple. Whip 1 cup whipping cream or use Cool Whip and fold in Jell-O mixture. Refrigerate.

Boiled Dressing

3 tablespoons butter

1 teaspoon salt

1 teaspoon dry mustard

1 teaspoon paprika

¼ teaspoon pepper

3 egg yolks

1 cup hot milk

¼ cup vinegar

On the top of a double boiler, mix salt, mustard, paprika, pepper. Blend in eggs and milk. Place over hot, but not boiling water and stir until thickened and smooth. Add butter and vinegar and stir until butter has melted. Cool and store in the refrigerator.

Molded Cranberry Salad

1	(3-ounce) package lemon Jell-O	¼	cup cooked salad dressing
1	cup boiling water	½	cup whipped cream
1	cup cranberry sauce	½	cup crushed pineapple, drained
1	cup chopped nuts		Crisp lettuce leaves

Dissolve Jell-O with boiling water. Add cranberry sauce and beat until smooth; cool. Add nuts and pineapple and turn into molds. Unmold on crisp lettuce and serve with combined boiled dressing and whipped cream.

Pearl Barnes Salad

1	(3-ounce) package lime Jell-O	1	tablespoon lemon juice
¾	cup boiling water	1	cup cottage cheese
1	(5-ounce) can evaporated milk	½	cup ground pecans
		½	cup chopped celery
1	(20-ounce) can crushed pineapple	½	cup mayonnaise

Mix Jell-O with boiling water and cool. Mix with rest of the ingredients and put in greased mold. Refrigerate until congealed.

Lemon Jell-O Vegetable Salad

1	(3-ounce) package lemon Jell-O	½	cup mayonnaise
1	cup boiling water	1	medium carrot, grated or finely chopped
1	(20-ounce) can crushed pineapple	1	cup chopped celery
1	(3-ounce) package cream cheese, softened	½	cup chopped nuts

Combine gelatin and water. Drain pineapple and measure juice and add water to make 1 cup. Then add to gelatin mixture. Chill partially. Mix softened cream cheese and mayonnaise and add to gelatin. Stir well. Add other ingredients. Pour into mold and chill until firm. Keep in refrigerator. Serves 10-12.

Cucumber Salad Mold

1	(3-ounce) package lime Jell-O	½	teaspoon salt
¾	cup hot water	2	tablespoons lemon juice
2	(3-ounce) packages cream cheese	¾	cup drained, chopped unpeeled cucumbers
1	cup mayonnaise	¼	cup finely sliced spring onions
1	teaspoon horseradish		

Dissolve Jell-O in hot water. Soften cream cheese and mayonnaise, stirring until creamy and well mixed. Add salt, lemon juice and horseradish. Add to lime Jell-O and beat with electric beater until smooth. Chill until partially set. Add cucumbers and onions. Turn into molds and refrigerate until congealed. Makes 5 molds or 6 small ones.

Grimes Tarragon Vinaigrette

2	cups good quality olive oil	½	tube anchovy paste
¾	cup tarragon vinegar	1	teaspoon Tabasco sauce
2	medium cloves garlic, pressed	2	teaspoons Worcestershire sauce
3	teaspoons Dijon mustard	1	teaspoon chopped tarragon, optional

Combine all ingredients and shake well. When refrigerated, the mixture congeals so, before using, bring dressing to room temperature. Use this as a marinade for vegetables, seafood or serve over mixed greens.

While I was growing up, Thousand Island or Blue Cheese dressings were a staple at my house. My mother was always whisking up some homemade creamy dressing. I don't believe I even knew what Italian or an oil and vinegar dressing was until I married my husband. As I have aged, I have learned to appreciate a dose of good quality balsamic vinegar on my salads. Be sure to try my famous Raspberry Dressing or the Grimes Tarragon Vinaigrette. They're both great. However, even though organic gourmet baby lettuces are more fashionable, there is still nothing better than a wedge of crisp iceberg lettuce smothered with homemade chunky blue cheese dressing!

Roger's Dressing

This was my mother-in-law's heart healthy salad dressing. My father-in-law, Roger Soles, former CEO of Jefferson-Pilot Corporation, always had this dressing ready and made for him at the Greensboro City Club. It's known as "Roger's dressing."

3 medium cloves garlic, minced

1 teaspoon salt

½ teaspoon paprika

½ teaspoon Accent (optional)

½ teaspoon dry mustard

½ teaspoon black pepper

1 teaspoon seasoning salt

3 tablespoons red wine vinegar

3 tablespoons lemon juice

¾ cup canola oil

Whisk all of the above ingredients in a bowl and pour into dressing bottle or any other airtight container. Will keep for weeks in the refrigerator. This could easily be doubled or tripled.

Mel's Raspberry Dressing

½	cup good quality raspberry vinegar	2	teaspoons smooth Dijon mustard
½	cup maple syrup	1-2	tablespoons chopped fresh tarragon
½	cup olive oil		Salt and pepper
½	cup canola oil		

Whisk all of the above in a bowl and transfer to airtight container. This will keep in refrigerator for up to two weeks. Take out of the refrigerator and let warm up a little before serving.

Delicious Blue Cheese Dressing

4	ounces good quality blue cheese	2	cups mayonnaise
	Additonal blue cheese for garnish	½	cup ketchup
2	cups half-and-half		Salt and pepper to taste

Mix together all of the above and pour into airtight container. Chill in refrigerator for 6 hours or more. Mixture will thicken as it chills. Garnish with additional blue cheese when serving over salad.

Bacon Dressing

¼	cup flour	2	cups water
1¼	cups sugar	¼	pound bacon, diced
	Salt	1½	teaspoons fat from bacon
1	cup vinegar		

Combine flour, sugar and salt. Mix well with part of the water. Heat vinegar and remaining water. Add flour mixture to vinegar-water mixture. Fry bacon and drain, saving 1½ teaspoons of the drippings. Add bacon bits to dressing, plus the bacon fat. Cook until thickened. Serve over fresh spinach or baby spinach. Makes 1 quart.

dressings

Thousand Island Dressing

1	cup Hellmann's mayonnaise	1	tablespoon minced fresh onion
¼	cup chili sauce (can substitute ketchup)	1	tablespoon minced chives
1	hard-boiled egg, grated	1	tablespoon minced fresh parsley
2	tablespoons pickle relish (sweet or dill)		Salt and pepper to taste

Mix ingredients and adjust seasonings to taste. Use immediately or cover and refrigerate.

Variation: Substitute ½ cup mayonnaise with ½ cup sour cream. Add 1 teaspoon Worcestershire sauce and a dash of Tabasco sauce.

Easy Thousand Island Dressing

1 cup Hellmann's mayonnaise

2 tablespoons chili sauce

⅓ cup milk

2 tablespoons sweet pickle relish

1 hard-boiled egg, chopped

Combine ingredients and chill. Makes 1⅔ cups.

Russian Salad Dressing

¾	cup sugar	1	teaspoon dry mustard
1½	teaspoons salt	2	teaspoons onion juice
2	tablespoons chopped green pepper	2	teaspoons paprika
½	cup canola oil	2	teaspoons Worcestershire sauce
⅔	cup vinegar		
1	can condensed tomato soup		

Mix in order provided. Boil 5 minutes, stirring constantly. Cool and serve. Refrigerate extra dressing.

A version of Thousand Island dressing, Russian dressing is one of my favorites. I especially like it on sandwiches.

French Dressing

1 can Campbell's tomato soup

¾ cup vinegar

½ cup oil

¼ cup sugar

2 tablespoons
Worcestershire sauce

3 tablespoons grated onion

1 teaspoon paprika

½ teaspoon dry mustard

Put all of the above
in a closed jar and shake
well before using.

Armand's French Dressing

1	egg yolk	6	tablespoons olive oil
¼	teaspoon dry mustard		Salt and pepper to
1	garlic clove, minced		taste
2	tablespoons vinegar or lemon juice		

This sauce is a vinaigrette that resembles a mayonnaise. Begin with the egg yolk and add ¼ teaspoon dry mustard and minced garlic, whisking together with 2 tablespoons vinegar or lemon juice and the garlic. Start beating with a wire whisk while slowly adding 6 tablespoons of oil of your choice. Add salt and pepper to taste.

Unlike a true mayonnaise, the result is a thin white sauce which coats greens more evenly than a true vinaigrette. You can add a small amount of heavy cream or sour cream to make the sauce even whiter and thicker.

Creamy Italian Dressing

1	cup Hellmann's mayonnaise	1	tablespoon water
2	tablespoons wine vinegar	1	teaspoon Worcestershire sauce
1	tablespoon lemon juice	½	teaspoon oregano
1	tablespoon canola oil	1	tablespoon sugar
		1	garlic clove, minced

Combine all ingredients and store in the refrigerator. Makes 1⅓ cups.

Creamy Balsamic Dressing

⅓ cup mayonnaise
⅔ cup sour cream
¼ cup buttermilk
⅛-¼ cup balsamic vinegar
2 cloves garlic, minced
2½ tablespoons grated Parmesan cheese

1 teaspoon Dijon mustard
½ teaspoon salt
½ teaspoon fresh ground pepper

Whisk mayonnaise and sour cream together in a large bowl. Add the remaining ingredients and whisk thoroughly. Chill.

Green Goddess Salad Dressing

½ cup Hellmann's mayonnaise
2 tablespoons milk
2 anchovies, minced
1 tablespoon tarragon vinegar

1½ teaspoons lemon juice
1 cup parsley leaves, minced
2 tablespoons chives, minced

Combine all the ingredients and store covered in the refrigerator. Makes ¾ cup.

Mayo Verde

Serve with asparagus, crudités or shrimp.

½ cup Italian parsley
2 tablespoons extra-virgin olive oil
2 tablespoons lemon juice

1 teaspoon Dijon mustard (or to taste)
½ cup mayonnaise

Wash and dry parsley. Put in blender with oil, lemon juice and mustard. Then stir into mayonnaise. You can add a little sugar to taste. If serving with shrimp, add lemon pepper and celery salt.

Basic Balsamic Vinaigrette

5 tablespoons olive oil

4 tablespoons balsamic vinegar

¼ teaspoon Dijon mustard

Salt and pepper to taste

Whisk together
and adjust seasonings.

Avocado Dressing

2 tablespoons sugar

2 tablespoons
Worcestershire sauce

2 tablespoons ketchup

2 tablespoons wine vinegar

2 tablespoons butter

Dash of salt

Bring to a boil, and pour
into avocado halves, placed
over top of lettuce. Sprinkle
with salt and pepper.

Basic Cooked Salad Dressing

2	tablespoons sugar	1	egg, slightly beaten
2	tablespoons flour	¾	cup milk
1	teaspoon salt	¼	cup vinegar
	Pinch cayenne pepper	1½	teaspoons butter
1	heaping teaspoon dry mustard		

Combine sugar, flour, salt, dry mustard and cayenne pepper in
the top of a double boiler. Blend in egg and milk. Place over hot,
not boiling, water and cook, stirring constantly, until thickened
and smooth. Add vinegar and butter. Stir until butter melts. Cool
and store in refrigerator. Makes about 1 cup.

Use in potato salad or in variations given below.

Mustard Dressing:
Add 2 tablespoons prepared mustard to 1 recipe cooked salad
dressing. Serve cold as a dressing for coleslaw.

Sour Cream Dressing:
Add ½ cup sour cream to 1 recipe cooked salad dressing. Beat
with a rotary beater or wire whisk. Use as a dressing for coleslaw
or potato salad.

Fruit Salad Dressing

⅓	cup sugar	1	teaspoon minced onion
1	teaspoon salt		
1	teaspoon dry mustard	2	tablespoons cider vinegar
1	teaspoon celery salt		
1	teaspoon paprika	1	cup oil

Mix first 7 ingredients in small bowl. Pour the oil in slowly, whisking
constantly. If too stiff, add more vinegar or lemon juice. Serve
over bowl of mixed fresh fruit.

dressings

pasta, rice and brunch

Old South Macaroni and Chesse

I received this recipe from the cook at a friend's family home in Union, South Carolina. Mrs. Toccoa Switzer and Dr. "Bubba" Switzer had invited me to lunch at their gracious Victorian home in Union, along with the Ambassador to the Court of St. James, whose wife was from Union. Mrs. Switzer's daughter, whose name is also Toccoa, had long talked about driving home in time for meals cooked by Dorothy Whitfield, who had been their family cook for many years. At that lunch, she served homemade country ham biscuits, succotash, and macaroni and cheese.

1	(8-10 ounce) box of elbow macaroni	6	eggs
	Salt and pepper	2½	cups milk
8	ounces sharp Cheddar cheese		Buttered cracker crumbs

Cook small box of macaroni according to directions and drain. Shred Cheddar cheese – approximately 2 cups or more. Grease a large casserole dish and layer macaroni, which has been sprinkled with salt and pepper, with shredded sharp Cheddar cheese, until it's close to the top of the dish.

Beat 6 eggs lightly with 2½ cups milk and pour on top of the macaroni until milk is level with the cheese.

Bake in a preheated 375 degree oven for 20 minutes. Take casserole out and sprinkle buttered cracker crumbs on top. Bake about 20 minutes longer until browned.

Perciatelli with Turkey

- Smoked turkey, cubed
- Cream of celery soup diluted with milk (1 can serves 3)
- Green and red bell peppers, cut in strips
- Mushrooms
- Green peas

Sauté peppers + mushrooms in olive oil. Add soup + heat through. Boil pasta, + combine with mixture + turkey. If serving immediately add peas.
If made ahead to serve as a casserole, steam peas + add just before serving.
If desired, add Italian parsley + sprinkle with Parmesan cheese!

Basic Macaroni and Cheese

2 tablespoons butter
½ cup unsifted flour
1 teaspoon salt
½ teaspoon dry mustard
¼ teaspoon pepper
2½ cups milk

2 cups grated Cheddar cheese
8 ounces elbow macaroni, cooked 6 minutes and drained
¼ cup fresh bread crumbs

In a 2-quart saucepan melt butter over low heat. Stir in flour, salt, mustard and pepper until smooth. Remove from heat. Gradually stir in milk until smooth. Stirring constantly, cook over medium heat about 10 minutes or until thickened. Remove from heat. Stir in 1½ cups of the cheese until melted. Turn macaroni into greased 2-quart casserole. Pour cheese mixture over macaroni; mix well. Mix remaining cheese and bread crumbs; sprinkle over top of casserole. Bake in 375° oven for 25 minutes or until topping is lightly browned. Makes 6 servings.

This macaroni and cheese dish was adapted from the Mueller's recipe printed on their elbow macaroni box many years ago. This is truly comfort food at its best.

Noodles Romanoff

2 tablespoons salt
4-6 quarts boiling water
1 pound broad egg noodles
4 cups sour cream
2 cups cream-style cottage cheese
2 medium onions, finely chopped

2 cloves garlic, minced
1 teaspoon salt
Dash pepper
2 teaspoons Worcestershire sauce
Paprika
½ cup Parmesan cheese

Add 2 tablespoons salt to rapidly boiling water. Gradually add noodles so that the water continues to boil. Cook uncovered, stirring occasionally until tender. Drain well. Combine noodles, sour cream, cottage cheese, onion, garlic, salt, pepper and Worcestershire sauce. Mix well. Turn into a 3-quart casserole dish and sprinkle with paprika. Bake in a 350° oven for 30 to 45 minutes. Serve noodles with freshly grated Parmesan cheese.

Chinese Fried Rice

This makes a nice Sunday night supper.

2 tablespoons oil

¼ cup diced green onion

½ cup cooked, diced pork or chicken

4 cups cooked rice

½ teaspoon salt

3 tablespoons soy sauce

2 eggs, beaten

In a large skillet or Dutch oven, heat oil until hot. Sauté green onion for a minute or so. Add cubed chicken or pork and toss around for a minute. Add rice, salt and soy sauce. Heat for a few minutes. Add beaten eggs and mix and toss until the eggs are cooked, about 2 minutes. Serves 4-6.

Variation: Add chopped green pepper and celery, along with thawed, frozen peas. You can also add 2 cups cooked, peeled shrimp.

Perciatelli with Turkey

1	green pepper, cut into thin strips	2	soup cans milk
1	red pepper, cut into thin strips	16	ounces perciatelli pasta or spaghetti
8	ounces fresh mushrooms, sliced	1	pound smoked turkey, cubed
2	olive oil	2	cups frozen green peas, thawed
2	cans cream of celery soup		Italian parsley
			Parmesan cheese

Sauté peppers and mushrooms in olive oil. Add soup and milk and heat through. Boil pasta according to directions and drain. Combine perciatelli with soup mixture and turkey. If serving immediately, add peas. If made ahead to serve as a casserole, steam peas and add just before serving. If desired, add Italian parsley and sprinkle with Parmesan cheese.

French Rice

1	(10.5-ounce) can onion soup, undiluted	1	(8-ounce) can sliced water chestnuts, reserve liquid
½	cup melted butter	1	cup uncooked white rice
1	(4.5-ounce) jar sliced mushrooms, reserve liquid		

Combine soup and butter, stirring well. Drain mushrooms and water chestnuts and reserve liquid. Add enough water to reserved liquid to make 1½ cups liquid. Add rice and other ingredients to soup mixture and stir well. Pour into lightly greased au gratin casserole dish. Cover and bake for 1 hour at 350°.

Summer Rice Salad

This is a delightful fresh summer salad.

1	cup uncooked long-grain white rice	2	ears fresh corn cut off cob
3	tablespoons extra-virgin olive oil	1	large tomato, diced or 1 pint cherry tomatoes, cut in half
2	tablespoons red wine vinegar	¼	cup diced sweet red onion
1	clove garlic, crushed	¼	cup packed basil leaves, sliced thin
	Salt and pepper to taste		

Cook rice according to directions. Remove from heat and let stand, uncovered, until it's cooled to slightly warm. Fluff with a fork. In a serving bowl, whisk together the oil, red wine vinegar, garlic, salt and pepper. Add the rice, corn, tomato, red onion and basil. Toss to coat and serve.

Gourmet Wild Rice Casserole

1	pound medium-hot pork sausage	2½	cups chicken broth
1	pound mushrooms, sliced	2	cups cooked wild rice (about ⅔ cup raw)
1	cup chopped onions or 1 cup chopped celery	1	teaspoon salt
¼	cup flour		Freshly ground pepper
½	cup heavy cream		Pinch of oregano, thyme and marjoram
			Chopped macadamia nuts

In a skillet cook sausage until cooked through and crumble. Remove meat and drain. Using some of the sausage fat, sauté mushrooms and onions. Return sausage to pan.

Mix flour and cream together until smooth. Add to meat mixture, along with chicken broth, and cook until thickened. Add rice and seasonings. Pour into buttered casserole dish, top with nuts and bake 30 minutes at 250°. This may be refrigerated or frozen until ready to bake.

Baked Wild Rice

1 box Uncle Ben's Rice with seasonings

¼ cup wild rice

1 medium onion, chopped

½ pound mushrooms, sliced

1 can water chestnuts, sliced

¼ cup butter

1 can Campbell's consommé

1 cup white wine

Pour contents of Uncle Ben's rice with seasonings into slightly greased casserole. Wash and drain wild rice and add to casserole. Sauté chopped onion and sliced mushrooms and slice can of water chestnuts. Add to rice mixture, stir in consommé and wine. Cover with foil tightly and bake at 325° for 1 hour, 20 minutes. You can prepare this early in the day and bake in the oven when desired.

Old-Time Rice Pudding

½	cup rice	1	teaspoon grated lemon peel
1	quart milk		
½	cup sugar	¼	teaspoon nutmeg
½	teaspoon salt	½	cup seedless raisins

Combine rice, milk, sugar and salt. Pour into a 1½-quart baking dish and bake in preheated 300° oven for 1 hour. Stir occasionally while baking. Add lemon peel, nutmeg and raisins and continue baking for a total of 1½ to 1¾ hours.

⅔ cup brown sugar may be used in place of the granulated sugar.

Baked Southern Cheese Grits

1	teaspoon salt	1½	cups grated sharp Cheddar cheese
4	cups water		
1	cup stone ground grits	4	eggs, slightly beaten
1	stick butter	½	cup shredded Cheddar cheese
1	cup milk		

Add salt to water and bring to a boil. Stir in grits slowly, keep at brisk boil. Remove from heat and stir in butter and milk. Cool to lukewarm. Beat in eggs and cheese and pour into a 2-quart buttered casserole. Bake at 350° for 1 hour or so. Sprinkle ½ cup grated cheese on top and cook 10 minutes more or until golden brown.

Carolina Grits Soufflé

Impress your Northern friends with
Carolina grits served in an elegant way.

2	cups chicken stock plus 1 cup water	¼	cup roasted garlic purée or 1 tablespoon minced fresh garlic
1	cup half-and-half	4	tablespoons butter
2	teaspoons salt		Salt, pepper and Tabasco to taste
1	cup white grits, stone ground	½	cup green onions, sliced thin diagonally
5	eggs, separated		
1½	cups sharp Cheddar cheese, grated		

Grease a 2-quart casserole or soufflé dish. In a 3-quart saucepan, bring the chicken stock, water, half-and-half, and salt to a boil. Stir in the grits, and reduce heat to medium. Cook, stirring often, until thick, smooth and creamy.

Beat the egg yolks, temper with a spoonful of hot grits, and then stir into the grits. Stir in the cheese, garlic purée and butter, and season with salt, pepper and Tabasco to taste. Cool at room temperature.

An hour before serving, preheat oven to 375°.

In a stainless steel bowl, beat the egg whites until they form stiff peaks. Gently fold the egg whites and sliced green onions into the grits mixture and spoon into the buttered soufflé dish. Bake 30-40 minutes, until the grits are set. Cover with foil if top gets too brown.

Serve immediately. Makes 8 servings.

Easy Grits Soufflé

1 package quick grits

2 eggs, beaten

½-1 cup sherry

2 cups grated
sharp Cheddar cheese

Salt to taste

2 tablespoons
Worcestershire sauce

Use quick grits and follow directions on package for 6 servings. To the cooked grits, add 2 eggs, beaten, sherry, grated sharp cheese, salt to taste and Worcestershire sauce.

Mix well and place in casserole dish. Cover with more grated sharp cheese and bake at 300° until thoroughly heated.

When reviewing all of my files, including my mother's and my husband's mother's, I found seven egg casserole recipes. No family should be without one good egg casserole recipe – especially for christmas morning or when you have house guests. It can be prepared the night before and popped into the oven when you start the coffee. Out of the seven, I chose the best three.

Katie's Breakfast Casserole

Refrigerate overnight

7-8	slices thin white bread, cubed	1	pound Neese's hot sausage
½	pound sharp Cheddar cheese, shredded	6	eggs
		2	cups milk
		½	teaspoon dry mustard

Cook sausage and drain. Grease a 13x9x2-inch casserole pan and put the cubed bread on the bottom of pan. Add layer of cheese, then sausage. Beat together eggs, milk, mustard and pour over the other ingredients. Refrigerate overnight. Bake in a slow oven, 325°, until slightly brown, about 40-45 minutes.

Jingle Bell Breakfast Casserole

Save some for Santa!

2	cups seasoned croutons	½	cup chopped onion, sautéed until limp
1½	cups shredded Cheddar cheese	6	eggs
1	(4-ounce) can mushroom pieces, drained	2½	cups milk, divided
		½	teaspoon salt
		½	teaspoon pepper
1½	pounds country sausage, browned and crumbled		Dash of Tabasco
		1	can cream of mushroom soup

Place croutons in greased 9x13-inch casserole pan. Top with cheese and mushrooms. Spread cooked sausage and onions over cheese. Beat eggs with 2 cups milk and seasonings. Pour over sausage. Cover and refrigerate overnight. The next day mix soup with remaining ½ cup milk and spread on top. Bake at 325° for 1 hour.

Variation: You can increase the amount of sausage to 2 pounds and the cheese to 2 cups for a slightly larger casserole. Also, try adding ½ teaspoon dry mustard to the mix.

Scrambled Egg Casserole

4	ounces Canadian bacon	12	eggs	
¼	cup green onions	1	(3-ounce) can mushroom pieces	
3	tablespoons butter	3	slices bread, make crumbs	
4	tablespoons butter, melted for topping	⅛	teaspoon paprika	

Cheese Sauce:

2	tablespoons butter	2	cups milk
2	tablespoons flour	1	cup Velveeta cheese, shredded
	Salt and pepper		

Make cheese sauce by melting 2 tablespoons butter, stirring in flour to make a roux. Add seasonings and gradually add 2 cups milk and cheese until thickened in a saucepan over medium heat. In large skillet, cook Canadian bacon and green onions. Add eggs and scramble just to set.

Fold the egg mixture and mushrooms into cheese sauce. Pour into a 7x12x2-inch casserole or double recipe and pour into a larger 19-inch casserole. Sprinkle paprika, 4 tablespoons melted butter and bread crumbs on top of casserole.

Cover and chill in the refrigerator for 8 hours or overnight. Bake uncovered for 30 minutes in a preheated 350° oven.

This is a different take on the traditional egg casserole. You wouldn't think scrambled eggs refrigerated overnight in a casserole could be good, but it is! And it's different.

Potato Round and Egg Casserole

1 pound sausage

1 cup sliced mushrooms

12 eggs

1 can cream of mushroom soup

1 can evaporated milk

1 (32-ounce) package frozen potato rounds

Grated Cheddar cheese

Brown sausage in frying pan. Remove sausage with slotted spoon and sauté mushrooms in sausage fat until soft. In bowl, beat eggs, soup and evaporated milk. Stir egg mixture into sausage and mushrooms. In a buttered 9x13-inch casserole dish, place frozen potato rounds. Pour egg/sausage mixture over. Top with grated Cheddar cheese. Refrigerate overnight. Remove from refrigerator and bake 45-50 minutes in preheated 350° oven.

Sausage and Cheese Vermicelli Casserole

1 box chicken flavored
rice vermicelli mix

½-1 pound Neese's hot sausage

1 cup chopped onion

½ cup grated cheese

1 cup cream of chicken soup

1 chicken breast, cooked and
shredded (optional)

Cook rice according to
directions. Brown sausage in
skillet. Place half of rice in
greased 2-quart casserole.
Layer sausage and chopped
onion on top of rice. Repeat
procedure. Sprinkle cheese on
top layer of sausage. Dilute
soup with ½ can of water and
pour over cheese. Bake in
350° oven for 45 minutes.

Gourmet Deviled Eggs

12	large eggs	2½	teaspoons prepared Dijon mustard
⅔	cup mayonnaise		
1½	teaspoons tarragon vinegar	⅓	teaspoon cayenne pepper
¾	teaspoon dry mustard	½	teaspoon curry powder

Salt and pepper to taste

Place eggs in a saucepan and cover with cold water. Bring to a boil over high heat for 5 minutes. Cover saucepan but turn heat off. After 15 minutes, remove eggs from pan and run under cold water.

Crack eggshells and peel eggs under running water. Halve the eggs lengthwise and scoop egg yolks out in a small bowl. Using a pastry cutter, cut up yolks until very fine. Add mayonnaise, vinegar, mustards, cayenne, and curry powder to bowl, and mix together until smooth. Season to taste with salt and pepper.

Spoon egg yolk mixture into the egg white halves. Sprinkle tops of eggs with paprika. Refrigerate immediately.

Hamburger Quiche

A meal in itself! Just add salad and bread.

2	pounds ground beef	1½	cups Cheddar or Swiss cheese, shredded
½	cup mayonnaise		
½	cup milk	½	cup sliced green onions
2	eggs		Dash of pepper
1	tablespoon cornstarch	1	unbaked deep pie shell

Brown meat in pan. Drain fat and set aside. Blend mayonnaise, milk, eggs and cornstarch until smooth. Stir in ground beef, cheese, onions and pepper. Pour into pie shell. Bake for 35-40 minutes in preheated 350° oven until golden and set. May be frozen after cooking.

Cheese Soufflé

3	tablespoons butter		Salt, pepper, nutmeg to taste
3	tablespoons flour		
1	cup milk	6	egg whites
4	egg yolks	1	cup finely grated cheese (Cheddar or Swiss)

Preheat oven to 400°. In a saucepan over low heat, make a roux by melting the butter in a saucepan, then adding the flour. Stir, cooking 3-4 minutes. Gradually add the milk while stirring constantly to prevent lumps from forming. Continue stirring over medium heat until mixture is really thick. Remove from burner, let cool slightly.

Whisk in egg yolks; season to taste. Beat egg whites until very stiff. Fold grated cheese and beaten egg whites into the egg yolk mixture. Spoon into a prepared soufflé dish by buttering the dish generously and dusting with grated Parmesan cheese like you would dust a cake pan. Bake 35-40 minutes or until top of soufflé is puffed and golden brown.

Swiss Alpine Quiche

2	cups shredded Swiss cheese	1¼	cups milk
2	tablespoons flour	3	eggs, slightly beaten
1	(10-ounce) package frozen chopped broccoli, thawed and drained	⅛	teaspoon salt
		⅛	teaspoon pepper
		1	unbaked pie shell, 9-inch
2	cups cubed cooked ham (about ½ pound)	1	cup sliced mushrooms, sautéed in butter, optional
3	tablespoons chopped onion		

Combine cheese and flour. Layer half of broccoli, ham and cheese in pie shell. Repeat layers. Sprinkle onion on top (and mushrooms if desired). In a small bowl, combine milk, eggs and seasonings. Pour over mixture in pie shell. Bake in a preheated 375° oven for 40-50 minutes or until knife inserted near center comes out clean. Let stand 5 minutes before serving.

Cheese Pudding

2 eggs

2 cups milk

Dry mustard

Worcestershire sauce

Salt to taste

2 cups diced cheese

4 slices white bread, buttered

Beat eggs. Combine the milk with mustard, Worcestershire sauce and salt to taste, and add to the beaten eggs. Place cheese and bread in layers in greased baking dish. Pour milk and eggs over bread layers and bake for 45 minutes – 1 hour in a preheated 350° oven. Can be prepared hours ahead and then baked when needed.

Variation: Add a generous sprinkling of poppy seeds to the top of the pudding before baking.

Homemade Maple Syrup

2 cups sugar

1 cup water

½ teaspoon maple flavoring

Boil sugar and water until sugar dissolves. Add flavoring. This makes a thin syrup, but good.

Buttermilk Pancakes

1	egg	1	tablespoon sugar
2	tablespoons vegetable oil	1	teaspoon baking powder
1	cup buttermilk	½	teaspoon baking soda
1	cup flour	½	teaspoon salt

Mix egg, oil and buttermilk. Mix dry ingredients, then add to buttermilk mixture. Stir gently. Pour batter onto hot griddle and flip pancake when lightly browned. Makes 6-8 medium pancakes. Serve with homemade maple syrup.

Deep Fried French Toast

1	pound loaf Challah bread	1	teaspoon vanilla
2	quarts vegetable oil	1½	tablespoons sugar
2	eggs	½	teaspoon salt
1	cup milk		Powdered sugar
			Maple syrup

Remove crusts from bread and cut bread into 1½-inch thick slices. Make slices smaller by cutting them on the diagonal. In a large electric frying pan, pour oil to 2 inches deep and heat until 375°.

While oil is heating, whisk together the eggs, milk, vanilla, sugar and salt. Dip bread in batter and let excess batter drip off. Do not let bread sit in batter. Fry bread in oil, turning frequently, until golden brown on all sides, about 2 minutes.

Transfer bread to paper towels to drain. Fry remaining bread wedges in same manner – making sure oil returns to 375° between batches. Dust wedges with powdered sugar and serve with maple syrup.

Chicken and Curry Sauce for Crêpes

2	tablespoons chopped onion	½	cup flour
2	tablespoons chopped celery	3	cups milk (or half milk/half chicken stock)
1	stick butter	1	cup cream
½	teaspoon salt	2	tablespoons sherry
1	tablespoon curry powder	3	cups cooked chicken, cut into large pieces

Sauté onions and celery in butter until onions are yellow. Add salt and curry powder and mix thoroughly. Add flour and cook until bubbly. Add milk and cream, stirring briskly until smooth and thick and cook until all the starchy flavor has disappeared. Add sherry and cooked chicken.

Chocolate Flecked Crêpes

1½	cups milk	1	tablespoon melted butter
3	eggs	¼	ounce Baker's semi-sweet chocolate
1	cup flour		

For chocolate crêpes, substitute 1 tablespoon cocoa for 1 tablespoon flour. Combine milk and eggs in a measuring cup; beat well. Place flour in a large mixing bowl and make an indentation in the center of the flour. Pour the milk/egg mixture in the well you made in the flour. With a whisk or electric beater, blend together to make a smooth mixture. Add melted butter and chocolate flecks.

Pour 2-3 tablespoons of batter on a hot buttered crêpe pan, swirling pan around to distribute batter evenly. Cook over high heat until the exposed side of the crêpe becomes dull. Flip crêpe out of the pan. When cool, fill crêpes. Crêpes will keep in the fridge for a few days or longer in the freezer.

Basic Crêpe Recipe

¾ cup all-purpose flour

¼ cup cake flour

½ teaspoon salt

2 whole eggs

3 egg yolks

1½ cups milk (or half-and-half)

Mix the dry ingredients together. Add the egg yolks and beat well to form paste. Add the milk and stir to form a thin batter. Grease a crêpe pan with a small amount of butter. Swirl 2-3 tablespoons batter around the pan. Place back on heat. Let cook until crêpe is not longer shiny. Flip crêpe out of pan. When cool, fill as you desire.

To make chocolate flakes:

Scrape a 1 ounce block of chocolate with a small paring knife, until you're made as many flakes as you need.

 Woodley's Coffee Cake

Perfect for dessert, not just for breakfast!

1	stick butter	2	cups flour
1	stick margarine	1	teaspoon baking powder
1½	cups sugar	½	teaspoon baking soda
2	eggs	¼	teaspoon salt
1	teaspoon vanilla	1	cup sour cream

Topping:

½	cup sugar	1	cup chopped pecans
5	teaspoons cinnamon		

Cream together butter, margarine and sugar. Add eggs, one at a time, then the vanilla. Add the flour which has been blended with baking powder, soda and salt, to the butter mixture alternately with the sour cream, beginning and ending with the flour.

Grease and flour a 8-inch or 9-inch tube pan. Add half of batter or less to pan. Sprinkle part of the topping over the batter, then add the balance of the batter and top with the balance of the topping. Bake for 1 hour in a preheated 350° oven.

Vanilla Breakfast Granola

As good for a snack as it is for breakfast!

	Nonstick vegetable oil spray	⅛	teaspoon cinnamon
4	cups old-fashioned oats	⅓	cup vegetable oil
1	cup sliced almonds	¼	cup honey
½	cup packed brown sugar	2	tablespoons sugar
¼	teaspoon salt	4	teaspoons vanilla
		1	cup raisins (optional)

Preheat oven to 300° and position rack on middle of oven. Spray large baking sheet with nonstick spray or line with parchment paper. Mix oats, almonds, brown sugar, salt and cinnamon in large bowl. Combine oil, honey and granulated sugar in small saucepan. Bring to simmer over medium heat. Remove from heat and add vanilla. Pour hot liquid over oat mixture and stir well. Using hands, toss mixture until thoroughly mixed.

Spread granola on prepared baking sheet and bake until brown, stirring occasionally, about 30 minutes. Transfer sheet to wire rack and cool completely. Break into small pieces and store in airtight containers. You can add raisins or dried cranberries to the granola at this point.

Streusel Coffee Cake

Makes a great hostess or house warming gift!

1	cup sugar	1⅔	cups all-purpose flour
½	cup Crisco shortening	1	teaspoon baking powder
2	large eggs		
1	cup sour cream	1	teaspoon baking soda
1½	teaspoons vanilla	½	teaspoon salt

Topping:

½	cup packed brown sugar	½	stick chilled butter, cut into pieces
¼	cup rolled oats	¼	cup chopped walnuts or pecans
½	teaspoon cinnamon		

For topping, mix brown sugar, rolled oats and cinnamon in a bowl. Add cold butter and rub together with hands until mixture is course. Mix in nuts. Set aside.

For cake, preheat oven to 350°. Butter and flour 8-inch square cake pan. With a beater, cream sugar and shortening in a large bowl. Add eggs one at a time, beating well after each. Beat in sour cream and vanilla. Sift flour, baking powder, baking soda and salt together into small bowl. Mix dry ingredients into butter mixture.

Spoon half of batter into prepared pan. Sprinkle half of topping over and swirl with tip of knife to marbleize. Spoon remaining batter over. Sprinkle with remaining topping. Bake for about 40 minutes. Cool for half hour and cut into squares and serve.

Peach Upside Down Coffee Cake

2 tablespoons butter

½ cup brown sugar, packed

⅓ cup toasted, slivered almonds

1 (16-ounce) can peach slices

2 cups biscuit mix

¾ cup milk

2 tablespoons oil

¼ cup granulated sugar

1 egg

2 tablespoons grated orange peel

Grease round 9-inch pan with butter. Sprinkle bottom with brown sugar and almonds. Drain peaches and arrange on top of mixture. Stir biscuit mix, milk, oil, sugar, unbeaten eggs and orange peel just until blended. Then beat well 30 seconds. Spread mixture over peaches and bake at 400° for 20-25 minutes. Cool and turn upside down on platter.

Old Salem Sugar Cake

This recipe was adapted from the old Moravian sugar cake recipes in Old Salem, North Carolina. In the south, the sugar cakes are plentiful around the holidays and are often given as Christmas gifts. Loaded with brown sugar and butter, they are yummy!

½	cup warm water	¼	cup dry instant mashed potatoes
½	teaspoon sugar	½	teaspoon salt
2	packages dry active yeast	½	cup melted butter
¾	cup warm water	2	eggs
2	tablespoons dry milk	3	cups flour
			Dash of nutmeg

Topping:

1	cup brown sugar	½	cup butter, melted and cooled
1	teaspoon ground cinnamon		

Mix ½ cup warm water, sugar and dry yeast together and set aside until the yeast bubbles. Mix ¾ cup warm water, dry milk, instant mashed potatoes, salt, melted butter and eggs with 1 cup of the flour on medium speed of an electric mixer. With a wooden spoon add 2 remaining cups of flour.

Place in greased bowl, turn to grease top. Cover and let rise until it doubles, about 1 hour.

Punch down and put in greased 17x12x1-inch (large jelly-roll) pan. Spread dough out to the end of the pan. Let rise 30 minutes. After dough has risen, make shallow indentations with your finger or thumb across cake and dribble cooled melted butter in the holes. Sprinkle with cinnamon and brown sugar and dribble butter all over. Let rise another 30 minutes and bake for 12-15 minutes in a 375° oven.

vegetables

Card 1 (top left)

Pressed from

is what's cookin'

Kissin wears out - cookin' don't

Good May '76

Book Club &
Sewing Group
Recipe from the
kitchen of
Elizabeth Lake

Serves ___

Broccoli Casserole

2 pk frozen Broccoli (I used one
chopped &
Cook and drain (I whole stalk
1 can cream mushroom cut up after
Soup - undilute's cutting)
2 eggs
1 cup Sharp grated cheese
3/4 Cups mayonnaise for 1 teas
2 TBs minced onion dehydrated onion
Salt & pepper to taste

Mix broccoli with sauce and
1/2 cheese ↑
Put in buttered casserole
over

Card 2 (bottom middle)

→ Top with cubed bread crumbs
Swishes around in marg-
arine
→ Add remaining cheese   1 Recipe
(Cheese first)   makes
350° - 30 min -   2 qts
units

Since we were having ↕ $0
two things - tried to
make this a little more
festive so added Bacon
crumbs (liberally) at last
minute

Taste at this point - I use
Hellman's mayonnaise so
added some lemon juice and
(hot) peppers -

6 servings?
I think

Card 3 (right)

Baked whipped Potatoes (Bid)

- 8 baking potatoes,
   boiled, then mashed
- 3/4 c. hot milk
- 2-3 oz. cream cheese
- 1 c. Sour cream
  2 TBs butter
  2 tsp onion Salt ; pepper
cream all; put in dish.
Dot w/ butter & paprika.
Bake, 350°, 20 minutes

Can layer Top w/
Parmesan

vegetables

In the first printing of this cookbook, some of my vegetable dishes were the most requested and most talked about in the entire book! Some of the readers' favorites included Country Green Beans (at least 30 people have told me they love this recipe), Ranch Squash Casserole, Mrs. Redhead's Broccoli Casserole, Mom's Creamed Potatoes and Majelle's Sweet Potato Casserole. They are all "winners" and easy to prepare.

Beginning in late April, Katie Redhead and I begin our twice weekly treks out to the local farmer's markets. Sometimes we're there before the farmers have set up their tents! It's so much fun to see our favorite farmers again and begin our personal relationships with each special farmer.

Vegetables have always played a large role in our families. Especially in the summer time when the produce stands and farmer's markets are in full swing. We're known for our vegetable plates and our children have grown up accustomed to eating vegetable plates for dinner. It's actually one of their favorite dinners – "cooked all day" country green beans, creamed potatoes, fried okra, sautéed fresh summer squash and onions, collard greens, stewed corn, crowder peas, fresh summer tomato slices and of course biscuits or cornbread!

When my children were very small, toddlers, we ate out frequently in Charlotte because we had renovated two houses and our kitchens were being replaced. Our favorite restaurants were diners since they were children friendly. The kids grew up loving collard greens because we introduced them to collards when they were two years old!

Thanksgiving at my house must have at least six or seven bowls of vegetables and vegetable casseroles on the table. It's hard to choose when you like so many! I hope you'll enjoy making vegetables for your family – the kind anyone can love.

 # Corn Pudding

One of our family favorites!

1	(14.5-ounce) can whole kernel corn	½	teaspoon seasoned salt
2	(14.5-ounce) cans cream style corn	½	teaspoon dry mustard
4	lightly beaten eggs	1	teaspoon instant minced onion
½	cup sugar	½	cup milk
5	tablespoons cornstarch	½	cup melted butter

Combine 3 cans corn with 5 slightly beaten eggs. In a small bowl, mix together the sugar, cornstarch, seasoned salt, dry mustard, and minced onion. Add this mixture into the corn mixture. Stir in milk and melted butter. Pour entire mixture into a buttered 3-quart casserole. Bake in a preheated 400° oven for 45 minutes – 1 hour. After about 20-30 minutes, stir mixture. Watch carefully after 45 minutes and don't let corn pudding burn.

Variation: Substitute 4 ears of fresh corn kernels cut from the cob, for the can of whole kernel corn.

Fresh Summer Corn Pudding

2	cups fresh corn	1	teaspoon salt
4	eggs	3	tablespoons sugar
4	cups milk	2	tablespoons butter
8	tablespoons plain flour		

Preheat oven 325°. Combine corn, eggs, milk. In separate bowl, mix flour, salt and sugar. Add to the corn mixture. Pour into large casserole dish. Dot with butter. Bake 1 hour, stirring 3 times in process of baking.

Stewed Corn

This is best when using fresh
summer corn, preferably Silver Queen.

6	ears corn			Salt and pepper
	Water		1	teaspoon sugar
4	tablespoons butter			

Cut kernels from cob, scraping thoroughly to get all of the corn's milk. In heavy small saucepan, heat corn with several tablespoons water, adding more water if corn is not very milky. Heat until corn starts to change color – but do not boil. Add butter, salt, pepper and sugar. Fresh summer corn will be ready in 15 minutes.

Variation: For creamed corn, substitute milk instead of the water.

I freeze and bag my summer corn to serve at Thanksgiving and Christmas dinners. To freeze, cook corn as directed, but only cook for about 5-10 minutes, just until the corn changes color. Do not season with butter or sugar. Salt and pepper is okay. Cool corn and pour 2-4 cups into freezer bags. Flatten bags and withdraw as much air as possible. Freeze.

When serving at a later date, thaw bags about halfway. Cook in heavy saucepan and add a little more water – the ice in frozen corn will add more. Season with butter, sugar and more salt and pepper. This should taste just like fresh summer corn.

Grilled Corn

6-8	ears corn with husks still on	½	cup melted butter
			Salt and pepper

Pull down leaves of husk without pulling them off. Remove the silks and brush corn with melted butter. Sprinkle with salt and pepper. Pull leaves back up on corn and wrap with twine to secure ends. Soak in warm water for about 10 minutes. This will prevent husks from burning when they go on the grill. Place corn on hot grill for 10-15 minutes, turning on different sides.

vegetables

Succatash

8	ears fresh summer corn, kernels cut from cob		Chicken broth to cover limas
1	cup (or more) fresh lima beans		Salt and pepper
		3	tablespoons butter

In a medium saucepan, place fresh lima beans. Add chicken broth or water just enough to cover limas but not too much. Bring to a low boil and simmer beans for 15-20 minutes. Beans should soak up the liquid. If at this point the liquid is still covering the beans, then drain some of the liquid. Add cut corn and continue simmering for another 15-20 minutes. Season with salt and pepper. Add butter near the end. You can add a little milk or a little more broth if you need.

You can use frozen lima beans for the same effect if you can't get fresh ones. Also, add chopped onion and chopped tomatoes to the lima/corn mixture to dress this up a bit.

Succatash is one of my favorite summer vegetable combinations. Since I freeze my summer corn and limas, I can make this dish in the winter and it's always welcomed. It's a great reminder that summer will be back soon!

Scalloped Eggplant

1	cup eggplant, cooked and drained	¾	cup milk
	Salt and pepper to taste	1	cup shredded sharp Cheddar cheese, divided
1	small onion, diced	1	cup crushed saltines
2	tablespoons butter		

Add all ingredients together except ½ cup shredded cheese. Put mixture in a small casserole dish and bake at 350° for 40 minutes. Remove from oven; sprinkle top with remaining ½ cup cheese. Return to oven and bake for an additional 20 minutes.

Scalloped Eggplant is a favorite dish of Martha Long, an avid eggplant lover.

On New Year's Day, I always prepare my traditional "good luck" lunch for my husband and his father. It's no secret in my house that I do not like collard greens. It's a taste that I have yet to acquire. But, as my teenage daughter says, "Mom, you're really missing out." She could eat them every single day if I would take the time to fix them.

Collard Greens

6-8 cups water (enough to cover ham hock)
1 ham hock
½-1 teaspoon red pepper flakes
½-1 teaspoon sugar
2 bunches collard greens

Start preparing seasoned water by placing ham hock in a large, tall Dutch oven. Cover ham hock with water by a couple of inches. Sprinkle red pepper flakes and sugar in water. Bring to a boil and rapidly boil for 15 minutes or so. Lower temperature and briskly simmer for another 1½ hours. Cover pot during most of the time – but check water level often – it will evaporate quickly. Keep adding water to keep water level above ham hock.

While water is simmering, wash collard greens well. Be sure to separate and remove all grit and dirt. Cut stems off and remove the very top leafy part of the collard, keeping 80 percent of the lower leaf. Stack leaves on top of each other and coarsely chop or slice greens.

After water has simmered for 1½ hours, remove cover and let water evaporate down a little more until ham falls off bone. Remove ham hock from water and cut meat off and put meat back into water. Discard any fat layers and bone. Add the collard greens to seasoned water. You don't want too much water – about equal level or less to the collards – they will shrink down immediately. Simmer in the seasoned water for about 20-30 minutes, maybe a little more, depending on your volume. You want the greens tender, but not mushy.

Serve with black-eyed peas, cornbread, rice and country ham.

Black-Eyed Peas

3-4	cups rehydrated black-eyed peas	1	cup onion, chopped
3	cups water		Several dashes red pepper flakes
4	ounces cooked country ham or smoked ham	2	large garlic cloves, minced

Put rehydrated black-eyed peas (you can find rehydrated peas in specialty grocery stores or soak dried beans overnight in water) in large saucepan. Add about 3 cups water, 4 ounces cooked country ham or smoked ham, chopped onion, several dashes of red pepper flakes and 2 large garlic cloves, minced in with the peas. Bring water to a boil. Reduce heat and simmer for about 30 minutes. Mix seasonings around with peas. Salt and pepper to taste. Enjoy.

Country Green Beans

These are the kind of green beans I grew up eating, the kind you get in roadside diners, cooked all day!

1	ham hock		Salt and pepper to taste
2	(15-ounce) cans of cut green beans or pole beans, drained, or		Vegetable oil
		1	teaspoon sugar
2	pounds fresh string beans, ends cut and strings pulled	4-6	peeled new potatoes, optional

Prepare seasoned water by placing ham hock in medium saucepan and covering with water. Add sugar to water and bring to a boil. Boil for 30 minutes to an hour, replacing water as it evaporates. When meat pulls off bone, remove ham hock and cut meat up. Replace meat to the water and add green beans. Bring to a boil and simmer green beans for 1-3 hours on low simmer, depending on how tender you like your beans. Add small trace of vegetable oil to further season water. Add peeled new potatoes to the beans for the last 45 minutes, if desired.

Sautéed Green Beans

1	pound thin green beans or haricots vert		Kosher salt and pepper
	Garlic salt or powder	2	tablespoons butter
	Dried thyme	2	tablespoons oil

If using thin green beans, cut hard end off and blanch in boiling water for 2 minutes. Drain. If using haricots verts, then you don't need to blanch. Heat oil and butter in a large skillet and sauté green beans with spices until green beans are limp and blackened. If using haricots vert, you will not need to sauté beans long. Regular green beans will take about 15-20 minutes. Enhance seasonings as you desire.

Traditional Green Bean Casserole

Thanksgiving would not be complete without a green bean casserole.

3	small packages frozen French style green beans or 3 (14.5-ounce) cans French style green beans	1	large can water chestnuts, sliced
		1	can cream of celery soup
		1	cup sour cream
1½	cups water	⅛	teaspoon pepper
1½	teaspoons salt	½	cup milk
		1	can Durkee French fried onion rings

Cook gently in boiling salted water the frozen green beans for about 4 minutes. Drain. If using canned green beans, drain well. In a buttered casserole dish, place a layer of green beans and a layer of water chestnuts. Repeat layers 4 additional times. In a separate bowl mix the cream of celery soup and sour cream with pepper and milk. Pour over the green bean/water chestnut layers. Bake at 350° for 25 minutes. Sprinkle French fried onions on top and bake about 10 minutes longer, until onions are browned.

vegetables

Majelle's Squash Casserole

An old Greensboro classic!

2	pounds yellow squash, sliced	1	cup sour cream	
¼	cup chopped onion	¾	cup shredded carrots	
1	can cream of chicken soup	1	(8-ounce) package herb stuffing	
		1	stick butter, melted	

Boil squash and onion in small amount of water for about 5 minutes and drain. In a small bowl, combine the soup and sour cream and gently stir in carrots. Fold in the squash/onion mixture and salt and pepper to taste. In another bowl combine the stuffing and melted butter. Spread half of the stuffing on the bottom of a long casserole dish. Scoop the squash mixture over top of the stuffing and top with more stuffing. You may not want to use all of the stuffing. Bake in a preheated 350° oven for 30-40 minutes, until bubbly and brown on top.

Ranch Squash Casserole

The key to this creamy casserole is the Ranch dressing.

2	pounds yellow squash, sliced	1	envelope Ranch buttermilk dressing	
1	cup sliced onion	1	cup shredded Cheddar cheese	
¾	cup mayonnaise	2	tablespoons butter, melted	
2	eggs, slightly beaten	½	cup fresh bread crumbs	
½	cup crushed unsalted saltine crackers			

Cook the squash and onion together in water until tender and drain well. In a bowl, mix the mayonnaise, eggs, saltines, Ranch dressing packet and shredded cheese together. Mash the squash with a fork and mix the additional ingredients together with the squash and pour into a casserole dish. Top with 2 tablespoons melted butter mixed with ½ cup bread crumbs. Bake for 20-25 minutes in a 350° oven.

Squash Stuffed Tomatoes

Prepare either squash casserole up to the baking point, but omit the stuffing if using Majelle's casserole.

Hollow out medium ripe tomatoes and fill 6-8 tomatoes with squash casserole. Place in a casserole dish or a cake pan, so the tomatoes will stand up. Place buttered bread crumbs on top of squash filling and bake in a 350° oven for 30 minutes. This is particularly good with grilled steak and potatoes.

Squash Gratin with White Cheddar Cheese

This is nice for company.

1 medium onion, thinly sliced

2 pounds yellow squash, thinly sliced

1 teaspoon salt and pepper

2 eggs

2 tablespoons sugar

½ cup milk

½ pound white Cheddar cheese, grated

1-2 tablespoons butter

Cook the onions and squash in a small amount of boiling water for 10-15 minutes or until fork-tender. Drain well. Arrange in a 2-quart baking dish. Add salt and pepper. Mix eggs, sugar, milk and cheese and pour over squash mixture. Dot with thin slices of butter. Bake in preheated 350° oven for 45 minutes. Cut into squares and then into diamonds to make a nice shape, if desired.

Squash Soufflé

A version of this squash soufflé has been around Greensboro for many, many years. It was very popular in the 60's and 70's.

2	pounds yellow squash		1¼	cups milk
½	onion, chopped		1¼	cups sharp Cheddar cheese, grated
1	teaspoon salt		1	egg, beaten
3	tablespoons butter, melted			Buttered bread crumbs or cracker crumbs
3	heaping tablespoons flour			

In a saucepan place sliced squash and chopped onion. Add water until just covered and add salt. Boil squash until fork tender. Drain squash well and mash squash and onion with a fork or masher. In a separate large saucepan, mix together melted butter and flour. Stir until smooth. Add milk and stir until it thickens. Add grated cheese and stir until the cheese melts, making a cheese sauce. Remove the pan from the heat and cook slightly. Add the beaten egg and cooked squash and onion to the cheese sauce. Add salt and pepper to taste.

Pour mixture into a double boiler and cook for about 45 minutes, stirring occasionally. Pour this into a lightly greased casserole dish and cover with buttered bread crumbs or buttered cracker crumbs. Bake in a 350° oven for 20 minutes or so until bubbly and brown on top.

Squash Fritters

2	cups grated squash		1	tablespoon grated onion
⅓	cup Bisquick mix		½	teaspoon salt and pepper
¼	cup grated Parmesan cheese or shredded Cheddar cheese		2-4	tablespoons butter

Combine all ingredients except butter. Melt butter in skillet and drop squash batter by tablespoons and cook until brown on both sides.

Vegetable Casserole

1   can French style green beans, drained
1   can white shoepeg corn, drained
½   cup celery, chopped
1   cup sharp Cheddar cheese, diced
½   cup onions, diced
1   can cream of celery soup
1   (8-ounce) carton sour cream
1   sleeve Ritz crackers
½   stick butter

Combine all ingredients except crackers and butter and pour into casserole dish. Top with crushed Ritz crackers, which have been tossed in melted butter. Bake 30-45 minutes in a 350° oven.

Variation: Add cooked chicken pieces to casserole for a main dish.

Mrs. Redhead's Broccoli Casserole

5-6   cups broccoli florets
1   can cream of mushroom soup
¾   cup mayonnaise
2   eggs
2   tablespoons minced onion
2   tablespoons minced fresh red pepper
   Salt and pepper to taste
1   cup sharp Cheddar cheese, grated
1   cup cubed or ground bread crumbs
3   tablespoons butter
3-4   slices crumbled cooked bacon

Cook broccoli until tender and drain. Mix soup, mayonnaise, eggs, onion, red pepper, salt and pepper and ½ cup grated cheese. Mix broccoli with this sauce and pour into buttered casserole dish. Add remaining cheese on top of casserole. Top with cubed bread crumbs that have been tossed with the 3 tablespoons of melted butter. Bake for 30 minutes in a 350° oven. Garnish with cooked crumbled bacon if desired.

Cabbage Casserole

1 medium head cabbage, cut into small strips

1 can cream of celery soup

2 cups grated sharp Cheddar cheese

1½ cups buttered bread crumbs

Cook cabbage in water over medium heat for 5-6 minutes. You can add some chopped onion and celery to this if you like. Drain well. In a buttered baking dish, layer half of cabbage, half of cream of celery soup and half of cheese. Repeat. Top with buttered bread crumbs and bake at 400-425° for 30 minutes or until casserole is heated through. This can easily be doubled.

Spinach and Rice Casserole

1 pound fresh spinach
or 2 boxes frozen
chopped spinach

1 cup hot cooked rice

1 cup grated Cheddar cheese
or ⅔ cup Cheese Whiz

¼ cup grated onion

2 tablespoons butter

1 cup buttered bread crumbs

If spinach is frozen, thaw,
drain and chop. If fresh,
chop. Mix hot rice with
cheese, onion and butter.
Fold in spinach. Turn into
a lightly buttered casserole
dish. Top with buttered bread
crumbs and bake at 350°
for 20-25 minutes.

Cheesy Artichoke Casserole

⅓	cup onion, minced	⅓	cup dry bread crumbs
2	cloves garlic, minced	½	pound Muenster cheese, grated
2	tablespoons extra-virgin olive oil	2	tablespoons fresh chopped parsley
4	eggs	¼	teaspoon dried oregano
1	(14-ounce) jar artichoke hearts, drained and finely chopped		

Lightly butter a small rectangular Pyrex dish. In a skillet, sauté onions and garlic in olive oil until soft; do not brown. Beat eggs and stir in chopped artichoke hearts, onions, bread crumbs, cheese, parsley and oregano. Pour into buttered casserole dish. Bake 30-35 minutes in preheated 325° oven.

Grandmother's Spinach Soufflé

1	(10-ounce) package frozen chopped spinach	½	cup Cheddar cheese
1	egg	3	tablespoons chopped onion
3	tablespoons butter	1	cup cracker crumbs
½	can cream of mushroom soup	2	tablespoons butter

Thaw frozen spinach and drain well with paper towels. Mix all ingredients except cracker crumbs and 2 tablespoons butter. Pour into small casserole dish and top with Ritz cracker crumbs that have been tossed in 2 tablespoons butter. Bake in a 350° oven for 30 minutes or until set.

Mom's Creamed Potatoes

3	pounds potatoes, russet, gold Yukon or white	1	large can evaporated milk
½	stick butter, soft or melted		Salt and pepper to taste

Peel and cube potatoes and boil in salted water for 20-30 minutes until tender. Drain potatoes well in saucepan and keep potatoes in pan. Remove from heat and salt and pepper potatoes well.

With an electric beater, beat potatoes on low speed until well crushed. Add soft or melted butter and beat. Slowly add evaporated milk and beat until smooth, until desired consistency is reached. You may not need the entire can of milk. Salt and pepper again and dot top of potatoes with a few dabs of butter. Cover pot and put back on stove (on no heat or on very low) until ready to serve. Serves 6-8.

Leftover Creamed Potato Cakes

Kids especially love these
fried creamed potato cakes for breakfast.

	Leftover creamed potatoes		Flour seasoned with salt and pepper
1	egg	⅓	stick butter

Spoon any leftover creamed potatoes (they're better if they're on the dry side, not too creamy) onto a sheet of plastic wrap and refrigerate. Remove when you're ready to make the potato cakes and add 1 egg to the mixture. Form into patties. Don't make them too big as they are hard to handle. Dredge in seasoned flour.

Heat butter in non-stick skillet until hot and add floured creamed potato cake. Fry on one side until brown and carefully flip. It may fall apart, but that's okay. Keep cooking on the back side until brown. Remove and serve immediately.

In my house, we never called these "Mashed Potatoes," They were always referred to as "Creamed Potatoes." I've probably eaten Creamed Potatoes 300 times in my life. We had them growing up a couple of times a week and I still fix them for my family every week, as well. Even when I eat at Le Cirque 2000 in New York, they know how much I like them and bring real Creamed Potatoes in a little copper pot with whatever dish I have ordered.

Kids Favorite Hash Browns

Kids love to spend the night at our house because I always make these hash browns. They think I'm going to so much trouble, but they're really easy!

3 medium russet potatoes

Peanut oil or
other vegetable oil

Salt

Heat about ¼-inch oil in cast iron skillet – I use a 9-inch pan. Any heavy skillet will do. Make sure oil is really hot. Peel and grate potatoes. Drain in colander while oil is getting hot. Drop grated potatoes in hot oil and spread around with spatula. Cook on both sides until brown – about 5 minutes per side. Remove and place on paper towel to drain. Salt and serve immediately.

Variation: Add some grated onion or chopped scallions to the grated potatoes for an extra kick.

Baked Whipped Potatoes

This has been made hundreds of times in our family.

8	baking potatoes	2	teaspoons onion salt
¾	cup hot milk	1	teaspoon salt
2	(3-ounce) blocks cream cheese	½	teaspoon pepper
1	cup sour cream	2	tablespoons butter for top
2	tablespoons butter		

Boil potatoes in salted water until tender. Drain. With an electric beater, whip potatoes with hot milk, cream cheese, sour cream, butter, onion salt, and salt and pepper. Pour into a Pyrex dish and sprinkle with paprika. Dot top of casserole with small slices of butter. Bake for 20-30 minutes in a 350° oven.

This can be refrigerated before cooking, but should be brought to room temperature before cooking. Serves 8-10.

Pennsylvania Dutch Potatoes

2	cups thin mashed potatoes		Pinch of pepper
2	eggs	1	tablespoon parsley
4	tablespoons butter	½	cup celery, diced
1	medium onion, diced	1	cup milk
1	teaspoon salt	7	pieces toasted or dry bread

Melt butter in a skillet and add onions and celery. Cook until soft, but not brown. Then beat eggs in milk. Mix all ingredients together and put into a buttered casserole dish. Dot with extra butter and bake 375° for 35 minutes or until brown.

World's Best Potatoes

6	large potatoes, peeled, boiled and cooled (do not cut up)	1½	cups sour cream
½	stick butter, melted	¾	cup chopped green onions
1	can cream of celery soup	1	cup grated Cheddar cheese
		½	cup crushed corn flakes

After potatoes are cooled, grate coarsely. Mix butter, soup, sour cream, green onions and cheese together. Grease a 9x13-inch baking dish. Spread this potato mixture into dish. Top with corn flakes and bake at 350° for 45 minutes.

Stuffed Baked Potatoes

This is always a favorite. Serve with grilled steak and a salad.

6	large baking potatoes	2-3	tablespoons chopped chives
1	stick butter	½	teaspoon pepper
4	tablespoons grated Parmesan cheese	1	teaspoon salt
5	slices bacon, cooked and crumbled	1	teaspoon granulated garlic or garlic powder
2	tablespoons sour cream		Paprika

Grease potatoes and bake at 400° for 45 minutes. Cut in half lengthwise. Spoon out potato centers while hot and put in mixing bowl. Reserve skins. Combine all remaining ingredients except paprika and add to the spooned out potatoes. Mix with electric mixer for 3 minutes at medium speed. Place mixture in reserved potato skins. Sprinkle lightly with paprika. Brown in hot oven approximately 4 minutes. Potatoes can be wrapped in plastic wrap and frozen before they are cooked in the oven. If potatoes are refrigerated, bake at 400° for approximately 20-25 minutes.

Variation: Cheddar cheese may be sprinkled on top of potatoes if desired.

Tater Tot Casserole

Follow the same instructions for World's Best Potatoes, but substitute the real potatoes for a (32-ounce) bag of frozen Tater Tots, which have been thawed. Place Tater Tots on bottom of a 9x13-inch casserole dish. Prepare sauce and spread over top of Tater Tots. Top with crushed corn flakes and bake in 350° oven for about 45 minutes.

My mother-in-law gave me this Betty Crocker Scalloped Potatoes recipe when I got married nearly 20 years ago. I had not used it for years and a friend, Gayle Koonce, recently gave it to me again. It's a great easy recipe. Betty Crocker suggested serving this with meat loaf, but it's delicious with any beef or chicken dish.

This Horseradish Potato Casserole recipe originally came from Melinda Holt in Charlotte, and was passed around to all of the neighbors on our street, especially when we'd have our famous annual progressive dinner party.

Betty Crocker's
Easy Scalloped Potatoes

6	medium potatoes – about 2 pounds	¼	teaspoon pepper
¼	cup finely chopped onion	¼	cup butter
3	tablespoons flour	2½	cups milk

Heat oven to 350°. Wash potatoes and remove skins. Cut potatoes into thin slices to measure about 4 cups. In greased 2-quart casserole, arrange potatoes in 4 layers, sprinkling each of the first 3 layers with 1 tablespoon onion, 1 tablespoon flour, ¼ teaspoon salt, dash of pepper and dotting each layer with 1 tablespoon butter. Sprinkle top layer with remaining onion, salt and pepper and dot with remaining butter.

Heat milk just to scalding; pour over potatoes. Cover and bake 30 minutes. Uncover and bake 60-70 minutes longer or until potatoes are tender. Let stand 5 to 10 minutes before serving.

Horseradish
Potato Casserole

7	large red potatoes	¼	cup Parmesan cheese
½	stick butter	½	cup Cheddar cheese
1	cup sour cream Salt and pepper to taste	1	small jar creamy horseradish
		5	slices bacon, cooked crisp

Boil red potatoes until barely tender. While still warm, grate potatoes with the skins. Mix potatoes with the butter, sour cream, salt, pepper, Parmesan and Cheddar cheeses, horseradish and crumbled bacon until blended. Mixture will be thick. Pour into large casserole dish. Sprinkle with paprika and bake for 45 minutes in a 350° oven.

Variation: Stuff this mixture into potato shells for horseradish stuffed potatoes.

Brown Sugar Glazed Sweet Potatoes

3-4 pounds sweet potatoes, peeled, cut into 1-inch pieces
⅔ cup packed brown sugar
6 tablespoons butter
1 teaspoon ground cinnamon
½ teaspoon salt
¼ teaspoon ground nutmeg
Pinch of ground ginger
2 cups miniature marshmallows
⅔ cup sliced almonds

Preheat oven to 375°. Arrange potatoes in a rectangular glass baking dish. Combine sugar, butter, cinnamon, salt, nutmeg and ginger in heavy small saucepan over medium heat. Bring to boil, stirring until sugar dissolves. Pour over potatoes; toss to coat. Cover dish tightly with foil.

Bake potatoes 45 minutes. Uncover and bake until potatoes are tender and syrup thickens slightly, basting occasionally, about 20-25 more minutes.

Increase oven temperature to 500°. Top potatoes with marshmallows and almonds. Return to oven and bake until marshmallows begin to melt and nuts begin to brown – about 3-4 minutes.

Grandmother's Sweet Potato Balls

3 cups cooked, mashed sweet potatoes
¼ cup butter
¾ cup brown sugar
2 tablespoons milk
¼ teaspoon salt
1 teaspoon grated lemon rind
½ cup crushed corn flakes
Large marshmallows

Mash sweet potatoes. Add butter, sugar, milk, salt and lemon rind. Mix well. Sprinkle a buttered baking dish with crushed corn flakes. Put half of potato mixture in dish. Cover with large marshmallows and add rest of potatoes. Cover with corn flake crumbs. Bake at 350° until marshmallows begin to ooze, about 20 minutes. Don't let marshmallows melt.

My friend
Ross Harris
gave me her mother's
Sweet Potato Casserole
recipe, which was
identical to my
mother-in-law's.
It's outstanding.

Majelle's
Sweet Potato Casserole

3	cups cooked mashed sweet potatoes	⅓-½	cup milk
1	cup sugar	1	stick butter, melted
2	eggs, well beaten	1	teaspoon vanilla
		½	teaspoon salt

Topping:

½	stick butter	1	cup brown sugar
½	cup flour	1	cup chopped pecans

Mix together all of the above ingredients except for topping in a food processor until smooth and creamy. Pour sweet potato mixture into a buttered 2-quart baking dish. Mix topping ingredients together and sprinkle on top of potatoes. Bake 350° for 30 minutes.

Fruity Sweet Potato Casserole

½	lemon, skin removed	½	cup melted butter
½	orange, skin removed	½	teaspoon salt
6	cups sliced sweet potatoes, cooked	½	cup shredded coconut
1	cup crushed pineapple	½	cup maraschino cherries
½	cup brown sugar		

Cut lemon and orange as thin as possible. Layer sweet potatoes, sliced orange, sliced lemon and pineapple. Make a syrup with melted butter, brown sugar and salt. Pour syrup over top of sweet potatoes. Top with coconut and cherries. Bake 30 minutes at 350°.

Mom's Asparagus Casserole

2	cans whole asparagus, drained	½	cup shredded Cheddar cheese
1	can cream of mushroom soup	⅓	cup fresh bread crumbs, fine
½	cup milk	2	tablespoons melted butter
1-2	hard-boiled eggs, sliced		

In a small casserole dish, layer ½ asparagus, ½ mushroom soup mixed with milk, and sliced egg. Continue with rest of asparagus, ending with mushroom soup mixture. Cover top with shredded cheese and bread crumbs on top. Sprinkle melted butter over bread crumbs. Bake at 350° for 30-40 minutes until bubbly and brown on top.

Variation: If you can get good fresh asparagus, use it instead of canned. You can substitute crushed saltine crackers for the bread crumbs if desired.

Marinated Vegetables

Clean out your pantry with this one!

2 cans French cut green beans
4 stalks chopped celery
1 large onion, chopped
1 or 2 cans artichokes, quartered
1 large can mushrooms

1 green pepper, chopped
1 small jar green olives, sliced
1 large jar pimientos, chopped
1 large can LeSeur peas
1 large can shoepeg corn

Marinade:

½ cup oil
1 cup vinegar
1 cup sugar

1 teaspoon salt
1 teaspoon dry mustard

Drain all canned veggies. Toss lightly in marinade. Marinate for 24 hours in refrigerator.

This Asparagus Casserole recipe is prepared every Christmas with our standing rib roast and every Thanksgiving with our turkey. Make sure you layer this in a fairly shallow casserole dish – you don't want it too thick. It doubles easily.

Creamed Asparagus

1 (1-pound) bunch fresh asparagus

½ cup sour cream

1 teaspoon sugar

2 teaspoons wine vinegar

¼ teaspoon paprika

½ teaspoon seasoned salt

½ cup toasted bread cubes

Cook asparagus and drain. Combine sour cream, sugar, vinegar, paprika and seasoned salt. Heat gently, but do not let come to a boil. Fold in the toasted bread cubes and spoon over asparagus.

Creamed Celery and Almonds

4 tablespoons butter

3 cups sliced fresh celery

1 cup slivered almonds

2 tablespoons flour

½ cup cream

⅛ teaspoon pepper

1 cup boiling chicken broth

3 tablespoons grated Parmesan cheese

In a large skillet, melt 2 tablespoons butter and sauté celery and almonds until celery is tender. Add remaining 2 tablespoons butter and blend in flour. Cook and stir for about 1 minute without coloring. Add cream, pepper and boiling chicken broth all at once stirring to blend. Increase heat to moderate high and cook, stirring until sauce comes to a boil and thickens. Spoon into 1-quart casserole dish and sprinkle with grated Parmesan cheese. Place under broiler until cheese browns.

Copper Pennies

5	cups sliced, peeled carrots	¾	cup salad oil
1	can tomato soup	1	scant tablespoon dry mustard
1	medium onion, sliced	2	scant tablespoons Worcestershire sauce
2	small green peppers, sliced round	1	teaspoon salt
1	cup sugar	1	teaspoon pepper
½	cup vinegar		

In a small saucepan, cook the sliced carrots in water until just tender. Drain. In a bowl, mix marinade by combining the tomato soup, sugar, salad oil, vinegar, salt, pepper, dry mustard and Worcestershire sauce. In another bowl place the sliced cooked carrots, onion and green pepper. Pour marinade over vegetables and marinate for 12 hours or more. This will store in the refrigerator for 1-2 weeks.

Glazed Carrots

4	medium carrots, julienned	1	tablespoon sugar or honey
1	tablespoon butter	½	teaspoon cinnamon

Julienne carrots ⅛ to ¼-inch thick by 1½ to 2 inches long. Place 1-inch water in medium saucepan and bring to boil over medium high heat. Place carrot strips in boiling water, cover and reduce heat to low. Cook 15-17 minutes. Drain liquid and add butter, sugar, cinnamon. Simmer carrots in this mixture over low heat until well glazed.

Marinated Tomatoes

3	large, ripe tomatoes, cut into ½-inch slices	2	tablespoons capers	
⅓	cup olive oil	1	clove, garlic, minced	
¼	cup red wine vinegar	1	teaspoon salt	
¼	cup finely chopped onion	1	teaspoon dried basil	
		¼	teaspoon ground black pepper	
			Chopped parsley	

Arrange tomatoes in a single layer in a shallow dish. Mix oil and rest of the ingredients except for the parsley. Spoon over tomatoes. Cover and marinate 3 hours. Garnish with parsley.

Escalloped Tomatoes

2	tablespoons chopped onion	½	teaspoon paprika	
1	tablespoon butter	3	tablespoons sugar	
1	(15-ounce) can chopped tomatoes or 2 cups fresh summer tomatoes, chopped	3	tablespoons tapioca	
		¾	cup sliced olives	
		¾	cup grated Cheddar cheese	
¼	teaspoon salt	½	cup buttered bread crumbs	

Brown onions in butter. Add tomatoes. Bring to a boil and combine salt, paprika, sugar, stirring constantly. Cook 5 minutes. Stir in tapioca. Pour into casserole dish in the following order:

Layer of tomatoes – Layer of cheese – Layer of olives – Repeat.

Top with buttered bread crumbs and bake in preheated 350° oven for 20 minutes. Serves 4-6.

Creamed Mushrooms

2 chicken bouillon cubes

¼ cup hot water

½ teaspoon salt

½ pound fresh mushrooms

2 tablespoons flour

½ cup half-and-half

½ cup fine dry bread crumbs

½ cup grated Parmesan cheese

¼ cup butter, plus 2 tablespoons

Dissolve bouillon in hot water. Cool. Wash and slice mushrooms; place in casserole. Melt 2 tablespoons butter in saucepan and stir in flour. Add bouillon mixture, half-and-half, and salt and pepper to taste. Cook mixture until thickened. Spoon this sauce over mushrooms. Combine cheese and bread crumbs and sprinkle over top. Dot with butter. Bake at 350° for 30-35 minutes.

Oven Roasted Vegetables

This is especially nice in the winter with a grilled steak or roast chicken.

4 carrots, peeled

4 potatoes, peeled

4 parsnips, peeled

4 shallots, peeled

4 tablespoons olive oil

1 clove garlic, minced

Salt and pepper

2 teaspoons
herbes de provence

Preheat oven to 400°.
Cut the carrots, potatoes, parsnips into uniform pieces. Combine all the vegetables and toss with olive oil, garlic and herbes de provence. Season liberally with salt and pepper and spread vegetables in a single layer onto a rimmed baking sheet. Roast for 45 minutes – 1 hour, until vegetables are soft and brown.

Baked Beans

1	pound dried beans	4	chopped onions
1	cup brown sugar	1	tablespoon mustard
1	cup ketchup or chili sauce		Bacon strips

Soak 1 pound of beans overnight in water. Cook until they are tender either in salted water or in ham broth. Cook to rather dry, not soupy, and mix in the brown sugar, ketchup or chili sauce, chopped onions and mustard. Put in baking pan. Cover with strips of bacon and bake at 275° for 6 to 8 hours or until brown. Take care not to let it get too dry.

Patio Beans

A wonderful combination of beans and flavors.

4	slices bacon	¼	pound sharp Cheddar cheese, cubed
1	medium onion, chopped		
1	(1-pound) can baked beans in tomato sauce	⅓	cup brown sugar
		⅓	cup ketchup
1	(1-pound) can kidney beans, drained	2	teaspoons Worcestershire sauce
1	(1-pound) can lima beans, drained		Parmesan cheese

Fry bacon until crisp. Sauté onion in bacon drippings. Combine in large casserole the beans, cheese, brown sugar and seasonings. Stir in the onion and bacon which has been crumbled. Sprinkle with Parmesan cheese. Bake at 350° for 30-40 minutes, until bubbly. Serves 6.

You can omit the cheese if you'd like. It's just as good. Play around with different combinations of beans, adding black beans as well.

Scalloped oysters

Drain 1 pint oysters.

Combine 6 tablespoons cream and the
  oyster liquor

Combine ½ c. dry bread crumbs
  1 c cracker crumbs

Pour over them ⅓ c. melted butter.

Plan to use two layers of oysters (no more)
and three layers of bread crumbs.
Grease a baking dish & cover it with
a layer of crumbs, then build up the
other layers of oysters & crumbs,
each layer of oysters with:
    Salt & paprika and pour ½
liquid over each layer. The top layer
of crumbs should be dry.

Bake 20 minutes in oven 400°

seafood

Living in North Carolina, I learned early on the joys of fishing on our coasts and cooking what you caught for dinner. My father taught me how to fish at an early age and I enjoyed many days and early mornings fishing with him. My job was to scale, clean and gut the fish so my mother could pan fry them that night. I didn't even mind! Flounder and pompano were my favorite fish growing up, although spot and stripe fish were more plentiful. Crabbing on the docks at Ocean Isle Beach was a kid's pastime, and we had so much fun bringing the clawing crabs home. Shrimp and oysters were abundant, but we usually just bought them – they were difficult to catch.

In those days, the beaches were wide, the days were long; we would get sunburned because you rarely wore sunscreen, and the best shells were there for the collecting. Calabash, North Carolina was only 30 minutes away, and we'd end the day with a plate of fried seafood that even a kid could like. Hushpuppies and slaw completed the meal, with sweet tea or Sun Drop.

Mel's Crab Cakes

In the South, there are many variations of the classic crab cake. My favorites are ones that do not include much breading, but rely on the great taste of crab to carry them.

2	tablespoons unsalted butter	1	teaspoon Tabasco sauce
2	teaspoons green spring onions, including green parts, minced	2	teaspoons Worcestershire sauce
		1	egg, beaten
2	tablespoons sweet onion, finely chopped	½	cup mayonnaise
		2-3	tablespoons finely chopped parsley
¼	cup minced celery	1	pound lump crabmeat, picked through
	Small handful fine bread crumbs		Juice from ¼-½ lime
1-2	tablespoons whole grain mustard or 1 tablespoon dry mustard	2	cups fresh bread crumbs, optional
		4	tablespoons oil or butter

In a skillet over low heat, melt butter and add minced onions and celery, sautéing until soft. Use a slotted spoon and transfer to a bowl to cool. Discard butter. To the cooled mixture, add bread crumbs, mustard, both sauces, beaten egg, mayonnaise, parsley and crabmeat, which has been sprinkled with the lime juice. Mix well. If the crab cakes are too wet to hold their shape, add a few bread crumbs to mixture.

Shape into 6 cakes about 3 inches by 1-inch thick or smaller cakes. Place crab cakes on a cookie sheet which has been lined with parchment paper and place in the freezer or refrigerator for a little while so they will firm up.

Dredge in bread crumbs or leave plain and fry over medium heat in 2-3 tablespoons oil or butter for 3 minutes a side until brown. If your crab cakes are really thick, then finish cooking them in a 375° oven for 5-10 minutes. Sauté half at a time so they are not too crowded in the pan. Drain and keep warm.

Serve with Rémoulade Sauce or homemade tartar sauce. Serves 4.

Rémoulade Sauce

1 cup mayonnaise

3 tablespoons Dijon mustard

2-3 tablespoons white wine vinegar

1 tablespoon paprika

2 tablespoons horseradish sauce

1 clove garlic, minced

⅓ cup green onions, minced

⅓ cup celery, minced

2 tablespoons finely chopped parsley

2 tablespoons ketchup

Salt and pepper to taste

Stir together and refrigerate. Enjoy with crab cakes or fried shrimp.

My mother's friend, Barbara McNeely, has been making these creamy crab cakes for years. Lots of people from Burlington will recognize this recipe.

Pawley's Island, South Carolina is located in the "low country" between Murrell's Inlet, South Carolina and Georgetown, South Carolina, about 2 hours north of Charleston. Pawley's Island is known for its shrimp and crab dishes and is home to some of the South's best restaurants.

Creamy Crab Croquettes

2	tablespoons butter		Salt and pepper to taste
2	tablespoons flour	1	pound crabmeat
2	cups cream	1	cup flour
2	hard-boiled eggs	2	eggs beaten
1	tablespoon minced parsley	2	cups saltine cracker crumbs

Make thick cream sauce by sautéing butter and flour in pan until light brown. Add cream and make a very thick sauce. Add chopped hard-boiled eggs, seasonings and crabmeat. Let stand overnight or chill 4 hours. Shape in croquettes and roll in flour, eggs and cracker crumbs. Fry in deep fat. Serves 4.

Pawley's Island Deviled Crab Casserole

1	pound lump crabmeat	1	egg, beaten
1	cup saltine cracker crumbs	1	cup mayonnaise
1	large stalk celery, finely diced	2	tablespoons prepared mustard
1	hard-boiled egg, finely diced	1	tablespoon Worcestershire sauce
		2	tablespoons dry sherry

Mix all ingredients. If mixture is too stiff, add more mayonnaise. Preheat oven to 350° and pour mixture into casserole dish. Bake 25-35 minutes, until top is golden brown. You can prepare this ahead by omitting the saltine cracker crumbs and mix in just before baking. Serves 4.

Variation: If preparing this as an appetizer in shells, you can eliminate the celery and add curry and celery salt. Heat only about 10-15 minutes.

Crabmeat Casserole

½ cup butter
⅔ cup flour
2⅔ cups milk
1 pound lump crabmeat
2 cups chopped celery
½ cup chopped green pepper
1 large jar pimientos, drained
⅓ cup slivered blanched almonds
4 hard-boiled eggs, chopped
2 teaspoons salt
1 cup shredded sharp Cheddar cheese
Buttered bread crumbs

Melt butter in a saucepan. Add flour and mix well for several minutes. Over low heat, slowly add milk. Raise heat a little and stir constantly until white sauce thickens. Add crabmeat, celery, pimiento, green pepper, almonds, hard-boiled eggs and salt. Pour into a 2-quart casserole dish and top with cheese and bread crumbs. Bake at 350° for 45 minutes. Serves 4-6.

Barbara's Crabmeat Au Gratin

This recipe dates back to the 1960's.

1 pound lump crabmeat
½ cup dry sherry
3 slices soft white bread
½ stick butter, melted
½ cup light cream
Juice of ½ lemon
Dash pepper
Salt to taste
1 teaspoon Worcestershire sauce
½ cup mayonnaise
1 cup grated cheese
1 cup fresh bread crumbs, buttered

Marinate crabmeat with sherry. Place soft bread in bowl and add cream, butter, lemon juice, Worcestershire sauce and mayonnaise. Blend well and season with salt and pepper. Toss crabmeat in and place in casserole dish or ramekins. Cover with shredded Cheddar cheese and add buttered bread crumbs on top. Bake 20-30 minutes until bubbly. Serves 4.

Crab Soufflé

12 slices stale bread, torn into small pieces

1 pound lump crabmeat

7 hard-boiled eggs, diced

2 tablespoons onion

2 tablespoons parsley

2½ cups mayonnaise

2½ cups milk

Salt and pepper to taste

2 cups grated Cheddar cheese

Combine bread, crabmeat, eggs, onion and parsley in a large bowl. Mix mayonnaise and milk together and pour over the crab mixture and blend. Season with salt and pepper. Put in greased casserole dish and cover with cheese. Bake in preheated 325° oven for 45 minutes. Serves 6.

Hawaiian Crab

1 onion, diced

2 tablespoons butter

2 large avocados, diced

1½ pounds lump crabmeat

½ cup grated Parmesan cheese

¼ cup bread crumbs

6 slices crisp bacon, crumbled

½ pint sour cream

½ cup melted butter

4 tablespoons chopped parsley

Season with salt,
pepper, cayenne pepper
and curry powder

Brandy

Paprika

Sauté the onions in butter.
Mix together all of the above
except Brandy and place in
shells. Top with additional bread
crumbs and dot with butter.
Pour 1 tablespoon Brandy over
each shell. Sprinkle with
paprika. Bake approximately
20 minutes at 350°.
Serves 6-8.

Crab Thermidor

4	tablespoons green pepper, chopped fine	½	cup light cream
½	cup onion, chopped fine	1	cup grated sharp Cheddar cheese
4	tablespoons butter	1	pound lump crabmeat
1	can Campbell's potato soup	3	teaspoons lemon juice
		2	tablespoons sherry

Sauté green pepper and onion in butter until soft. Add soup and cream to pan and mix thoroughly on medium heat but do not boil. Add cheese, crabmeat, lemon juice and sherry. You may add curry powder if desired. Heat thoroughly and serve over top of Pepperidge Farms Patty Shells or other puff pastry shells. Serves 4.

Marinated Shrimp

½	cup tarragon vinegar	1	whole garlic clove
4	tablespoons horseradish mustard	1	cup salad oil
1	teaspoon salt	½	cup green onions with tops, finely minced
	Dash of ground pepper	½	cup celery, finely minced
1	tablespoon paprika		
2	tablespoons tomato ketchup	1-1½	pounds cooked shrimp
½	teaspoon cayenne pepper		

Mix vinegar, mustard, salt, pepper, paprika, ketchup, cayenne pepper and clove of garlic mashed well through sieve. Then add oil, beating thoroughly. Add green onions and celery. This dressing should be poured over cooked shrimp and marinated at least 3-4 hours. Serves 4-6.

Presidential Shrimp Creole

2	slices bacon	1	(15-ounce) jar Heinz cocktail sauce
1½	cups onions, chopped	2-3	splashes Worcestershire sauce
1½	cups green peppers, chopped	1	tablespoon sugar
1½	cups celery, chopped	3-5	pounds shrimp, peeled and deveined
2	(28-ounce) cans diced tomatoes		Hot rice
1	(6-ounce) can tomato paste		

In a large Dutch oven cook bacon until crisp. Remove bacon but leave the grease and sauté the onions, celery and green peppers until soft. Add tomatoes, tomato paste and cocktail sauce. Simmer for ½ hour or more.

Add Worcestershire sauce and sugar. Add the shrimp about 10 minutes before serving, simmering just long enough to cook the shrimp. Serve over hot rice. Sprinkle crumbled bacon and chopped parsley on top if desired. Enjoy!

I received this recipe from Dorothy Singleton, a great low country cook from South Carolina. She prepared this version of shrimp Creole for a special dinner for the President of Latvia, Vaira Vice-Freidberga, at the Debordieu home of my good friend, former Ambassador Bonnie McElveen-Hunter. I was privileged to have been a guest that weekend.

Shrimp Gumbo

1	cup butter	4	pounds cooked shrimp
3	tablespoons flour		Salt
2	cloves garlic, minced		Parsley
1	large onion, sliced		Bay leaves
1	pound okra, chopped		Tabasco sauce to taste
5	cups water		

Heat butter over low heat in a Dutch oven and stir in flour. When this starts to brown, add onion, okra and garlic and cook until soft. Add the cooked, shelled shrimp and water. Let simmer slowly for 45 minutes. Add seasonings and adjust for taste. Simmer at a very low temperature as the shrimp will overcook if you let them boil. Serves 10-12.

Gourmet Shrimp Creole

The memory of this dish remained with me for nearly ten years. As I was testing over five different shrimp Creole recipes, I kept remembering this particular one which was prepared by a friend, Melanie Ketner, ten years ago. When I called her and asked if she still had the recipe, she told me that it was her mother-in-law's and that she indeed still had it. I prepared it that same night and remembered why I liked it so much.

¼	cup bacon grease	1	cup water
¼	cup flour	5	teaspoons salt
1½	cups onions, chopped	1	teaspoon pepper
1	cup green onions, chopped	½	teaspoon cayenne pepper
1	cup green peppers, chopped		Dash of Tabasco sauce, or more
1	cup celery, chopped	2-3	bay leaves
1	pound fresh mushrooms, sliced	1	teaspoon sugar
3	garlic cloves, minced	1	teaspoon dried thyme
1	(6-ounce) can tomato paste	1	teaspoon curry powder
2	(16-ounce) can chopped stewed tomatoes	1	teaspoon Worcestershire sauce
		3	teaspoons lemon juice
1	(8-ounce) can tomato sauce or more if desired	2	pounds fresh shrimp, peeled and cleaned
		½	cup parsley, chopped for garnish

Make a roux of flour and bacon grease. Add onions, green onions, green pepper, celery and mushrooms and sauté until tender, about 15-20 minutes. Add garlic and continue cooking a few more minutes. Add tomato paste, chopped tomatoes (I use Hunt's stewed tomatoes with onions, celery and green peppers), tomato sauce, water, salt, pepper and other seasonings. Simmer, covered for 1 hour.

Add shrimp and cook until done, 5-15 minutes. This dish is better if make early in the day or the day before so the flavors will blend. However, if time will not allow, it is still delicious right after it is prepared. Correct the seasonings and serve over rice garnished with parsley. Serves 8-10.

New Orleans Jambalaya

An easy version of jambalaya.

1	pound andouille sausage, sliced	5	garlic cloves, minced
½	cup oil	½	teaspoon salt
2	medium onions, chopped	1	pinch cayenne pepper
1	bunch green onions, bulbs plus 3 inches green tops, chopped	2	pounds shrimp, peeled and deveined
½	cup celery, chopped	2	(15-ounce) cans diced tomatoes
1	teaspoon fresh thyme leaves	1	(6-ounce) can tomato paste
2	bay leaves	½	lemon, quartered
		3	cups cooked white rice

Cook sausage in oil until light brown. Add onions, green onions, green pepper, celery, thyme, bay leaves, garlic, salt and cayenne pepper. Cook 5 minutes longer. Add shrimp, tomatoes with liquid, tomato paste and lemon quarters. Simmer slowly, uncovered, tossing often until shrimp are pink. Remove bay leaves and lemon. Stir in rice or serve over rice. Makes 8 servings.

Shrimp and Artichoke Casserole

2	cans marinated artichoke hearts	1	tablespoon Worcestershire sauce
1	pound fresh shrimp, cooked	⅓	cup dry sherry
1	pound mushrooms		Salt and pepper to taste
4½	tablespoons butter	¼	cup Parmesan cheese
4½	tablespoons flour		Paprika and parsley to garnish
1½	cups milk		

Drain artichokes and arrange in a buttered flat baking dish. Spread cooked shrimp over artichokes. Sauté sliced mushrooms in 2 tablespoons butter for 6 minutes. Add to baking dish. Make cream sauce of butter, flour and milk. Add Worcestershire sauce, sherry and salt and pepper and pour over shrimp and vegetables. Bake in preheated 350° oven for 30 minutes. Serves 4-6.

This Jambalaya dish ranks as one of my top ten dishes to prepare. I love the way it smells while everything is cooking. It's so easy yet fun to make. It's always a showstopper at covered dinners and a favorite for a Sunday or weeknight dinner.

This recipe originally did not call for any shrimp. If you don't like or are allergic to seafood, eliminate the shrimp and increase the sausage to 1½ pounds and the chicken to 1½ pounds.

Shrimp, Sausage and Chicken Jambalaya

2	bay leaves
1	teaspoon garlic powder
1½	teaspoons salt
¼	teaspoon cayenne pepper
½	teaspoon white pepper
¼	teaspoon black pepper
1½	cups chopped onions, divided
1½	cups chopped green pepper, divided
1½	cups chopped celery, divided
3	cloves garlic, chopped
½	stick butter
	Tabasco sauce to taste

1-1½	pounds andouille sausage, sliced
1	tablespoon chopped fresh garlic
4	boneless, skinless chicken breasts, cut up
1	pound fresh shrimp, shelled, cleaned
2	cups rice
5-6	cups chicken stock, divided
1¼	cups tomato sauce
1	(15-ounce) can petite diced tomatoes
1	(15-ounce) can Hunt's stewed tomatoes with celery, onions and green peppers

Mix the bay leaves, garlic powder, salt, cayenne powder, white pepper and black pepper in a small bowl. If you like spicy dishes, then increase the cayenne to ½ teaspoon and the white pepper to 1 teaspoon. Sauté 1 cup of the onions, green pepper and celery in the butter in a large wide saucepan or large covered skillet. Add the seasoning mixture, Tabasco sauce if desired, and the chicken and sausage. Cook over medium high heat for 10-15 minutes or until the sausage has browned, stirring constantly.

Add the garlic and more butter if needed. Add the rice and reduce the heat to medium or medium low. Simmer, stirring constantly for about 5-10 minutes.

Stir in 4 cups chicken stock, tomato sauce, remaining onions, celery and green peppers. Bring to a boil and then reduce heat to low. Simmer, covered, for about 15 minutes until the rice is absorbed. Add the shrimp and tomatoes and cook covered another 5 minutes, or until rice is cooked and liquid is absorbed. I always have to add a little more broth – 1-2 cups more. I like my jambalaya a little on the soupy side. Serve with garlic French bread.

Let stand for about 5 minutes and scoop out into serving bowls. Remove the bay leaves before serving. Serves 8-10.

seafood

Shrimp Étouffée

A New Orleans classic!

1	stick butter	1	tablespoon paprika
2	medium onions, chopped	1	teaspoon salt
1	stalk celery, finely chopped	1	teaspoon black pepper
4	garlic cloves, minced		Dash cayenne pepper
1½	teaspoons minced jalapeño pepper	2	pounds shrimp, shelled and deveined
2	tablespoons flour	1	bunch green onions, chopped
1	(14-ounce) can Italian chopped tomatoes, juices reserved	¼	cup chopped parsley
			Hot cooked rice

In a skillet, melt butter and add onions and celery and cook until onions soften. Add the garlic and jalapeño pepper and cook for a couple of minutes. Add the flour and heat, stirring constantly, for about 3-4 minutes.

Stir in the tomatoes and juice, paprika, salt, black pepper and cayenne pepper. Bring to a simmer and cook for 5-10 minutes. Add the shrimp and heat on medium heat until they turn pink, about 3-5 minutes. Stir in the green onions and parsley and serve over cooked rice.

Shrimp Thermidor

¼	cup chopped onion	½	cup grated cheese (or more) – sharp Cheddar
2	tablespoons chopped green pepper		
2	tablespoons butter	2	teaspoons lemon juice
1	can cream of potato soup	1½	cups cooked shrimp, split lengthwise
¾	cup light cream		

Cook onion and pepper in butter until tender but not brown. Add soup and cream. Heat slowly, stirring constantly until blended. Bring just to a boil. Add cheese and stir to melt. Add lemon juice and shrimp. Heat thoroughly and serve in pastry shells (Pepperidge Farms). Serves 4.

Skewered Shrimp Scampi

4-5 jumbo shrimp per person

½ stick butter

4 cloves garlic, minced

1-2 tablespoons
fresh chives, minced

¼ cup lemon juice

Soak wooden skewers
in water for 30 minutes. Peel
shrimp, leaving tails on. Skewer
4-5 jumbo shrimp on each
skewer. Combine remaining
ingredients. Marinate shrimp
for 1-2 hours. Place shrimp
on a hot grill. Baste with the
garlic/butter mixture. Turn after
1 minute. Baste again. Serve
when shrimp are pink.

Shrimp Newberg

1½	pounds fresh shrimp, peeled		Dash cayenne pepper
2	tablespoons butter	3	tablespoons flour
¼	teaspoon salt	⅛	teaspoon black pepper
¼	teaspoon dry mustard	4	tablespoons dry sherry or Vermouth
1½	cups whipping cream	2	egg yolks, well beaten
	Dash Tabasco sauce		Puff pastry shells

In the top level of a double boiler, melt butter. Gradually add flour, blend well. Add salt, pepper, cayenne pepper, Tabasco sauce and dry mustard. Blend together, cooking on low, for 2 minutes. Gradually pour in the cream, stirring constantly, for about 1 minute. When well blended, remove from heat and cool.

Place beaten egg yolks in a large bowl. Gradually add cooled sauce to egg yolks, stirring constantly. Return mixture to top of double boiler, stirring, while keeping water in the lower portion of the double boiler at a low boil or simmer. Add shrimp and sherry or vermouth and heat, stirring about 2 minutes. Do not allow to boil! Serve over puff pastry shells. You can also serve over hot cooked rice.

Pan Roasted Shrimp with Garlic

1	pound shrimp, peeled		Dash of dried red pepper flakes
4	tablespoons extra-virgin olive oil	½	teaspoon salt
4	large garlic cloves, pressed through sieve	4	tablespoons dry white wine
		2	tablespoons chopped fresh parsley

Peel and devein shrimp. Butterfly the shrimp. In a large frying pan, warm the olive oil over medium heat and add the garlic and Tabasco sauce. Sauté over low heat – do not brown the garlic. Add the shrimp and sauté about 2 minutes, turning once and cooking 2 more minutes. They should be white/pink. Add the wine and stir for an additional minute. Remove from heat and sprinkle with parsley. Serve hot with rice or pasta. Serves 3-4.

seafood

Garlic Broiled Shrimp

2	pounds fresh shrimp	1	bunch green onions, diced
½	cup melted butter	¼	cup fresh parsley, chopped
½	cup olive oil		Black pepper to taste
1½	tablespoons lemon juice		
3	cloves garlic, minced		

Devein and butterfly shrimp, leaving tails on. Mix melted butter, olive oil, lemon juice, garlic, green onions and parsley in shallow dish and add shrimp and toss. Cover and marinate at least 30 minutes. Broil shrimp under high broiler 3-4 minutes. Turn over and repeat. Serve with drippings. This is good with pasta or rice and a green vegetable. Serves 6-8.

Wild Rice and Seafood Casserole

2	packages Uncle Ben's Wild Rice (discard seasonings)	½	cup dry white wine
4	tablespoons butter	½	teaspoon salt
1	onion, finely chopped	½	teaspoon garlic salt
1	pound medium whole mushrooms	¼	teaspoon crumbled dried tarragon or 1 teaspoon fresh
	Juice of ½ lemon	3	tablespoons Parmesan cheese
2	tablespoons flour	1	pound cooked shrimp
1¼	cups chicken broth	½	pound crabmeat
1	tablespoon parsley		

Preheat oven to 350°. Cook rice without seasonings. Melt 2 tablespoons butter in large skillet. Add onions and stir. Add whole mushroom caps and stems to pan and sprinkle with lemon juice. Cook gently until tender.

In another pan melt 2 tablespoons butter and blend flour to make roux. Cook for few minutes and add chicken broth and wine, stirring until thick. Season with salt, garlic salt and tarragon. Stir in Parmesan cheese.

Mix ¾ of the sauce, wild rice, mushrooms and seafood. Reserve a few shrimp for garnish. Spoon into 2-quart casserole. Garnish with seafood. Pour the rest of the sauce over the casserole and cover. Bake 45-60 minutes. Sprinkle with chopped fresh parsley before serving. Serves 8-10.

Gourmet Lobster Tails

6-8 small lobster tails or 4 large ones, frozen or fresh

Melted butter

Thaw lobster tails, if frozen. Preheat broiler. Cut tails down through the middle of hard shell with kitchen shears. With a knife, cut through flesh but not underside membrane. Pull flesh out and lay on top. Brush with melted butter and place approximately 4 inches from broiler.

Broil for about 8 minutes. Lobster is done when meat is opaque.

If you prefer to boil the lobster tails, do not cut meat out first. Boil for about 15 minutes and serve with melted butter. Serves 4.

Variation: Prepare a marinade-like the "Garlic Broiled Shrimp" recipe and marinate lobster tails before broiling.

Scalloped Oysters

1 pint oysters, liquid reserved

6 tablespoons cream

½ cup dry bread crumbs

1 cup cracker crumbs

⅓ cup melted butter

In a small bowl combine oyster liquid with 6 tablespoons cream. In another small bowl, combine bread crumbs with cracker crumbs. Plan to use 2 layers of oysters (no more) and 3 layers of bread/cracker crumbs, then build up the other layers of oysters and crumbs.

Season each layer of oysters with salt and paprika and pour ½ cream liquid over each layer. The top layer of crumbs should be dry.

Bake for 20 minutes in a preheated 400° oven. Serves 4.

Shrimp and Crabmeat Casserole

1½	pounds cooked shrimp, peeled	½	cup diced celery
½	pound crabmeat	⅔	cup flour
1	can sliced water chestnuts	½	teaspoon salt
		½	teaspoon garlic salt
4	ounces sliced mushrooms	¼	teaspoon paprika
		⅛	teaspoon cayenne pepper
½	cup melted butter		
½	cup diced green pepper	2	cups milk
½	cup diced onion	1	can cream of shrimp soup

Combine shrimp, crabmeat, water chestnuts and mushrooms. In a large saucepan, sauté green pepper, onion and celery in melted butter. When vegetables are tender, add flour and seasonings. Stir, cooking 1-2 minutes. Add milk gradually stirring constantly.

Stir in cream of shrimp soup. Heat until blended. Combine milk/ soup mixture with shrimp and crabmeat.

Turn into a lightly buttered casserole dish. Let cool, and refrigerate or freeze. Can be frozen for up to 6 months. Bake in a preheated 350° oven for 35-40 minutes. (If casserole has been frozen, bring to refrigerated or room temperature before baking.) Serve over hot rice. Serves 8-10.

Variation: You can add 1 cup of chicken broth if you like to the casserole to make this more saucy. Or you can serve over puff pastry shells. You may also substitute lobster bisque for the cream of shrimp soup. To add a richer taste, add 3 hard-boiled eggs, sliced, and 2 tablespoons sherry to the sauce.

seafood

Chinese Shrimp Casserole

3	cups cooked rice	4	tablespoons butter
½	pound crabmeat	1	pound fresh shrimp
1	(10-ounce) package frozen green peas, thawed	1	can cream of mushroom soup
		1	soup can mayonnaise
1	cup celery	1	(3-ounce) can Chinese noodles
½	cup chopped green pepper		
		1	small package slivered almonds
½	cup onion, chopped		
¼	cup parsley	2	tablespoons butter

Mix rice, crabmeat and peas in a large mixing bowl. Set aside. In a large skillet, sauté celery, onions, green pepper and parsley in 4 tablespoons of butter until soft. Add shrimp and cook until shrimp are pink, about 5 minutes. Cool and add the rice mixture.

Stir together the cream of mushroom soup and mayonnaise. Add seasonings and fold into the rice and seafood mixture. At this point it can be refrigerated.

Just before baking, fold in the Chinese noodles. Sprinkle slivered almonds on top which have been lightly sautéed in 2 tablespoons of butter. Bake in a preheated 375° oven for 30-40 minutes.

Variation: Instead of the cream of mushroom soup/mayonnaise mixture, substitute cream of celery soup, 1 cup of half-and-half and ¼ cup dry sherry.

When my children were small, this casserole was served at both of their christening brunches. It's a great bridal shower casserole as well. It can easily be doubled or tripled to serve large crowds.

Salmon Mousse

1 envelope unflavored gelatin

2 tablespoons lemon juice

½ cup boiling chicken broth

½ cup mayonnaise

¼ cup milk

2 tablespoons
chopped parsley

1 tablespoon
minced green onion

1 teaspoon prepared
Dijon mustard

¼ teaspoon black pepper

7 ounces cooked salmon

½ cup shredded cucumber

Celery leaves

Fresh dill weed

Soften gelatin in lemon
juice in a large bowl. Add
broth and stir to dissolve
gelatin. Add all ingredients
except salmon and cucumber.
Beat until well mixed. Chill
30 minutes or until slightly
thickened. Beat until frothy.
Fold in the salmon. Turn into
mold. Chill 3 hours until firm.
Serve on leaf lettuce with
green olive for the "eyes."
Serve with good crackers
or Melba toast.

Shrimp and Grits

1½	pounds fresh shrimp	1½	tablespoons lemon juice
6	slices bacon		Tabasco sauce
	Peanut or vegetable oil		Chopped parsley for garnish
8	ounces sliced mushrooms		Salt and pepper to taste
1	cup sliced green onions		Cooked grits or cheese grits
2	cloves garlic, minced		

Peel and clean the shrimp. Dice the bacon and cook until crisp in a large skillet. With a slotted spoon remove the bacon and set aside. Add enough oil to the bacon fat to sauté the shrimp. Stir and add the mushrooms in about 2-3 minutes. Add the green onions and minced garlic. Season with the lemon juice, Tabasco sauce, parsley and salt and pepper. Serve over grits or cheese grits.

Variation: You can add sliced andouille sausage, before the mushrooms.

Salmon with Dill Sauce

4	salmon fillets	½	teaspoon prepared mustard
4	tablespoons butter	¾	cup bottled clam broth
1	tablespoon flour	1	egg yolk
¼	teaspoon salt	1	tablespoon lemon juice
¼	teaspoon pepper	1	tablespoon chopped fresh dill

Salt and pepper salmon and broil in hot broiler 4 inches from top for 6 minutes. Meanwhile, make sauce for salmon. In a small saucepan, melt butter and add flour, stirring for about 1 minute. Add salt, pepper, mustard and clam broth, stirring until smooth. In another bowl, put egg yolk, lightly beaten. Pour sauce into egg yolk and stir; then pour mixture back into saucepan. Keep warm and add lemon juice and chopped dill. Serve with salmon. Serves 4.

Flounder Florentine

2	large flounder filets	½	cup grated American cheese
1	package frozen chopped spinach	¾	teaspoon salt
1	teaspoon grated onion		Dash of pepper
4	tablespoons butter	4	hard-boiled eggs
4	tablespoons flour	½	teaspoon prepared mustard
	Salt and pepper to taste	2	teaspoons cream
2	cups milk		

Place a large sheet of aluminum foil on a flat pan or shallow baking dish. Place the largest filet in the center of the foil. Cook spinach 1 minute. Drain. Chop the spinach and season it with the onion, a little butter, salt and pepper. Spoon it over the first fish filet and cover it with the second filet.

Prepare a white sauce with the butter, flour and milk. Add the grated cheese, salt and pepper. Pour over the fish filets. Bring the foil up over the fish, sealing the edges with double folds to make a package. Be sure to have a seal about 2 inches above the bottom of the pan so that the juices will not leak out.

Place in a 425° oven and bake 30 minutes. During this time, prepare 4 hard-boiled eggs. Remove yolks and mash with the mustard, salt, pepper and cream to moisten. Fill egg whites with this yolk mixture. Remove fish from the oven and fold back the foil. Arrange eggs around fish. Spoon a little sauce over each egg. Return to oven with foil open for 10 minutes to brown very lightly. Serve at once with rice and vegetables. Serves 4.

Herb Stuffed Fish

1 pound white fish filets

1 can Campbell's
New England Clam Chowder

½ cup milk

1 cup herb seasoned
stuffing mix

2 tablespoons butter

4 ounces Velveeta
cheese, sliced

In a shallow baking dish arrange fish filets on bottom. Combine soup and milk and pour over fish. Top with stuffing mix and dot with butter. Bake in preheated 350° oven for 25 minutes or until done. Top with cheese slices and continue baking until cheese melts.

Tuna Cashew Casserole

1 (3-ounce) jar
chow-mein noodles

1 can condensed cream of
mushroom soup

¼ cup water

1 can chunky style tuna
(about 1 cup)

¼ pound cashew nuts

1 cup celery, finely diced

¼ cup minced onions

Dash pepper

Salt

Heat oven to 325°. Set
aside ½ cup chow mein
noodles. In a 1½-quart
casserole dish, combine
rest of noodles with next
7 ingredients. Taste; add
salt if nuts were unsalted.
Sprinkle reserved noodles
over top. Bake for 25 minutes.
If preferred, bake in
6 individual casseroles or
scallop shells. Serves 6.

Heavenly Fish

1½	pounds fish fillets	2	tablespoons mayonnaise
1	tablespoon lemon juice	2	tablespoons chopped green onion
⅓	cup grated Parmesan cheese	¼	teaspoon salt
3	tablespoons butter, softened	⅛	teaspoon Tabasco sauce

Pat fish dry with paper towel. In a 2-quart shallow casserole, arrange fillets with thickest meaty areas to outside edge of dish. Brush fillets with lemon juice and let stand for 10 minutes or more. Cover fish and bake at 350° for 15 minutes. Take out and cover fish with cheese/mayonnaise mixture and put back into oven for 10 minutes. Serve with rice and vegetables. Serves 4.

Golden Gate Tuna

½	pound mushrooms, sliced	⅛	teaspoon thyme leaves
½	cup sliced onion		Salt to taste
½	cup slivered green pepper	½	cup sour cream
2	tablespoons salad oil	4	quarts boiling water
3	(7-ounce) cans chunk-style tuna, drained	12	ounces medium egg noodles (about 6 cups cooked)
2	(11-ounce) cans condensed cream of tomato soup	½	cup coarsely chopped filberts
½	cup milk	⅓	cup butter

Sauté mushrooms, onion and green pepper in heated oil. Stir in tuna, soup, milk, thyme and salt to taste. Heat to serving temperature; stir in sour cream. Meanwhile, add 1½ tablespoons salt to rapidly boiling water. Gradually add noodles so that water continues to boil. Cook according to package directions; drain. Serve tuna mixture over noodles. Garnish with chopped parsley. Serves 8.

poultry

Country Captain

2 large chicken breasts, split and skinned

flour, salt, and pepper

shortening

1 onion, finely chopped

1 green pepper, chopped

½ clove garlic, minced

1½ teaspoon curry powder (more or less to taste)

¾ teaspoon salt

¼ teaspoon pepper

1 can tomatoes (20 ounces)

¼ teaspoon each chopped parsley and thyme

cooked long grain rice

¼ cup currants or raisins

¼ cup toasted, blanched almonds.

Dredge chicken in flour, salt, and pepper. In large skillet, brown chicken in shortening; remove to oven-proof casserole and keep hot. Meanwhile, add onion, green pepper and garlic to remaining shortening in skillet; cook and stir until vegetables are tender. Add curry powder, ¾ teaspoon salt, pepper, tomatoes, chopped parsley and thyme. Bring to a boil, pour over chicken.

Bake covered at 350 degrees for about 45 minutes or until chicken is tender.

Remove chicken to large heated platter and around it, pile the cooked rice. Add currants or raisins to sauce mixture and pour over rice. Sprinkle with almonds, garnish with additional parsley.

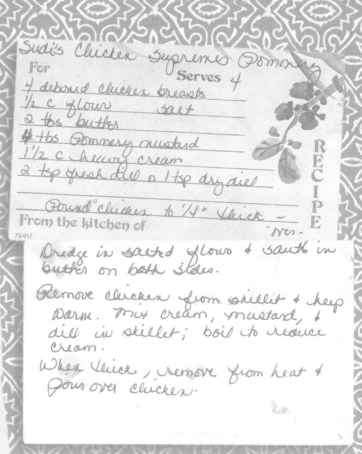

Sudi's Chicken Supreme Pommery

For   **Serves 4**

4 deboned chicken breasts

½ c flour   salt

2 tbs butter

4 tbs Pommery mustard

1½ c heavy cream

2 tsp fresh dill o 1 tsp dry dill

Pound chicken to ¼" thick —

RECIPE

From the kitchen of

75-917

'ver.-

Dredge in salted flour & sauté in butter on both sides.

Remove chicken from skillet & keep warm. Mix cream, mustard, & dill in skillet; boil to reduce cream.

When thick, remove from heat & pour over chicken.

poultry

Chicken Scallopine
(for 1)

1-2 Ts shallots or onion   2 TBS
Chicken breast 3-4
1 TB butter   2 then   3
1 Tsp olive oil
3-4 sliced mushrooms 1pkg
1 TB marsala, or white wine   1/3 cup
lemon juice   1 lemon

Pound chicken lightly between
wax paper; sprinkle w/ S & P.
Heat butter & oil till foamy.
Cook shallots & m'rooms 1 min. ð58.
Add chicken - cook 5 mins. ð
until springs back to Touch.
Remove. Put wine in skillet,
Let bubble. squeeze in
lemon. Let part. of it boil
away. Pour remainder over
chicken.

Chicken Pot Pie.

2 cups cut up chicken.
(2 boil 4 breast pieces
til tender & reserve
1 cup of broth.)
1 lg. pieces of celery
or 2   sautéd in butter.
1 can cr. mushroom soup

use folded pie crust (in
with canned rolls usually)
fold out one shell in
pie pan. Scatter chicken
& celery. add broth &
soup mixed together —
Put top crust on pie —
Bake 375° — about an hr.
til brown —

CHICKEN PIE

4 cooked chicken breasts

1 1/3 Cups chicken broth
1 can chicken soup
½ cup each celery and onion (optional. can also use mush-
                                                    rooms
1 stick butter

1½ cup each of milk and bisquick

cook breasts and reserve broth to use. Saute celery/
onion/ mushrooms in 2 Tbs. of butter. Pour broth
Cut up chicken in bottom of casserole dish.

Add sauted celery,etc if using . Add celery soup.
On top pour bisquick/milk that has been mixed.
Bake 45-60 minutes about 400 degrees.

If taking with me, I mix the chicken, broth and
vegetables together in zip bag. Take along the
can of soup and bisquick with me. Assemble there.
Serves 6-8.

# Chicken Pie

4	cooked split chicken breasts, meat pulled or 1 oven roaster, simmered until tender	½	large onion, chopped (can use 2 bunches green onions if you have them)
1	chicken bouillon cube	¾	cup celery, chopped (about 4 small stalks)
1	can cream celery soup or cream of mushroom soup	½	stick butter
			Salt
1½	soup cans chicken broth	2	pastry sheets, Pillsbury foldout

Gently simmer chicken breasts or roaster in water and bouillon for 1 hour, until meat is tender and pulls easily off the bone. Reserve broth. When slightly cooled, pull meat off the bone with a fork an shred into small pieces.

In a small skillet, sauté the chopped onions and celery until tender in ½ stick of butter. In a small saucepan, heat the cream of celery soup with 1½ soup cans of chicken broth until well mixed.

In a 9-inch pie plate, fold out one of the pastry shells. Place chicken meat on top of the pastry shell and salt and pepper well. Pour sautéed celery and onion (with leftover butter in pan) over top of the chicken. Pour the soup mixture over top of the chicken until covered. You can cover the pie completely with the second pastry shell, pressing down on the ends to secure edge. Be sure to pierce top with sharp knife 7-10 places to let the steam escape. Or, cut pastry into shapes (I like to use hearts or stars) and overlap shapes on the top. Broth will show through and that's okay.

Bake in hot oven 375° for about 45 minutes – 1 hour.

Vegetable Chicken Pie

Follow the same procedure as with the chicken pie. However, after placing the chicken and sautéed onions and celery in the pastry shell, add 1 peeled, chopped carrot, 1 peeled potato cut into small cubes and about ¼ cup frozen peas. Add ½ cup frozen corn or fresh corn cut off the cob, if desired. Follow everything else as directed above.

There are two schools of thought on chicken pie – all white meat with no vegetables, or a more traditional pot pie with peas, carrots, corn and potatoes. Personally, I prefer the all meat version and add my own vegetables to the plate, but sometimes it's easy to throw the vegetables in. Here are both versions.

Easy Chicken Pie

4	chicken breasts	1	stick butter
1⅓	cups chicken broth	1½	cups Bisquick
1	can cream of celery soup or cream of mushroom soup	1½	cups milk
			Salt and pepper
			Celery salt

Stew chicken breasts gently in water or chicken broth until tender. Reserve broth. Tear chicken into pieces and put in a 13x9x2-inch Pyrex dish. Pour 1⅓ cups broth over chicken. Salt and pepper chicken and sprinkle celery salt to taste. Spread soup all over. Cut 1 stick of butter and dab over soup. Mix Bisquick and milk together in small bowl and pour over chicken. Bake in 350° oven for 1 hour.

Variation 1: You can add 2 cubed potatoes, 2 ears of corn – kernels removed, ½ cup carrots and chopped celery and onion which has been sautéed. Pour butter and Bisquick mixture over as directed above.

Variation 2: You can add chopped blanched broccoli and sliced mushrooms to the chicken.

Variation 3: Instead of cream of celery soup, you can use cream of chicken soup or cream of onion.

Chipped Beef Chicken

1	large jar chipped beef	1	cup sour cream
4-6	boneless chicken breasts	1	can cream of mushroom soup
6	slices bacon		

Cover bottom of casserole dish with chipped beef – about 1 layer. Place 4-6 boneless chicken breasts (which have been wrapped with 1 piece of bacon) on top of the chipped beef. Mix together the sour cream with the cream of mushroom soup and spread over chicken and chipped beef. Bake covered for 1 hour in a 350° oven. After 1 hour, uncover and continue baking another ½ hour. Serve with hot rice and vegetables.

Grilled Barbecued Chicken

2	whole chickens, cut into quarters or 8 chicken breasts		Salt
		1	stick butter or 1 cup olive oil

Wash chicken well and pat dry. A couple of hours before cooking, liberally salt chicken. When ready to grill, melt butter or have 1 cup olive oil ready in a bowl. To grill, set grill at medium high and place chicken on grill bony side down (skin side up). Immediately brush top side with butter or oil. After 15 minutes, turn chicken and baste with butter or oil again.

Turn heat to low and cook for about 30 minutes covered. Turn chicken and baste with butter a couple of times during the grill time; 5 minutes before removing chicken from grill, baste both sides of chicken liberally with barbecue sauce. Save extra sauce to serve at the table.

Chicken Scaloppine

3-4	boneless, skinless chicken breasts	8	ounces sliced mushrooms
2	tablespoons chopped shallots	⅓	cup Marsala wine or other white wine
3	tablespoons butter		Juice of 1 lemon
2	tablespoons olive oil		

Pound boneless chicken lightly between waxed paper; sprinkle with salt and pepper. In a large skillet, heat butter and olive oil until foamy. Cook shallots and mushrooms for a couple of minutes. Add chicken and cook for about 5 minutes, or until it springs back to touch. Turn chicken and continue cooking 3-4 more minutes. Remove chicken from pan. Put wine in skillet and heat to bubbling. Squeeze in juice of 1 lemon and let it reduce for several minutes. Pour sauce over chicken and serve with rice or noodles.

Barbecue Sauce

1 sliced onion

2 tablespoons oil

2 tablespoons dark brown sugar

Salt

Several dashes Tabasco sauce

½ cup water

2 cloves garlic, minced

In a small saucepan, gently sauté onion in oil for 5 minutes or until soft, but not brown. Add all other ingredients and cook over medium heat for about 30 minutes. You may strain the sauce if you want a smooth sauce or serve as is.

Variation: Recipe may be doubled. If you do not want to grill the chicken, you may place the chicken pieces in a large roasting pan or casserole dish and pour barbecue sauce over chicken, cover and bake at 325° for 2 hours.

Bubba's Baked Barbecued Chicken

6-8	chicken pieces		3	tablespoons Worcestershire sauce
⅓	cup oil		2	tablespoons prepared mustard
¾	cup ketchup or small can tomato sauce		2	teaspoons salt
½	cup water		½	teaspoon black pepper
½	cup vinegar			
3	tablespoons sugar			

Mix all ingredients and pour over chicken pieces which have been placed in a large frying pan or electric skillet. Cover chicken with sauce and cook over low heat until cooked through. If cooking in the oven, prepare the same way.

Mom's Fried Chicken

	Vegetable oil		1	cup seasoned flour, divided
6	chicken pieces (I use breasts)		½	cup milk
	Salt and pepper to taste			

In an electric skillet or large cast iron skillet, heat oil to 350°. Use enough oil to cover bottom of pan about ¼-½-inch thick. You won't be deep frying the chicken. While oil is heating, rinse and dry chicken pieces. You can keep the skin on or take off. Salt and pepper chicken. Divide the flour into two bowls of about ½ cup flour which has been seasoned to your liking. Pour milk in third bowl. When oil is hot, dip chicken in flour, then milk, then other bowl of flour and place in skillet breast side down.

Cook until chicken is light brown, about 10 minutes per side. After you have turned the chicken and cooked for 10 minutes or so, cover the skillet and cook for 5-10 minutes. Then remove the lid and continue frying until browned and fork tender. Remove from pan and drain on paper towels until ready to eat. Serve hot or at room temperature.

Sarah's Oven Fried Chicken

Vegetable oil	¼-⅓ cup flour
Flour	Water or chicken broth
Salt, pepper, paprika	Salt
6-8 chicken pieces	

Put enough oil in the broiler pan to have ⅛-inch coverage of oil. Heat pan with oil at 500°. Meanwhile, flour chicken by shaking the pieces in a bag of seasoned flour. Carefully take out the pan of scalding hot oil, and arrange the chicken in the pan. Reduce the temperature to 400°. Cook the chicken for 30 minutes, turn and cook 30 minutes longer. Serve with Chicken Gravy.

Chicken and Dumplings

1½	cups self-rising flour	½	cup chicken broth
2	tablespoons shortening	1	large fryer or hen
		1	stick butter

Boil chicken in generous amount of water until tender, adding salt and pepper to taste and add butter. Once tender, remove chicken from pot and strain broth. Measure at least 2 quarts and put back into pot. Pull meat from chicken in pieces and reserve.

In a bowl, mix flour and shortening and add warm chicken broth to make a firm dough. Cover and let stand 5 or 10 minutes. Divide in 3 parts and roll each part very thin on a floured board. Bring measured chicken broth in large pot to a full boil.

Cut dough into 2-inch strips and break strips about 1½ inches long, drop into boiling broth 1 piece at a time. Cook uncovered at least 10 minutes, reduce heat and cook 20 more minutes covered. Add chicken meat and serve in large bowl or serving dish.

Chicken Gravy

¼-⅓ cup flour

Chicken drippings left in pan

Water or chicken broth

Salt and pepper

To make chicken gravy, mix about ¼-⅓ cup flour to the drippings left in the pan after chicken is removed. Stir until dripping absorbs the flour. Add water or broth until desired consistency, stirring constantly over medium heat. Add salt and pepper to taste.

Back in the 80's clay pots were popular ways of preparing chicken and other meats. If you still have a clay pot, pull it out and try this version of roasted chicken and vegetables.

Clay Pot Chicken

1	(3-pound) whole chicken roaster	¼	cup dry vermouth
1	tablespoon butter	¼	cup chicken broth
1	large onion, finely chopped	½	teaspoon salt
2	cloves garlic, chopped	½	teaspoon pepper
2	carrots, finely chopped	2	tablespoons chopped parsley
2	stalks celery, chopped	1	tablespoon cornstarch dissolved in 2 tablespoons water, optional
3	tablespoons lemon juice		

Soak pot for 30 minutes in water. Drain water off and rub butter over chicken. Salt and pepper well. Place vegetables in pot and chicken on top of vegetables. Add lemon juice, vermouth, broth and parsley. Salt and pepper entire pot. Cover with clay pot cover and bake in 450° oven for 1½ hours. Pour pan juices in a pan and bring to boil on the stove. Stir in the dissolved cornstarch and keep stirring until thick. Cut chicken in pieces and serve on platter. Pour sauce over.

Day's Jalapeño Chicken

4-6	chicken breasts, cooked – meat torn into pieces, broth reserved	1	small jar chopped pimientos, drained
1	cup celery, chopped	1	large jar Cheese Whiz
1	cup onion, chopped	1	(16-ounce) can English peas
½	green pepper, chopped	8	ounces or more spaghetti, cooked in broth
1	(10-ounce) can Rotel tomatoes with jalapeños		

Sauté celery, onion, peppers. Cook spaghetti in chicken broth and drain. In a large bowl, mix spaghetti with sautéed vegetables. Add Cheese Whiz and mix in all other ingredients. Add salt and pepper to taste. Bake at 350° until bubbly, about 20-30 minutes.

Baked Chicken and Rice

1	small box of uncooked minute rice	1½	cans chicken broth mixed with both soups
1	can cream of mushroom soup	5-6	chicken pieces on the bone (you can use all breasts if you wish)
1	can cream of celery soup	1	package dry Lipton onion soup mix

Grease a 9x13-inch casserole dish well. Cover bottom of dish with uncooked minute rice. Mix the two soups together with 1½ cans chicken broth and pour over rice. Lay chicken pieces on top of this. Sprinkle 1 package of dry Lipton onion soup mix over chicken. Cover tightly with aluminum foil and bake for 3 hours at 300-325°. Do not open foil while the chicken is cooking.

Country Captain

2	large chicken breasts, split and skinned	1	(20-ounce) can chopped tomatoes
	Flour, salt and pepper	¼	teaspoon chopped parsley
	Vegetable oil	¼	teaspoon chopped thyme
1	onion, finely chopped		
1	green pepper, chopped		Cooked long-grain white rice
½	clove garlic, minced		
1½	teaspoons curry powder	¼	cup raisins or currants
¾	teaspoon salt	¼	cup toasted, blanched almonds
¼	teaspoon pepper		

Dredge chicken in flour, salt and pepper. In a large skillet, brown chicken in oil. Remove to a large casserole dish and keep hot. Meanwhile, add onion, green pepper and garlic to remaining oil in skillet. Cook and stir until vegetables are tender. Add curry powder, salt, pepper, tomatoes, chopped parsley and thyme. Bring to a boil, and pour over chicken. Bake covered at 350° for 45 minutes or until chicken is tender. Remove chicken to a large platter and pile hot cooked rice around it. Add raisins or currants to sauce mixture and pour over rice. Sprinkle with almonds and garnish with parsley.

Bride's Chicken Casserole

An old Burlington favorite!

4 cups cooked chicken
(about 3 large breasts)

1 can French
style green beans

1 can white
whole kernel corn

¼ cup green pepper, chopped

¼ cup onion, chopped

½ cup celery, finely chopped

1 cup Cheddar cheese

1 cup sour cream

1 can cream of celery soup

1 sleeve Ritz crackers

1 stick butter, melted

Chop chicken breasts into small pieces. Mix all ingredients except Ritz crackers and butter and pour into a large buttered casserole dish. Crush Ritz crackers in a bowl and pour melted butter over it and mix until well coated. Sprinkle buttered crackers on top of casserole and bake at 350° for about 45 minutes. Serve with rice.

Chicken-Wild Rice Casserole

2	(3-pound) whole broiler fryer chickens	1	pound fresh mushrooms
1	cup water	¼	cup butter
1	cup sherry	2	(6-ounce) packages long-grain and wild rice with seasonings
1½	teaspoons salt		
½	teaspoon curry powder	1	cup commercial sour cream
1	medium onion, sliced		
½	cup sliced celery	1	can cream of mushroom soup

Place chickens in deep pot or Dutch oven; add water, sherry, salt, curry powder, onion, and celery. Cover and bring to a boil; reduce heat and simmer for 1 hour. Remove from heat; strain broth.

When chicken is cool, remove meat from bones and discard skin. Cut meat into bite size pieces. Slice mushrooms and sauté in butter for about 5 minutes, stirring. Reserve a few caps for garnish, but sauté along with sliced mushrooms.

Measure chicken broth and use as part of liquid for cooking rice, following directions on package. Don't overcook rice. Combine chicken, mushrooms and cooked rice in large 3½ or 4-quart casserole. Blend in sour cream and mushroom soup and toss with chicken-rice mixture. Arrange reserved mushroom caps on center of casserole. Cover and refrigerate if desired. To heat, bake covered at 350° for 1 hour. Makes 8-10 servings.

poultry

Chicken Quesadillas

These are perfect for children and grown-ups alike!

3½	cups shredded cooked rotisserie chicken (Buy the grocery store cooked chicken.)	2	tablespoons butter
		2	large garlic cloves, minced
¼	teaspoon salt	2	cups Monterey Jack cheese (with or without peppers)
½	teaspoon pepper	8	(7-inch) flour tortillas
1	large onion, chopped	2	tablespoons oil

Pull chicken meat from Rotisserie chicken with a fork. Shred the chicken into small pieces. Sprinkle the chicken with the ½ teaspoon salt and ¼ teaspoon pepper. Reserve the other ¼ teaspoon salt and pepper. Cook onions with remaining salt and pepper in butter until tender. Do not brown. Add garlic and cook on low heat another minute or so. Transfer to a bowl and add chicken to onion and garlic. Add cheese to bowl and stir. Toss around to coat chicken.

Lay tortilla flat and spread ½ cup mixture on half of tortilla, then fold over to form a half-moon. Press firmly around the edge. Put together the other quesadillas in the same manner. Heat a large non-stick skillet with oil on medium until pretty hot and place tortillas in pan – you'll probably be able to get 2-3 in a pan at a time. Cook for about 2 minutes and turn quesadilla over and continue cooking until cheese is melted. Transfer to a plate and tent to keep warm until rest of the quesadillas are cooked. Cut in half and serve with black beans, tomato salsa and rice.

Chicken and Asparagus Cassolettes

2	cups cooked white rice	⅓	cup milk
1	small jar chopped pimientos	1	can cream of mushroom soup
1	bunch cooked asparagus	½	teaspoon salt
		⅛	teaspoon black pepper
2	cups diced cooked chicken	½	cup grated sharp Cheddar cheese

Grease 4 (10-ounce) individual baking dishes. Place ½ cup cooked rice in each dish. Divide the pimiento between the four dishes. Halve the asparagus spears and divide between dishes. Top with chicken. Mix together the soup, milk, salt and pepper. Pour over the chicken. Divide the cheese between the baking dishes, sprinkling it on top. Cover and store in the refrigerator. Remove and allow dishes to come to room temperature and bake for 30 minutes in a 350° oven. You can use a 1½-quart casserole dish and layer entire amounts of rice, asparagus, chicken, soup and cheese.

Chicken Noodle Supreme

3	chicken breasts, cooked and cubed	1	can cream of chicken soup
1	(8-ounce) package wide egg noodles	1	soup can chicken broth
1	green pepper, finely chopped	1½	cups grated Cheddar cheese
1	can whole kernel corn		Bread crumbs or Ritz cracker crumbs
1	large jar pimientos	½	stick butter melted

Cook noodles in large saucepan with cream of chicken soup and 1 soup can of chicken broth mixed together for about 10 minutes or until they are tender. Mix together with the cooked chicken pieces, green pepper, canned corn, pimientos and cheese. Pour into a large casserole dish and sprinkle with buttered Ritz crackers or bread crumbs. Bake for 30 minutes in a 350° oven.

Stir-Fried Lemon Sesame Cashew Chicken

This is one of our favorites!

3	chicken breasts, cut into small pieces	3	carrots, sliced thin
½	cup lemon juice	1	green pepper, sliced thin
1	bunch green onions		Optional: broccoli, red pepper or asparagus
¼	cup chicken broth	¼	cup cashews
¼	cup honey	1-3	tablespoons oil, depending on number of vegetables cooking
¼	cup dry sherry or Vermouth		
4	tablespoons soy sauce		

Marinate chicken in marinade for an hour or more. In a small bowl, mix together chicken broth, honey, sherry or vermouth, lemon juice and soy sauce. Stir fry green onions and then carrots, green pepper and any other vegetables in 1 tablespoon oil. You may need to add 1-2 more tablespoons of oil to the pan and heat. Add chicken and stir fry until cooked. Add chicken broth mixture and sprinkle with cashews. Heat a few more minutes and serve over rice or noodles.

Lemon Sesame Marinade

Zest of 1 lemon

1 slice ginger

⅛ cup dry sherry or vermouth

½ teaspoon oil

½ cup parsley, chopped

2 cloves garlic

1 teaspoon lemon juice

½ teaspoon sesame oil

1 teaspoon cornstarch

Mix all ingredients together and marinate chicken for 1 or more hours.

Chicken Supremes Pommery

As a new bride this was one of my husband's favorite elegant dinners.

4	boneless, skinless chicken breasts	4	tablespoons Pommery mustard
½	cup flour	1½	cups heavy cream
	Salt	2	teaspoons fresh chopped dill or 1 teaspoon dried dill
2	tablespoons butter		

Between sheets of waxed paper, pound chicken to ¼-inch thick. Dredge chicken breasts in salted flour and sauté in butter on both sides, about 5 minutes per side. Remove chicken from skillet and keep warm. Mix cream, mustard and dill in skillet; boil to reduce cream and thicken. When thick, remove from heat and pour over chicken. Serve with hot rice and vegetables.

Easy Chicken
à la King

3 cups cooked chicken meat

1½ cans cream of celery soup

6 eggs, hard-boiled and cut

½ cup green pepper, chopped

Onion seasoning to taste

Seasoning salt to taste

Salt and pepper

½ cup mushrooms, sliced

1 cup celery cooked
with the chicken

Mix all of the ingredients
and heat in a chafing dish for
company. Serve over pastry
shells or toast.

Chicken à la King

*When I was a child this was a Sunday night favorite because
we served it over puff pastry shells – that was the best part.*

2	tablespoons butter	3	cups chicken, cooked and cubed
½	cup green pepper, finely chopped	1	stick butter, room temperature
1	cup sliced mushrooms	3	egg yolks
2	tablespoons flour	1	teaspoon onion juice
½	teaspoon salt	1	teaspoon lemon juice
2	cups whole milk or half-and-half	½	teaspoon paprika
			Toast or pastry shells

In the top of a double boiler, heat 2 tablespoons butter – on direct heat at first, you will put it on the double boiler later. Add green peppers and mushrooms and cook for about 5 minutes. Stir in flour and salt and cook until light brown and frothy, constantly stirring. Gradually stir in milk or half-and-half and continue heating until sauce has thickened, stirring often.

Remove the pan from direct heat and set over hot water in double boiler. Add the cooked chicken and stir. Cover pan and let stand, keeping water in the bottom boiler hot, but not boiling. You want this mixture to stay warm. Meanwhile, in a mixing bowl, cream the softened butter and beat in egg yolks, lemon juice, onion juice and paprika. Pour this egg/butter mixture into the chicken mixture in the double boiler, and continue stirring until the sauce thickens at little. Serve hot over toast or in pastry shells.

Chicken Divine

1	large whole broiler-roaster chicken or		Dash Worcestershire sauce	
4	large chicken breasts		Salt, pepper and paprika to taste	
2	celery stalks	½	pound grated Cheddar cheese (1 cup or so)	
¼	onion	1	large bunch broccoli, cooked crisp tender	
5-6	tablespoons butter			
5-6	tablespoons flour	½	sleeve Ritz crackers, crushed	
1	quart milk			
	Garlic salt and onion salt to taste	¼	stick butter, melted	

Stew a large roaster chicken with the celery and onion until tender – about 1 hour. Pull meat off the bone in large pieces. In a saucepan make a thick white sauce by melting 5-6 tablespoons of butter and adding flour and blending until smooth. Add milk and continue heating until sauce is thick. Season sauce with garlic salt, onion salt, Worcestershire sauce, salt, pepper and paprika. Once thick, add about 1 cup grated cheese and blend until cheese is melted.

In a large casserole dish layer the chicken pieces on bottom. Cut broccoli in large spears and layer on top of the chicken. Pour cheese sauce over chicken and broccoli. Top with crushed Ritz crackers that have been mixed with melted butter and heat in a 350° oven for 30-40 minutes until sauce has bubbled over the broccoli.

Stuffed Chicken Breasts

4	bone-in chicken breasts	½	cup frozen chopped spinach, thawed
1	cup crabmeat		Thinly cut lemon slices
½	cup shredded Swiss cheese		Melted butter, garlic salt and black pepper

Wash chicken breasts and pat dry. Carefully cut a slit in the side of each chicken breast to form a deep pocket. Put aside. In a bowl, combine thawed spinach, crabmeat and Swiss cheese. Stuff cheese mixture in pockets in chicken. Brush both sides of chicken with melted butter. Cut thin slices of lemon and slide lemon slice under the skin on top of the crabmeat mixture.

Place chicken in a shallow casserole dish skin side up and sprinkle with garlic salt and pepper. Cover with foil and bake for 45 minutes at 350°. Remove foil and broil for a few minutes until the skin is browned.

Variation: Add or substitute chopped artichoke hearts, chopped cooked broccoli or add wild rice and walnuts.

Baked Chicken Jambalaya

2	tablespoons oil	2½	cups stewed tomatoes
1	cup onion, finely chopped	1	cup raw white rice
1	cup green pepper, finely chopped	1½	cups chicken broth
2	cloves garlic, chopped	1	tablespoon chopped parsley
1	cup diced cooked chicken	¼	teaspoon chili powder
1	cup diced cooked ham	1½	teaspoons salt
2	cups andouille sausage, sliced	¼	teaspoon pepper
			Frozen green peas, defrosted

Cook rice according to directions and put aside. Preheat oven to 350°. Put oil in large skillet and heat. Cook sausage for 10 minutes. Add onion, green pepper and garlic. Cook slowly, stirring until onion and pepper are tender. Add chicken and ham and cook another 5 minutes.

Add tomatoes with their liquid, the cooked rice, broth, parsley, chili powder, salt and pepper and peas. Turn mixture into a large casserole dish. Cover and bake for 15-20 minutes.

Roast Turkey or Chicken

1	(6 to 8-pound) roasting chicken or 1 (12 to 16-pound) turkey	⅓	cup chopped fresh tarragon
1	cup butter, softened		Salt
½	cup finely chopped shallots	½	onion, halved
		2	stalks celery
		1	carrot, cut into pieces

Preheat oven to 400°. Wash fresh chicken or turkey in cold water, cleaning well and removing any giblet pieces in the inside of the bird. Pat dry and salt and pepper chicken or turkey well. Stuff ½ onion, 2 stalks celery and 1 carrot in the inside of the bird. In a small bowl, mix the butter, shallots, and tarragon together. Spread the butter mixture up under the breast skin, working your way under the skin. Massage butter into bird. Spread rest of butter over top of bird over breasts and around legs. Place turkey or chicken breast side up on a roasting rack in the middle of a heavy duty roasting pan.

For chicken, roast in a hot oven for 15 minutes. Turn heat down to 325° and continue cooking for about 1 hour more. A (6 to 8-pound) chicken should be ready by that time. If chicken is closer to 8 pounds, it might take another 10 minutes or so. If chicken is smaller than 6 pounds, it will probably be ready in 1 hour total (45 minutes from time heat was turned down).

For turkey: roast in hot oven for 15 minutes. Open oven and place an aluminum foil tent over turkey breast to keep from browning too much. Place meat thermometer through the foil "breast plate" in the thickest part of the breast, not touching the bone. Turn down heat to 350° and return turkey to oven. Continue cooking at 350° for 2-2½ hours. Do not open oven door except to check thermometer at the end or better yet, use an instant read thermometer that you can read outside of the door. Remove turkey when thermometer reads at about 165-170°. The temperature will go up after you remove it and the tent of foil will keep it warm. Do not carve turkey for at least 20-30 minutes. You want the juices to stay in the bird – if you cut it too quickly, they will run out.

Serve with Turkey Gravy and Corn Bread Dressing.

Turkey Gravy

For thin gravy use 1 tablespoon each fat and flour for each cup liquid.

For thick gravy use 3 tablespoons fat and 3 tablespoons flour for each cup liquid.

For liquid, use water, milk or broth from cooked giblets.

After turkey has cooked, pour drippings from pan into a measuring cup. Measure drippings and pour calculated amount back into roasting pan. Place over very low heat and stir in desired amount of flour. Be sure to blend flour and fat well with a gravy whisk. Cook until bubbly, stirring constantly. Remove pan from heat and add liquid – either broth or milk. Pour lightly into pan all at once. Put back on heat and cook until thick, stirring constantly. For giblet gravy, stir in cooked, diced giblets and 1-2 hard-boiled eggs, chopped. Salt and pepper to taste.

Leftover Turkey Casserole

1 cup cooked
leftover turkey, chopped

1 can cream of chicken soup

1 cup celery, chopped

1 teaspoon onion, minced

½ cup mayonnaise

2 hard-boiled eggs, chopped

½ cup almonds

½ cup cracker crumbs

Potato chips

Lightly toss together all
ingredients except potato chips.
Turn into casserole. Cover with
potato chips. Bake at 350° for
about 30 minutes.

**Variation: Add 1 tablespoon
lemon juice and pimientos
to casserole. Add grated
cheese to potato chips.**

Turkey Tetrazzini

½	pound spaghetti		2	tablespoons Worcestershire sauce
1	cup diced celery			
1	cup green pepper, chopped		2	cups chopped cooked turkey
¼	cup onion, chopped		½	pound sharp Cheddar cheese, grated
½	pound mushrooms, sliced			
½	cup butter		¾	cup Parmesan cheese, grated
¼	cup flour		1-1½	cups bread crumbs, buttered with ½ stick melted butter
2	cups milk			
2	teaspoons salt			
¼	teaspoon pepper			

Cook spaghetti and drain. Make the sauce by sautéing the celery, pepper, onion and mushrooms in butter in a large saucepan or skillet. Sauté vegetables until onion is transparent. Add the flour and blend well. Add the milk, all at once. Cook and stir constantly until thick. Blend in cheese, salt and pepper, Worcestershire sauce and turkey. Stir until cheese melts. Don't overheat.

In a large casserole dish (or small ones if you like) place a thick layer of noodles and pour sauce over top. Sprinkle buttered bread crumbs with Parmesan cheese on top. Bake in a 350° oven for 15-20 minutes if baking right after casserole is assembled. If you refrigerate or freeze, then you will need to allow extra time for baking, approximately 40 minutes.

Variation: Instead of 1 quart milk, stir in 2 cups chicken broth and blend until thickened and smooth. Add 1 cup cream, along with 2 tablespoons dry sherry. You can add pimientos to the mixture instead of using green peppers.

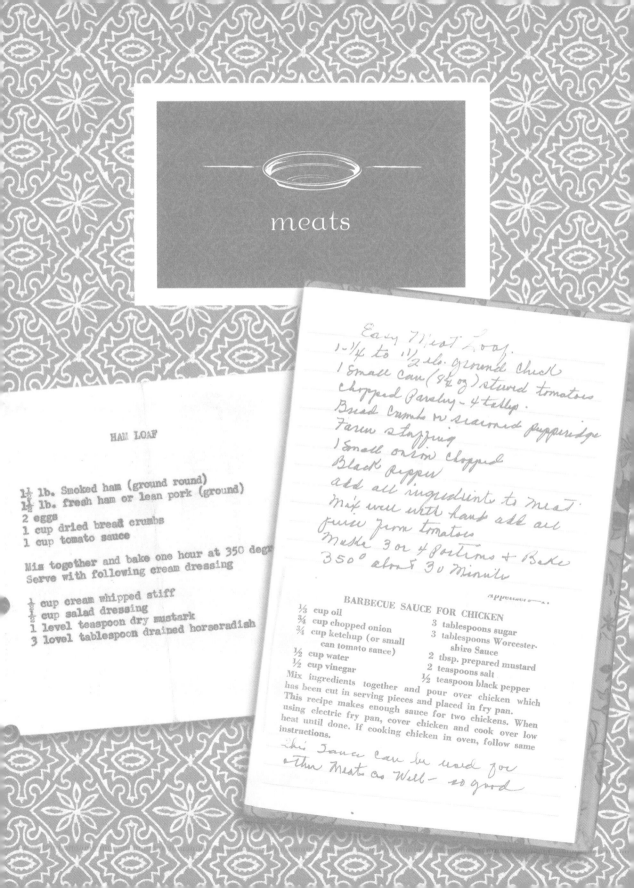

meats

Easy Meat Loaf

1-1/4 to 1-1/2 lb. ground chuck
1 small can (8½ oz) stewed tomatoes
chopped Parsley — 4 tablsp.
Bread crumbs or seasoned Pepperidge
Farm stuffing
1 small onion chopped
Black Pepper
add all ingredients to meat.
Mix well with hand add all
juice from tomatoes
Make 3 or 4 Portions & Bake
350° about 30 Minutes

HAM LOAF

1½ lb. Smoked ham (ground round)
1½ lb. fresh ham or lean pork (ground)
2 eggs
1 cup dried bread crumbs
1 cup tomato sauce

Mix together and bake one hour at 350 degr
Serve with following cream dressing

½ cup cream whipped stiff
½ cup salad dressing
1 level teaspoon dry mustark
3 level tablespoon drained horseradish

BARBECUE SAUCE FOR CHICKEN

⅓ cup oil
¾ cup chopped onion
¾ cup ketchup (or small can tomato sauce)
½ cup water
½ cup vinegar
3 tablespoons sugar
3 tablespoons Worcestershire Sauce
2 tbsp. prepared mustard
2 teaspoons salt
½ teaspoon black pepper

Mix ingredients together and pour over chicken which has been cut in serving pieces and placed in fry pan. This recipe makes enough sauce for two chickens. When using electric fry pan, cover chicken and cook over low heat until done. If cooking chicken in oven, follow same instructions.

This Sauce can be used for
other Meats as Well — so good

meats

As a child I grew up eating beef or chicken most every night. We were a meat and two vegetable family. Friday night was almost always reserved for a big family steak on the grill. Hamburger, pot roast, country style cube steak, meat loaf and Sunday roast beef were staples each week. Pork chops, fried chicken or fish might provide an alternative. Potatoes or rice complimented the beef with peas, green beans or a salad, and bread, usually biscuits, completing the meal. My father taught me to love rare steak and hamburgers – back in a time when it was safe to eat your ground beef rare.

Those are good memories – family suppers where we actually talked about important things and Sunday meals after church with lots of relatives dropping by for Sunday afternoon visits. It represented a slower time – a nice quality of life.

Many of my friends shy away from eating much beef, but I still to this day vary our family meals with a mean pot roast, prime rib, steaks on the grill, hamburgers, country style steak, beef stews and meatloaf. And as my mother did, I nearly always serve creamed potatoes and broccoli, asparagus or green beans. You'll see some sophisticated beef dishes listed as well – those are usually reserved for holidays and company.

Lee's Stuffed Beef Tenderloin

Impress your guests with this special dish!

1	cup green onions, chopped
4	garlic cloves, minced
8	ounces mushrooms, sliced
¼	cup butter
¼	cup chopped parsley

1	whole beef tenderloin, trimmed
¼	teaspoon seasoned salt
¼	teaspoon black pepper
1	(4-ounce) package crumbled blue cheese

Marinade:

¼	cup olive oil
½	soy sauce
1½	cups Worcestershire sauce

1	cup good quality cooking Sherry or red wine
	Garlic powder

Sauté onions, garlic and mushrooms in butter. Add parsley and set aside. Butterfly trimmed tenderloin lengthwise to within 1-inch of the other side. Sprinkle beef with salt and pepper. Spoon mushroom mixture along the opened beef and top with blue cheese. Fold meat over and tie securely with kitchen twine.

Place tenderloin in a large pan and pour marinade over. Baste every few hours for 8 hours or place in a 2 gallon Ziploc bag and roll beef over. Optional: Press crushed peppercorns onto both sides.

Grill over medium heat, tented, until 140° or medium rare, or bake in a 350° oven to the same temperature. Let set 10 minutes before slicing.

Easy Beef Tenderloin

1 whole beef tenderloin, trimmed

Salt and pepper

Liberally salt and pepper beef tenderloin on all sides. Tuck small piece of tenderloin under large piece. Preheat oven to 400° and heat tenderloin 10 minutes per pound for medium rare. Let the beef rest for 15 minutes before slicing. If the small piece is too rare, cut it off and heat some more. Slice in thin slices and serve while warm or at room temperature on rolls with horseradish sauce.

Standing Rib Roast
is one of my favorite
holiday dishes and always
one of the best! Even after
working in the kitchen all
Christmas day, this never
ever fails to taste good to
me. If given the option,
buy Hereford beef, the
best you can get. It will
make a difference.

Yorkshire Pudding

*This is another recipe
from my friend David Grimes –
it was his mother's.*

2 eggs

1 cup all-purpose flour

1 cup milk

½ teaspoon salt

3 tablespoons
Roast Beef drippings

Preheat oven to 350°.
In a bowl, beat eggs, milk, flour
and salt until smooth. Pour
roast beef drippings into a
10-inch pie plate and tilt to
coat bottom and sides of pan.
Pour the batter in pan on top of
drippings. Bake for 25 minutes
or until deep golden brown.
Slice and serve with standing
rib roast, gravy and
mashed potatoes.

Mel's Christmas Standing Rib Roast

1	(9 to 9½-pound) standing rib roast (about 4 ribs) Kosher salt	1	stick butter
		6-7	garlic cloves, minced
		1	tablespoon freshly ground black pepper

Beef Jus:

½ stick butter   ½-¾ cup dry red wine
2½ cups beef broth

I always ask for the first cut of the standing rib roast. It's a little larger than the end of the standing rib. Get your butcher to cut meat away from rib bones and tie back together. Take standing rib roast out of the refrigerator about ½-1 hour before putting in the oven. Preheat oven to 450°. Place roast – bone side down, fat side up – in a heavy roasting pan. Sprinkle entire rib roast with kosher salt (I use kosher or fleur de sel) and rub into fat and meat on top and sides.

Soften 1 stick of butter in a bowl and add 6-7 crushed garlic cloves and 1 tablespoon freshly ground black pepper. Mix together until all 3 ingredients are blended. Reserve 1 tablespoon for the beef jus you'll make later. With the spoon scoop small amounts of the butter out of the bowl and spread all over the roast. Use the back of the spoon to spread and press the butter down. Insert a meat thermometer in the widest part of the prime ribs, being sure that the thermometer does not touch the bone.

Place pan in the oven with the largest side facing the back. Heat in 450° oven for 15 minutes. Then lower heat to 325-350° and continue cooking for about 2-2½ hours. Take the roast out when the meat thermometer reads 125°. Remove roast from roasting pan and place the roast on a large platter. Tent with aluminum foil to keep warm. Do NOT cut roast for at least fifteen minutes – even longer – you want the juices to stay in the meat. If you cut the roast too soon, all the juices will run out onto the platter.

While the roast is standing, drain all but about 2 tablespoons of fat from the roasting pan, being careful to keep the little bits from leaving. Put the roasting pan over two burners and add 2½ cups beef broth and ½-¾ cup dry red wine. Boil until there is about 1½ cups liquid is remaining – about 10 minutes. Add ½ stick butter and 1 tablespoon of the reserved garlic butter and melt into the reduced jus. Pour into a gravy boat and serve with the prime rib.

Slice prime rib and serve with jus. This will make enough for 8-12 people, maybe more.

meats

 # Childhood Pot Roast

1	(2 to 3-pound) boneless chuck roast (or bone in)	2	additional cans beef broth
2	tablespoons flour	1	cup red wine, optional
2	teaspoons salt	6	whole small onions or shallots, peeled
¼	teaspoon pepper	4	carrots cut up in large pieces
3	tablespoons oil		
½	cup onion, chopped	4	medium potatoes, peeled and cut in half or 8 small new potatoes, peeled and left whole
½	cup celery, chopped		
1	package Lipton onion soup mix, optional		
1	can beef broth		

Combine flour with salt and pepper. Rub outside of meat with this mixture. Heat oil in a large wide heavy pot or Dutch oven – one of the largest pots you have. Or, use a large electric skillet. It must be heavy or beef will burn. Add roast and brown slowly over moderate heat. Turn meat to brown on all sides.

Add chopped onion and celery and Lipton's onion soup sprinkled over roast. Add 1 can beef broth. Cover pot tightly and cook over very low heat for about an hour or more. Add additional beef broth and red wine after roast has cooked for an hour or so. You want enough liquid with the roast so that it comes up about halfway to the roast – not covering it. You want vegetables to be in liquid.

After meat has been cooking for about 1½-2 hours, add cut potatoes, carrots and small whole onions or shallots. Try to get them in the liquid around the roast. Season entire pot with plenty of salt and pepper when you add the vegetables. Simmer for another 1½ hours or more, for a total of 3-4 hours. Pot roast will be fork tender. Serve roast on a large platter surrounded by the vegetables. Serve with rice.

To make the pot roast "fancier", add whole mushrooms near the end of cooking time. You can add tomatoes for a more "ragoût" feel. Season with herbs such as rosemary or thyme if desired.

An easy short cut to this recipe is to brown meat as directed in the recipe. Place browned roast in very large Pyrex dish with all the vegetables, Lipton soup, water or broth, salt and pepper and cover tightly with foil. Place in 300° oven for 3-4 hours. Check roast to see if tender – be careful when pulling back foil – steam will build up.

Crockpot Roast

To prepare Pot Roast in the crockpot, brown meat as directed above. Place in crockpot and cover with the sautéed chopped onions and celery and soup mix. Cover with 1 can beef broth and cook on low for 3 hours. After 3 hours, remove meat and place peeled new potatoes, shallots and carrots in broth.

Add more beef broth and up to 1 cup red wine. Place pot roast back in crockpot and simmer on low for another 4 hours or more. Turn heat up to high for another 2 hours, until meat is tender. If you start around 9:00-10:00 AM, dinner will be ready by 6:00 PM.

Pot roast is truly one of my favorite dishes and one of the most well received meals when I take it to someone's house, primarily because no one prepares this anymore and it reminds them of their childhood. If you cook this on top of the stove, it does take a lot of work, but you can do other things in between checking on the roast. You don't have to stand over it. There are so many ways to adapt this recipe, so experiment!

Easy Beef 'n Cheese Casserole

2 tablespoons oil

1 onion, chopped

2 pounds ground beef

1 (11-ounce) jar of spaghetti sauce with mushrooms

1 pound linguine noodles or thin spaghetti noodles, cooked and drained

1 pound sharp Cheddar cheese, grated

Seasoning salt

Sauté onions in oil and add ground beef. Cook until meat isn't pink, stirring constantly, and crumbling. Add spaghetti sauce and heat. Mix noodles, meat sauce and ½ cheese and seasoning salt in large casserole dish. Sprinkle with remainder of cheese over top. Cover with foil and bake at 325° for 30-45 minutes. Uncover for last 10 minutes. Serves 8-10.

Company Beef Casserole

1	pound spinach noodles	½	cup sour cream
1½	pounds ground beef	⅓-½	cup minced onions or scallions
1	tablespoon butter		
	Salt and pepper	1	tablespoon green pepper, minced
3	(8-ounce) cans tomato sauce	2	tablespoons parsley, chopped
1	(8-ounce) carton large curd cottage cheese	2	tablespoons butter
1	(8-ounce) package cream cheese	½	cup Cheddar cheese, grated

Cook noodles according to package directions. Brown ground beef in 1 tablespoon butter. Add salt and pepper to taste. Stir in tomato sauce. Remove from heat. In a bowl, combine cottage cheese, cream cheese, sour cream, onions, green pepper and parsley.

In a 2-quart casserole dish, layer noodles and cheese mixture, alternating with each layer. Pour in 2 tablespoons melted butter. Top with meat and tomato mixture. Bake in a 350° oven for 30 minutes. Add grated Cheddar cheese to top and bake an additional 5-10 minutes, just until cheese is melted. Do not overcook or cheese will get hard. This is best made a day ahead and then baked. Serves 8.

Note: Sometimes I make this into two smaller casseroles and freeze one of them.

Hamburger Stroganoff

½	cup finely chopped onion	1	teaspoon pepper
¼	cup butter	1	cup sliced mushrooms
1	pound ground beef	1	cup cream of chicken soup
2	tablespoons flour	1	cup sour cream
1	teaspoon salt		

Cook the onion in butter in a saucepan over medium heat. Add the beef and cook, stirring, until beef is light brown. Add the flour, salt, pepper, mushrooms and soup and cook for 5 minutes. Add the sour cream and simmer for 15 minutes longer. Serve over rice and garnish with paprika.

meats

Country Style Steak with Gravy

1½	pounds cubed steak	½	teaspoon pepper
½	cup flour	½	cup shortening
½	teaspoon salt		

Mix flour, salt and pepper. Flour meat and melt shortening in skillet until hot, then add floured meat. Brown on each side for 5-8 minutes. Remove meat and put in a baking dish. Pour prepared gravy (see gravy recipe on sidebar) over meat and bake uncovered in a preheated 325° oven for 45 minutes. Serve with mashed potatoes and green beans.

 # Grandmother's Meatloaf

This recipe is at least 80 years old!
You'll probably want to double this recipe.

1	pound ground chuck	1	teaspoon salt
2	slices bread, torn into cubes		Dash black pepper
⅓	cup milk	1½	teaspoons Worcestershire sauce
½	cup chopped onion	1	egg, beaten
¼	cup chopped celery	1	(8-ounce) can tomato sauce, divided
⅛	cup chopped green peppers		

Meatloaf Sauce:

½	of the tomato sauce above	½	teaspoon dry mustard
4	teaspoons brown sugar		Dash nutmeg

Soak bread in milk in large bowl. Add rest of the ingredients to the soaked bread and mix together well. Keep ½ of the tomato sauce for topping. Bake without topping in 350° oven for 30-45 minutes. Make topping and spoon over meat loaf and bake for another 15 minutes. This recipe can easily be doubled. Serve with scalloped potatoes and a salad and French bread. Serves 3-4.

Variation: Instead of all ground beef, substitute ½ pound of ground veal or ground pork and ½ pound of ground beef. You can substitute ketchup for the tomato sauce and omit the bread and milk. You can also add one small can of chopped tomatoes to the meatloaf mixture.

Country Style Steak Gravy

4 tablespoons drippings from fried cube steak

½ cup seasoned flour, from coating steak

1 teaspoon salt to taste

3 cups half milk and half water

Pour drippings from skillet. Return 4 tablespoons of drippings to skillet and add ½ cup flour and 1 teaspoon salt, plus additional flour if needed. Brown over medium heat, loosening brown crusty bits from the skillet. Stir until smooth.

After browning, remove from heat and stir in half milk and half water mixture. Return to heat. Stir and simmer until well mixed but thin – it will thicken in the oven.

Beef Stroganoff

1½ pounds round steak

Flour, salt, pepper
for dredging

Oil for browning

8 ounces fresh
mushrooms, sliced

½ cup onion, chopped

2 cloves garlic, minced

1 can beef broth

1-2 cups sour cream

Cut 1½ pounds round
steak into thin 2-inch strips.
Dust with seasoned flour and
brown meat in large skillet with
oil. Add mushrooms, chopped
onion and garlic and brown
lightly. Stir in 1 can beef broth.
Cover and cook 1 hour on
medium simmer. After an hour,
or until beef is tender, stir in
sour cream. Cook over low
heat for about 5 minutes.
Serve over rice or noodles.

Uncooked Noodle Lasagna

*A real time saver! Prepare this
lasagna the night or morning before serving.*

1	medium onion, chopped	1	small can tomato paste
½	green pepper, finely chopped	1	(15-ounce) carton cottage cheese, large curd
½	teaspoon garlic powder		
1½	pounds ground chuck	8	ounces Swiss cheese, cut into small pieces
½	teaspoon oregano		
2	large cans chopped tomatoes, drained		Heavy shredded Parmesan cheese
1	(15-ounce) can tomato sauce	1	box lasagna noodles, uncooked

In a large saucepan, combine onion, green pepper, garlic powder
and ground beef. Cook until beef is browned and drain grease,
keeping beef mixture in the saucepan. Add oregano, chopped
tomatoes, tomato sauce and tomato paste. Simmer 1 hour. While
sauce is hot, layer sauce, dots of cottage cheese, and sprinkle with
Swiss and Parmesan cheese, then the uncooked noodles. Repeat
for 3 layers total, but only 2 layers of noodles, topping for the third
layer the sauce, cottage cheese, Swiss and Parmesan cheeses.

Cover and place in the refrigerator overnight. Remove and let
set at room temperature for 30 minutes or so if you have time.
Bake lasagna covered at 350° for 30-40 minutes. Uncover and
bake another 5-10 minutes. Let stand 5 minutes before serving.
This will cut nicely into squares for serving.

Traditional Lasagna

3	tablespoons olive oil	1	tablespoon basil, crumbled
½	cup onion, chopped		
¼	cup green pepper, chopped	1	teaspoon salt
		½	teaspoon black pepper
4	cloves garlic, minced	½	pound cooked lasagna noodles
1	pound (or more) ground beef		
		8	ounces grated mozzarella cheese
3	cups canned puréed plum tomatoes		
		2	cups ricotta cheese
3	tablespoons butter, melted	1	cup freshly grated Parmesan cheese
1	teaspoon oregano		

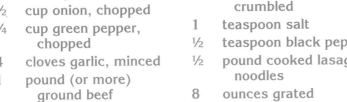

Heat oil in skillet and add the onions, green pepper and garlic and cook gently until vegetables are light brown. Add the beef and cook until it is no longer pink and is crumbled. Add the puréed tomatoes and add to the meat mixture, simmering 15 minutes. Add butter, oregano, basil, salt and pepper and simmer for another 30 minutes – partially covered. Preheat oven to 375°.

Assemble the lasagna by drizzling some sauce over the bottom of a shallow baking dish. Layer the noodles over the sauce, sprinkle some mozzarella and spread a layer of ricotta cheese. Make another layer of noodles, sauce, mozzarella and ricotta. Finish with noodles and sauce. Sprinkle Parmesan cheese over entire top and bake for at least 20 minutes until lasagna is bubbling.

Italian Meatballs with Spaghetti Sauce

The secret of Italian spaghetti is in the spices. You can experiment with different types such as: oregano, basil, rosemary, fennel or Italian seasoning. You may also add mushrooms or green peppers.

Meatballs:

2 pounds ground beef or 1 pound ground beef and 1 pound ground pork
Salt and pepper to taste
1-2 cloves garlic, minced

Fresh parsley or dried parsley flakes
2 eggs
2 teaspoons grated Parmesan cheese
4-5 slices of dried bread
Vegetable oil

Add salt and pepper to beef. Mince garlic finely and add to meat. Cut parsley finely and add to meat. Add eggs and grated cheese together and mix into meat. Grate dried bread and add to mixture until completely blended. Roll into meatballs and fry in oil until brown.

Spaghetti Sauce:

2 medium onions, chopped
Olive oil
1 small can tomato paste
2-3 cans water

1 quart canned tomatoes or 2 medium cans tomatoes
Small amount of salt
1 teaspoon dried Italian seasoning

Dice onions finely and fry in small amount of olive oil until golden. Add tomato paste and 2-3 cans water, depending on how thick you want the sauce to be. Stir well. Add chopped tomatoes, spices and meatballs. Cover pan and simmer sauce for 1 hour.

Beef Spaghetti

1	pound ground beef	1	(8-ounce) can tomato sauce
1	onion, finely chopped	1	jar commercial meaty spaghetti sauce
½	green pepper, finely chopped		Oregano to taste
1	small can tomato paste		
1	tomato paste can of water		

Cook ground beef until it crumbles. Remove beef from pan, but use fat to cook pepper and onion. Add more oil if too dry. Cook onion and pepper slowly until soft. Add cooked hamburger back to pan and add tomato paste with an equal amount of water. Add tomato sauce, commercial spaghetti sauce (we like Chef Boy-ar-dee meat sauce) and oregano. Simmer on low heat for about 1-2 hours (it will stick). The longer it cooks, the softer the beef becomes. Serve hot over cooked spaghetti, topped with freshly grated Parmesan cheese.

This Beef Spaghetti makes a very thick, flavorful spaghetti sauce. It was adapted from a friend's recipe. She brought this to my house when I had surgery and was especially well received by the children.

Woodley's Spaghetti

¼	pound bacon	2	(28-ounce) cans tomatoes, whole, undrained, chopped
4	onions, chopped	1	(15-ounce) can tomatoes, chopped
3	green peppers, chopped	2	(6-ounce) small cans tomato paste
3	cloves, garlic, minced		Salt and pepper to taste
1½	pounds ground round		
½	pound ground pork		

Cut bacon fine with scissors and brown in a large stock pot. Chop onions, green pepper and garlic. Add to bacon, cook until onions are clear. Add ground beef and pork until meat separates. Add tomatoes and tomato paste, salt and pepper to taste. Bring to a boil, then simmer 4 hours to thicken. If too thick, add water and keep simmering until consistency is right. Serve over cooked spaghetti noodles and serve topped with freshly grated Parmesan cheese. Serves 12-16.

Stuffed Peppers

*This is an elegant dish that is easy
to prepare. You rarely see it served anymore.*

6	large green peppers	½	teaspoon seasoned salt
¼	cup butter	½	teaspoon black pepper
½	cup chopped onions	½	cup fine dry bread crumbs
1	pound ground beef or veal, cooked	2	tablespoons grated Parmesan cheese
1	cup cooked rice		
2	tablespoons chopped parsley	2	tablespoons melted butter

Cut thin slice from stem end of pepper. Remove seeds and cook, covered in small amount of boiling water, 3-5 minutes. Drain and sprinkle inside of green pepper with salt. Cool. Sauté onion in butter, combine with cooked beef or veal, rice and parsley. Season with salt and pepper. Stuff green peppers with mixture. Mix bread crumbs with melted butter and Parmesan cheese. Sprinkle over top of each green pepper. Bake 375° for about 30 minutes.

Pepper Steak

1½	pounds round steak	1	teaspoon salt
¼	cup vegetable oil	½	teaspoon black pepper
2	cloves garlic, crushed	½	cup puréed tomatoes
3	small onions, sliced	1½	cups cold water
	Pinch of thyme	3	medium green peppers
2	tablespoons sugar		

Cut meat into 1-inch cubes. Heat oil in heavy skillet and add meat. Brown slowly, stirring often, for about 20 minutes. Add crushed garlic and sliced onions during last minutes of browning. Add other seasonings, puréed tomatoes and ½ cup of the water. Cover and simmer until meat is tender, about 1 hour, stirring occasionally and adding remaining water gradually as liquid evaporates. Add green pepper, which has been cut into 1-inch cubes, and cook 15 minutes longer. Serve hot with noodles, rice or whipped potatoes.

Swedish Meatballs with Sour Cream

½	pound ground round steak	¼	teaspoon black pepper	
½	ground veal	2	teaspoons Worcestershire sauce	
2	eggs, beaten	4	tablespoons butter	
2	slices bread, soaked in milk and wrung out	1½	cups sour cream	
2	tablespoons butter	¼	cup heavy cream	
½	cup minced onion	1½	teaspoons Dijon mustard	
2	tablespoons capers	2	teaspoons dill seed	
2	teaspoons salt	½	teaspoon salt	

Combine meats well and add 2 beaten eggs and soaked bread. Melt butter in a skillet and sauté onion until brown. Add to the meat mixture. Then add the capers, salt, pepper and Worcestershire sauce. Combine all of this well and shape into 2-inch balls. This can be done in advance and refrigerated until ready to cook.

In a heavy cast iron skillet, sauté the meatballs in 4 tablespoons butter. When they are browned and cooked through, remove the meatballs and drain fat from skillet. Mix and heat in the same skillet sour cream, heavy cream, dill seed, and salt. Don't let the sauce boil. Spoon sauce over meatballs and serve with rice. Makes 6-8 servings.

Corned Beef Casserole

1	(8-ounce) package medium thin egg noodles	1	can mushroom (or cream of chicken) soup
1	(12-ounce) can corned beef, diced	1	cup milk
¼	pound grated sharp cheese	½	cup chopped onions
		¾	cup buttered bread crumbs (not too fine)
		1	small can green peas
		1	small jar pimientos

Cook noodles, drain. Add beef, cheese, soup, milk and onions, peas and pimientos. Mix together in large bowl and pour into greased 2-quart casserole dish. Top with buttered bread crumbs. Bake at 350° for 45 minutes.

Hot Dog Chili

1½ pounds ground beef

1 medium onion, diced fine

1 can tomato paste

3 cans water

½ cup ketchup

1 teaspoon vinegar

1½ tablespoons chili powder

1 teaspoon salt

Do not brown hamburger ahead. Combine all ingredients in a large saucepan, adding 1 can water at a time and blend. Cook over medium to low heat slowly for 1½ hours.

I've seen the chili put into the blender to grind up a little and returned to the saucepan if you want a finer chili.

Veal Parmigiana

½	cup onion, chopped	⅔	cup grated Parmesan cheese
1	tablespoon oil		
2	(8-ounce) cans tomato sauce	2	pounds veal cutlets, about ¼-inch thick or pounded to ¼-inch thick
2	garlic cloves, crushed		
½	teaspoon oregano	¼	cup oil
1	bay leaf	½	pound thinly sliced mozzarella cheese
2	eggs		
⅓	cup bread crumbs		

Sauté onion in 1 tablespoon oil in a saucepan. Add tomato sauce, garlic and seasonings. Simmer for about 15 minutes. Remove bay leaf. Beat eggs in separate dish. In another dish combine bread crumbs and ⅓ cup Parmesan cheese. Dredge cutlets in egg and then crumb mixture. In large skillet heat oil and brown cutlets on both sides.

Place cutlets in 13x9x2-inch Pyrex dish. Pour half of tomato sauce mixture over cutlets. Top with thinly sliced mozzarella cheese. Cover with remaining sauce. Sprinkle remaining ⅓ cup Parmesan cheese on top and bake in 350° oven for 45 minutes.

Veal Scaloppine

1½	pounds scaloppine veal	3	tablespoons butter
	Seasoned flour with grated Parmesan cheese	1	beef bouillon cube
		¼	cup boiling water
		3	tablespoons white wine

Pound veal medallions very thin. Dredge in seasoned flour with grated Parmesan cheese added. In a skillet, sauté the medallions in butter until lightly browned – about 2-3 minutes per side. Remove veal to a warm platter. In ¼ cup boiling water, dissolve 1 beef bouillon cube. Add this to the skillet that you cooked the veal in. Stir in 3 tablespoons white wine, scraping pan well. Pour sauce over meat and serve with rice or pasta.

meats

Osso Buco

2	whole veal shanks cut into 3-inch pieces	1	teaspoon dried rosemary
	Flour for dredging	¾	cup dry white wine
3	tablespoons olive oil	3-4	tablespoons tomato paste
2	tablespoons butter	4	garlic cloves, finely chopped
½	cup onion, finely chopped		
1	medium carrot, chopped	2	tablespoons chopped parsley
½	cup celery, finely chopped	1	teaspoon salt
			Fresh ground pepper
1	small can crushed tomatoes	2	lemon slices
		1	cup beef broth

Dredge shanks in flour. Brown in 3 tablespoons hot oil and butter for about 10 minutes. Brown on all sides and remove. In same pot, sauté chopped vegetables and rosemary. Add more oil if needed and cover if necessary until carrots are soft – about 10 minutes.

Blend wine with tomato paste and add to vegetables. Reduce wine to half and scrape up bits. Stir to prevent burning or sticking. Add parsley, garlic, salt and pepper, lemon slices and broth. Put shanks and all vegetables in casserole. Cover and roast at 350° for 1-1½ hours. If roast is not fork tender at this point, cook longer. Before serving, remove lemon. Add broth and tomatoes if needed.

Orange Pork Chops

¼	cup orange juice	½	teaspoon dry mustard
½	teaspoon salt	⅛	cup brown sugar
⅛	teaspoon pepper	3	pork chops

Mix ingredients and pour over pork chops. Bake at 325° for 30 minutes to an hour – until pork is cooked through.

My father gave me my grandmother's recipe for country ham that he had kept in her handwriting for over 40 years. It said "Receipt for cooking country hams." My grandparents who lived in Staunton, Virginia really knew how to cook hams. My father would always bring us a real Virginia country ham home for Thanksgiving or Christmas. I remember it soaking in the kitchen sink for a day or so.

Fried country ham is one of my favorites. We have fried country ham every single Christmas morning. Growing up we used to have it for a light Sunday supper with biscuits. My father-in-law has a farmer friend that he gets his ham from and he has it sliced and I always make it with redeye gravy on Christmas and on New Year's Day with black-eyed peas, rice and collard greens.

Grandmother Genie's Receipt for Cooking Country Hams

1	whole country ham	Ground cinnamon
	Brown sugar	Ground cloves
	Powdered sugar	

For a ham 1 year or older, soak for 24 hours in cold water. Clean by scrubbing with a brush. Put in large pot with fresh cold water, covering completely. Allow to come to a boil. Boil slowly for 3-4 hours accordingly, about 20 minutes for each pound. Let ham stay in liquid until it cools. Then take ham out and pull off skin. Cover with brown sugar, a little powdered sugar, cinnamon and cloves. Put in baking pan and bake about ½ hour. Let brown well. If there is a good deal of fat on top after taking off skin, cut some of the fat off before baking. Serve hot or cold.

Fried Country Ham

Country ham slices

Have country ham cut in slices about ⅛-inch thick or thinner. Place in a cold, heavy frying pan (cast iron is the best) and turn heat to low and cook the ham on one side until the fat is transparent. Turn over and cook again on the other side. It'll take about 15 minutes if it's thick and a little less if it's real thin. If you cook it too long, it'll get hard.

Redeye Gravy:

After ham is cooked, remove from pan and keep warm. Add to the pan a little water – maybe ½-1 cup and let boil for 3-5 minutes. Scrape up bits in pan.

Add 1-2 tablespoons brewed coffee to water and simmer. I usually add the ham back into the redeye gravy and cover and simmer or just turn heat off if everything else is not ready. Remove ham from pan and pour redeye gravy in a small pitcher to pour over ham or even better, southern style grits.

Ham Loaf

1½	pounds smoked ham (ground)	2	eggs
1½	pounds fresh ham (ground)	1	cup dried bread crumbs
		1	cup tomato sauce

Mix together and bake for 1 hour at 350°. Serve with the following cream dressing:

Cream Dressing:

½	cup cream, whipped stiff	2	level teaspoons dry mustard
½	cup Miracle Whip	3	level tablespoons drained horseradish

Mix whipped cream, Miracle Whip, dry mustard and horseradish together and chill. Serve with ham.

Crockpot Pork Barbecue

This is better served the next day
after the flavors have had a chance to rest.

½	can Coca-Cola	1	(5-pound) pork shoulder or Boston butt

Sauce for Pork:

1	minced onion	½	cup water, mixed with vinegar to make 1 cup
2	cloves garlic, minced	1	cup ketchup
1	stick butter, melted	1	tablespoon Worcestershire sauce
	Juice of ½ lemon	1	teaspoon Tabasco sauce
	Grated peel of lemon	½	teaspoon chili powder
1	cup brown sugar		
½	cup vinegar		

Season pork shoulder with salt and pepper and brown on all sides in a heavy Dutch oven or a large skillet. Remove from pan and place in crockpot. Pour ½ can of Coke in the crockpot over the pork shoulder or Boston Butt. Cook all night on low in the crockpot. The next morning, pull off the fat and pull the meat apart with a fork and put into a large roasting pan. Make sauce by combining all of the sauce ingredients and pour over the pork and let cook slowly for at least an hour on the stove. Serve with hushpuppies and coleslaw.

Ham Salad

Leftover baked or boiled country ham

Mayonnaise

Salt and pepper to taste

Take leftover country ham and cut in small pieces – usually baked country ham will break apart fairly easily. Mix with mayonnaise until consistency is how you like it. Salt and pepper ham mixture to taste. Keep in airtight jar and spread on white bread to make sandwiches.

Glazed Ham

1 small (5-pound) Swift ham

¼ cup orange juice

1 cup brown sugar

2 teaspoons vinegar

2 tablespoons mustard

Score and cook ham for 1 hour at 325°, fat side up. Mix orange juice, brown sugar, vinegar and mustard together and pour over top of ham and cook for 35-45 more minutes. Slice and serve with rice or potatoes and green beans.

Pork Marinade

1½ cups dry red wine

⅔ cup brown sugar

½ cup vinegar

½ cup ketchup

½ cup water

½ cup vegetable oil

3 tablespoons soy sauce

4 cloves garlic, minced

2 teaspoons curry powder
or to taste

1 teaspoon ground ginger

½ teaspoon
freshly ground pepper

Barbecue Sauce
for Ribs

¼ cup vegetable oil

1 medium onion, minced

¼ cup vinegar

1 cup tomato sauce

1 cup water

1 teaspoon salt

⅛ teaspoon cayenne pepper

2 teaspoons Angostura bitters

To prepare the barbecue
sauce, heat the oil in a
saucepan and add the onion,
cooking until onion is tender.
Add all other ingredients
and mix well.

Festive Pork Roast

1 (5-pound) boneless rolled pork roast	2 teaspoons cornstarch

Combine ingredients for Pork Marinade. Place meat in a plastic bag and cover with marinade. Seal bag and set in a shallow dish. Marinate in refrigerator for 6-8 hours (or overnight), turning occasionally. Drain meat, reserving 2½ cups marinade. Pat meat dry and place on rack in shallow roasting pan. Roast in 325° oven for 2½ hours or until meat thermometer registers 170°.

Blend cornstarch into reserved marinade; cook, stirring, until thickened and bubbly. Brush roast frequently with sauce during last 15 minutes of cooking. Heat remaining sauce and pass with meat. Serves 12.

Martha Long's Oven Barbecue Ribs

6-8 pounds spareribs

Have the spareribs cut into serving pieces and figure on 1 pound per person. Put them in an open roasting pan in a hot (450°) oven for 30 minutes. In the meantime, prepare the barbecue sauce and cover the ribs with it. Reduce the oven temperature to 350° and bake for 1 hour. Cover the ribs with foil for the first 30 minutes of the baking time at 350°, then remove the cover and let the sauce glaze and reduce in quantity.

This recipe was originally published in 1961 in the cookbook Let's Eat at Home by Dallas Morning News food editor Julie Benell. Martha suggests serving the ribs with slaw made with shredded cabbage, real mayonnaise and plain French's mustard. Angostura bitters can be found in many grocery stores or gourmet supermarkets in the cocktail mix section.

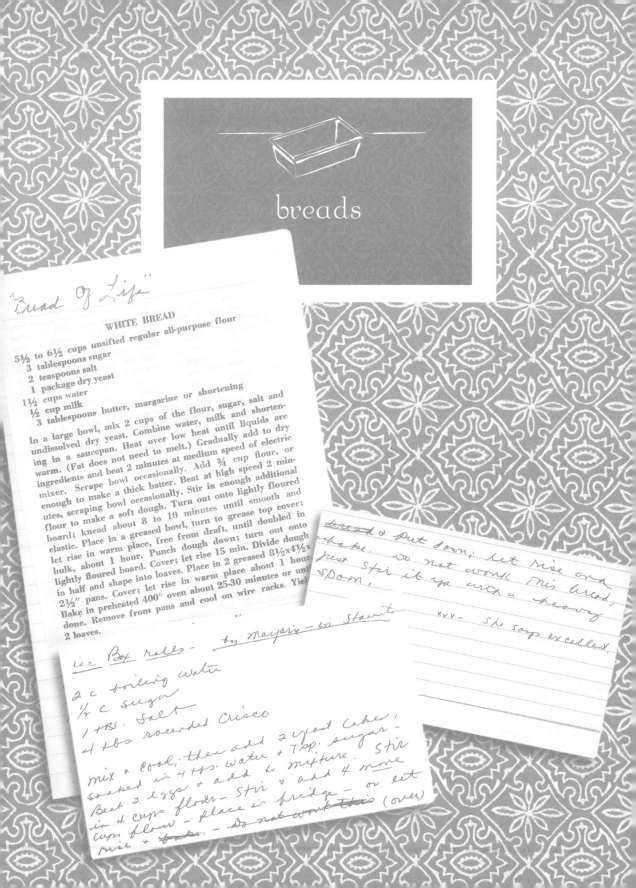

breads

"Bread Of Life"

WHITE BREAD

5½ to 6½ cups unsifted regular all-purpose flour
  3 tablespoons sugar
  2 teaspoons salt
  1 package dry yeast
1½ cups water
  ½ cup milk
  3 tablespoons butter, margarine or shortening

In a large bowl, mix 2 cups of the flour, sugar, salt and undissolved dry yeast. Combine water, milk and shortening in a saucepan. Heat over low heat until liquids are warm. (Fat does not need to melt.) Gradually add to dry ingredients and beat 2 minutes at medium speed of electric mixer. Scrape bowl occasionally. Add ¾ cup flour, or enough to make a thick batter. Beat at high speed 2 minutes, scraping bowl occasionally. Stir in enough additional flour to make a soft dough. Turn out onto lightly floured board; knead about 8 to 10 minutes until smooth and elastic. Place in a greased bowl, turn to grease top cover; let rise in warm place, free from draft, until doubled in bulk, about 1 hour. Punch dough down; turn out onto lightly floured board. Cover; let rise 15 min. Divide dough in half and shape into loaves. Place in 2 greased 8½x4½x 2½" pans. Cover; let rise in warm place about 1 hour. Bake in preheated 400° oven about 25-30 minutes or until done. Remove from pans and cool on wire racks. Yiel
2 loaves.

bread & put down; let rise and
shape. Do not work this bread,
rest stir it up with a heavy
spoon.

xxx- She says excellent.

ice Box rolls -   by Marjorie - in Staunton
2 c boiling water
½ c sugar
1 tbs. Salt
4 tbs. rounded Crisco

mix & cool; then add 2 yeast Cakes
soaked in 4 tbs. water & Tsp. sugar.
Beat 2 eggs & add to mixture. Stir
in 4 cups flour- Stir & add 4 more
cups flour - place in fridge - or let
rise & bake. - do not work this (over)

breads

Bubba made white bread until she was in her 90's. One of my fondest memories was when I stopped by her apartment when she was around 90 years old. I had brought her a couple of ripe summer tomatoes. In her kitchen was some of her homemade white bread. We sliced the tomatoes, slathered the bread with mayonnaise and ate our tomato sandwiches in her little kitchen. It's one of my last memories of being with my grandmother before she went to a nursing home.

Living in the south, you know all about biscuits. One of my best childhood friend's family has made a fortune from selling just that – biscuits. If you're in North Carolina or Virginia, you have to stop at a Biscuitville and try a real biscuit. When I left North Carolina at the age of 18 to attend college in Washington, DC, no one at school had ever heard of a biscuit. As a treat to my roommates and friends, I would bring bags of Biscuitville biscuits back.

Growing up, we would have country ham biscuits for supper – sometimes we still do! – or biscuits with pork tenderloin gravy (my aunt would can the pork tenderloin) or chipped beef gravy. Buttered biscuits were served with most family suppers. During holiday dinners, my grandmother always made the bread, usually yeast rolls or more delicate angel biscuits and my mother put them in her silver biscuit tin or bread basket lined with a pretty linen towel.

In Greensboro, there is one famous biscuit maker, Ella Barham. Ella has been making biscuits and yeast rolls for over 60 years. She is absolutely famous for her party-sized ham biscuits. She spent the day with me, trying to pass on her legacy of biscuit making. What a joy and thrill it was for me. I hope you'll enjoy them as much as the hundreds and hundreds of folks from Greensboro have.

# Perfect White Bread

1	package dry yeast	2	teaspoons salt
¼	cup warm water	2-3	tablespoons butter
	Pinch of sugar	6	cups sifted all-purpose flour
2	cups milk, scalded		
3	tablespoons sugar		

Soften yeast in warm water with a pinch of sugar. Combine hot milk, sugar, salt and butter in a large bowl. Butter will melt. Cool to lukewarm. Stir in 2 cups of sifted flour, beating well with an electric beater. Add yeast/water mixture and continue beating. Add the rest of the flour by cup-fulls, beating in between. You'll have to use a heavy spoon to mix in the last cup of flour. Make sure all of the flour is incorporated.

Transfer dough to a greased bowl. Cover with a towel and leave in a warm place for about an hour or more, until dough is doubled in size. Punch dough down and knead out on a floured surface until smooth, about 1 minute. Do not over knead.

Cut dough into 2 portions and shape into loaves. Place in 2 buttered bread pans. Cover again and let rise until doubled in size, about 45 minutes. Do not let bread rise too long – it will then sink and be hard. Bake in a 400° oven for about 20 minutes. Remove from oven and when bread has cooled a little, remove from the pans and cool on wire racks. Enjoy!

Angel Biscuits

5	cups all-purpose flour	2	teaspoons salt
⅓	cup sugar	1	cup Crisco
1	teaspoon baking soda	1	package dry yeast
3	teaspoons baking powder	2	cups warm buttermilk
		2	tablespoons warm water

Dissolve yeast in 2 tablespoons warm water. In a large bowl, sift flour, sugar, baking powder, sugar and salt. Cut in shortening. Add yeast mixture and buttermilk to dry ingredients. Knead enough to hold together. Roll dough to ½-inch to ¾-inch thickness. Cut with biscuit cutter. Arrange on baking sheet. Bake in preheated 400° oven for 15-20 minutes. You can store the dough in the refrigerator.

This is the white bread my grandmother used to make. It's perfect for sandwiches, especially tomato sandwiches with lots of mayonnaise.

These light Angel Biscuits are perfect for Thanksgiving or other special occasions. You must make the dough the night before serving and keep dough in the refrigerator until the next day.

Buttermilk Biscuits

To make fluffy buttermilk biscuits, substitute buttermilk for the plain milk and add a pinch of soda. Roll the biscuits out thicker, about ½ to ¾-inch thick, and cook a little longer. Serve hot with butter.

It was a wonderful day when Ella Barham spent the day at my house, passing on the legacy of her biscuit making to a devoted student and fan. Ella is famous in Greensboro for her little party sized country ham biscuits. Her biscuits melt in your mouth. No one does them better than Ella and I am grateful that she chose to share her recipe and techniques with me.

Ella's Famous Ham Biscuits

6	cups Red Band self-rising flour		Melted margarine to brush tops
12	large tablespoons Crisco	2	sticks butter, softened
2	cups milk	2	pounds thinly sliced country ham

Measure 6 cups self-rising flour in a large mixing bowl. Place 12 large tablespoons (serving spoon size) of Crisco in the center of the flour and start blending the Crisco and flour together by using your hands to incorporate the shortening with the flour. Work this together until the mixture resembles coarse crumbs. You want the mixture to stay together if you squeeze a small handful. Adjust Crisco or flour if necessary.

Start adding milk to the flour/Crisco mixture, blending with a mixing spoon. The dough should completely incorporate all of the flour. This will appear pretty moist. You don't need to knead the dough at this time. The dough can rest for a while like this. When you're ready to proceed, prepare the rolling surface by sifting some of the flour out. I use a dough cloth and rolling pin sock, which helps the dough from sticking.

Work in small batches – you'll use 5 or 6 batches for this amount of dough. Place a small amount of dough on the floured surface and roll dough around in the flour. Press down and gently roll out until it's about ⅓-inch thick. Using a small "party size" round cutter, cut biscuits one at a time and remove to cookie sheet. Place biscuits side by side so that they touch.

Using a fork, make 3 indentations across the top of the biscuits. Brush tops with melted margarine or butter. Bake in a preheated 450° oven for 10-12 minutes. If the biscuits feel done, but have not browned, then place them under a broiler for a minute or so until lightly browned.

While the biscuits are still hot, cut them with a knife in half and spread a small dab of softened butter between the halves. Place on a cool cookie sheet until you're ready to stuff with the country ham – or you can enjoy the biscuits without the ham. To make ham biscuits, cut the thinly sliced ham in small pieces and place 2-3 layers of ham in the biscuit. Store ham biscuits in an airtight container. They can be refrigerated or frozen at this point.

To serve the ham biscuits, reheat on a cookie sheet for 5-6 minutes at 375°, a little longer if they have been frozen. Enjoy all the compliments you will receive and thank Ella Barham for sharing her treasure. Makes about 7-8 dozen small biscuits.

Dorothy Singleton's Biscuits

2	cups self-rising flour	⅔-1	cup Crisco
1½	tablespoons sugar	⅔	cup 2% milk

In a large mixing bowl, put flour and sugar and blend. Make a well in the center of the flour. Place the Crisco in the center. With the back of a large tablespoon, start mixing a little of the flour with the Crisco. Slowly add a little milk and blend the Crisco mixture with small amounts of the flour. Continue adding more milk, blending a little more flour in each time, until all the flour is mixed in. This procedure will take about 5 minutes or more.

On a floured surface, knead the dough a couple of times and roll out dough to ½-inch thick. Cut with a round 2-inch or 3-inch biscuit cutter. Bake on a non-greased cookie sheet for 20 minutes at 400°. Serve biscuits hot with butter.

During the weekend that Dorothy prepared dinner for the President of Latvia, she also made her delightful homemade biscuits. I watched her and was surprised at her technique, but quickly incorporated it into my biscuit making routine.

Cheese Biscuits

1¾	cups sifted all-purpose flour	¾	cup finely grated sharp Cheddar cheese
1	teaspoon salt	¼	cup butter
	Dash of cayenne pepper	¾	cup milk
3	teaspoons baking powder		

In a medium mixing bowl sift together the flour, salt, cayenne pepper and baking powder. Add cheese and toss well to mix. Cut in butter with a pastry blender until mixture resembles cornmeal. Make a well in center and add milk. Stir quickly until ball of dough comes off the sides of bowl – about 30 seconds. On a floured surface, knead 2 or 3 times. With a floured rolling pin, roll out to ¼-inch thickness. Cut into 2-inch rounds. Place, 1-inch apart, on light greased cookie sheets. Bake in preheated 425° oven about 16 minutes. Do not overcook. Makes 2½-3 dozen biscuits. Split biscuits, butter and fill with rounds of baked or country ham.

Notes About Using Yeast

First of all, it is so important to always use fresh yeast. I have made so many loaves of bread that did not rise because my yeast was old. If you're not sure if the yeast is bubbling or foaming enough, it probably isn't. You'll have much more success using fresh yeast.

If you buy yeast in a jar (bulk), keep it refrigerated at all times. You'll still need to replace it periodically, but it will last longer in the refrigerator than on the pantry shelf.

I have started using rapid rise yeast in a lot of my bread recipes. Sometimes this is called "bread machine" yeast. I like it and it speeds things along. It can be mixed right into the flour, etc. and doesn't have to be rehydrated with warm water and sugar like regular active dry yeast.

During my first printing, an elderly lady wrote me asking why some yeast breads use milk and some use water. The answer is both are fine, but milk produces a softer bread (country white bread) and water produces a harder, crustier bread (French bread or pizza dough).

Ella Barham's Yeast Rolls

Small Batch:		Large Batch:	
1	yeast package	4	yeast packages
¼	cup warm water	¼-½	cup warm water
	Pinch of sugar		Pinch of sugar
⅔	cup water	2⅔	cups water
⅓	cup Crisco	1⅓	cups Crisco
¼	cup sugar	1	cup sugar
½	teaspoon salt	2	teaspoons salt
1	large egg	4	large eggs
2½	cups Pillsbury all-purpose flour	10	cups Pillsbury all-purpose flour, sifted

In a heavy Dutch oven (not a tall one) heat water and Crisco until Crisco is melted. Remove from heat and let cool until water is lukewarm.

In a small bowl, mix the salt and sugar together. Using ¼-½ cup warm water, temper yeast in water until yeast is bubbly and foamy.

When the water/Crisco mixture has cooled to lukewarm, pour the sugar/salt into the water and beat with an electric beater. Add the eggs and continue beating. Pour the yeast mixture in and beat more. Start adding the sifted flour in batches. You will need to finish mixing with a strong spoon. Move the flour into the dough until the consistency is firm, but not too much. Brush the top of the dough with melted margarine, making sure the top and sides are covered. Let the dough rise in the pan until it is doubled in bulk.

Meanwhile, butter the cookie sheets or jelly-roll pans. Sift additional flour out on a rolling surface. I use a pastry cloth.

When the dough has risen, punch it down a couple of times with your spoon or hand. You don't have to knead too much. Fold the dough over and grab sections, small amounts at a time. Roll each small batch of dough in the sifted flour and using a rolling pin, roll out to about ½-inch thick. Cut rolls with a 1½-inch round cutter. Brush the top with melted margarine and fold roll over in half. Press roll down with your fingers (the yeast makes it want to puff out). Place rolls close together on buttered pan. When the folded rolls have filled the jelly-roll pan, brush roll tops with melted margarine.

Let the rolls rise again until they have doubled in size. This will only take about a half an hour. Bake the rolls right away. Don't let the rolls sit too long after they have risen. Bake in a 400° oven for about 12-15 minutes. The smallest proportion makes about 2 dozen rolls.

Mel's Sweet Potato Biscuits

4	cups all-purpose flour	1	cup butter, cold and cut into small pieces
2	tablespoons baking powder	1⅓	cups cooked mashed sweet potatoes
⅓	cup sugar	1	scant cup buttermilk
2	teaspoons salt		
	Pinch of baking soda		

Combine flour with baking powder, salt, sugar and baking soda. Mix together with a whisk to incorporate and fluff flour. Cut in cold butter with a pastry blender until crumbly – about 5-7 minutes. After cooking sweet potatoes (I like mine to still be warm and moist in the cooking pan), whisk together sweet potatoes and buttermilk; add to dry ingredients, stirring just until moistened. You might need to add a little more flour – this dough will be wetter than normal.

Turn dough out onto lightly floured surface and knead 3-4 times. Keep flour on your hands. Pat or roll dough to ½-inch thickness. Cut biscuits with a 1½-inch round biscuit cutter and place biscuits on a lightly floured or greased cookie sheet. You may always use a larger size cutter – I just like the smaller size – they're great for parties.

Bake in a preheated 425° oven for 10-12 minutes or until biscuits are golden brown on top. Slice biscuits while hot and spread a dab of soft butter on both sides. Place 2 small pieces of thinly sliced country ham between the biscuits. Be careful if you have your ham shaved, as it will dry out quickly. Store in airtight container or place in foil trays and cover with saran wrap tightly. These will freeze nicely and are great for gifts. Reheat in a 350° oven for 5 minutes or so. Makes about 2-3 dozen biscuits.

I spent several years tweaking this sweet potato biscuit recipe. People request them all the time. Serve these sweet potato biscuits with shaved country ham or smoked turkey breast with chutney.

Bubba's Refrigerator Rolls

½	cup sugar	2	dry yeast packages ·
1	teaspoon salt	¼	cup warm water
1	cup shortening	2	beaten eggs
2	cups boiling water	8	cups flour

Mix sugar, salt, shortening and boiling water. Let cool. Dissolve yeast packages in ¼ cup warm water and add to above cooled mix. Add eggs and beat. Add 4 cups flour and beat thoroughly. Add the other 4 cups of flour and beat. You may have to finish with a spoon. Do not knead. Cover tightly and refrigerate. Remove 2 hours before serving time. Shape into rolls and let rise until light. Bake in preheated 400-450° oven for 15 minutes.

Shawpuck Rolls

*This recipe was written on
an old, torn piece of parchment paper.*

½	cup mashed potatoes	½	cup sugar
1	cup scalded milk	1	teaspoon salt
1	tablespoon sugar	¼	cup shortening, melted
1	package dry yeast	2	beaten eggs
2	cups all-purpose flour	2	cups all-purpose flour

Combine potatoes, milk and 1 tablespoon sugar. Cool to lukewarm. Add yeast and 2 cups flour, beating thoroughly. Add sugar, salt, shortening, eggs and 2 cups flour. Knead lightly. Let rise until doubled and place in greased bowl in refrigerator overnight. Roll dough on floured surface to ½-inch thickness or shape into balls. Place 3 balls in muffin tins and let rise until double. Bake in preheated 400° oven 15 minutes.

breads

Parkerhouse Rolls

¾	cup milk	2	packages active dry yeast
¼	cup butter, cut up	4-5	cups bread flour
¼	cup sugar	2-3	tablespoons melted butter
2	teaspoons salt		
¾	cup warm water		

In a saucepan, heat milk, sugar, salt and cut-up butter until lukewarm In a large bowl, sprinkle the yeast over warm water. Stir to dissolve and add the lukewarm milk mixture and 3 cups of flour. Beat until smooth. Stir in enough of remaining flour to make a soft dough.

Knead on floured board for 5 minutes. Place in buttered bowl, turn and cover. Let rise until dough has doubled. Punch down and turn out and divide dough in half. Roll out each half ¼ to ½-inch thick. Cut into rounds 2-3 inches.

Take a dull knife and grease slightly. Brush tops with melted butter and take knife off center and fold small side over large side so that the edges meet. Place rolls, touching one another in rows in buttered jelly-roll pan. Cover and allow to rise until doubled. Bake at 375° for 12-15 minutes. Makes about 2½ dozen.

These may be made ahead and cooled. Wrap in foil to reheat.

Corn Muffins

2	eggs	1	cup plain cornmeal
1	cup sour cream	1	teaspoon salt
⅓	cup oil	3	teaspoons baking powder
1	small can cream style corn		

In a large bowl, beat eggs and blend sour cream, oil and corn into the eggs. Add dry ingredients. Pour or spoon into 12 greased muffin tins and bake in preheated 375° oven for 20-25 minutes until brown. Cool in pan.

Biddy's Cornbread

1	cup unsifted all-purpose flour	⅓	cup sugar
1	cup yellow cornmeal	1	cup buttermilk
1	tablespoon baking powder	¼	cup salad oil
¾	teaspoon salt	2	eggs

Pour 2 tablespoons oil or bacon fat into 9-inch cast iron skillet and place in preheated 425° oven for 10 minutes or so. Meanwhile, in a large bowl, combine dry ingredients. In a another small bowl, combine buttermilk, oil and eggs and beat. Pour liquid into dry ingredients and mix just until moist. Remove pan from oven and pour cornbread batter into hot pan. Bake in preheated 425° oven for 12-15 minutes.

To make cornbread muffins, fill mini muffin tins ¾ full and bake about 10 minutes. I even dot the tins.

cornbread has always been cooked in our family. Biddy is my mother's childhood nickname and thus the name of this recipe. Be sure to make this in a cast iron skillet.

Buttermilk Hush Puppies

2 cups self-rising flour

2 cups self-rising white cornmeal

1 teaspoon sugar

½ teaspoon salt

½ teaspoon pepper

1 large onion, grated

2 cups buttermilk

1 large egg

Vegetable oil

Combine flour, cornmeal, sugar, salt and pepper in large bowl. Beat egg and buttermilk and add to dry ingredients. Heat 3 inches vegetable oil to 375° in deep fryer or Dutch oven. Drop hush puppy batter by level tablespoons into oil, fry in batches 6 minutes or until golden. Drain on paper towels. Makes about 50 hushpuppies.

Pal's Spoonbread

¼	cup melted butter	4	eggs
¼	cup white cornmeal	½	teaspoon sugar
1½	cups boiling water	1½	teaspoons baking powder
½	cup all-purpose flour		Pinch of salt
1½	cups whole milk		

Pour melted butter in 8-inch baking pan. Put cornmeal in bowl. Mix well. Stir in flour, milk, eggs, sugar, baking powder and salt, mixing until smooth. Pour in pan. Bake in preheated 350° oven for 30-35 minutes until firm and golden brown. Makes 9 servings.

Bubba's Cornbread Dressing

1	recipe Biddy's cornbread (5-7 cups, crumbled)	2-3	tablespoons butter
		1	large onion, finely chopped
6-7	cups white bread crumbs	1½	cups celery, finely chopped
	Salt and pepper to taste	2	eggs, slightly beaten
2½	cups chicken broth	½	cup parsley, chopped

Prepare recipe of Biddy's cornbread and let it sit out until it is stale – up to 2 days. Reduce amount of buttermilk in recipe to make it less moist if you like. You should have about 6-7 cups of cornbread crumbs. Prepare fresh bread crumbs with stale white bread, measuring about 6-7 cups. Sometimes I use several different kinds of bread. You can make this ahead and freeze.

Sauté the onion and celery with butter in a large heavy pan, cooking until soft. In a large bowl mix the stale cornbread with the white bread crumbs, and salt and pepper liberally. Start mixing the bread mixture with chicken broth, mixing with your hands. You want the stuffing to be wet, but not soggy. Add the sautéed celery and onions, 2 eggs slightly beaten, and combine well. Lastly add the parsley. Keep mixture fairly loose, not packing too tightly.

Pour into 2 small greased casserole pans, pie plate or one large casserole dish. Mixture can also be made into patties and placed on cookie sheet. If putting into casseroles, bake in a 325° oven for 1 hour or until set and slightly crunchy on top. If making patties, cooking time will be about ½ hour.

Bubba always brought the cornbread stuffing or dressing to our Thanksgiving dinners and it was the best. Over the recent years, recipes have sought to fancy up Thanksgiving stuffing, adding all kinds of things to jazz it up. When it is made simply, there really isn't any need to change it.

Bubba's Spoonbread

2	cups boiling water	2	eggs, separated
1	teaspoon salt	⅔	cup evaporated milk
¾	cup white cornmeal	1	teaspoon baking powder
3	tablespoons butter		

Preheat oven to 375°. Put cornmeal in boiling water and let thicken, then add butter. Cool. Add egg yolks and milk and fold in egg whites. Pour into lightly greased small baking dish and bake for 40 minutes.

This Banana Nut Bread recipe came from my friend Toccoa Switzer. It was her grandmother's and I've been using it for nearly 20 years.

Toccoa's Banana Nut Bread

½	cup butter	1	teaspoon baking soda
1	cup sugar	2	cups sifted flour
2	eggs	½	cup nuts, finely chopped
3	crushed very ripe bananas		

Cream butter and sugar and add eggs one at a time. Crush bananas with fork on side of the bowl and let slide in. Sift flour and soda together and add to banana mixture. Add nuts – I usually use pecans or walnuts. Pour into greased and floured loaf pan. Bake in preheated 325° oven for 1 hour.

Zucchini Bread

3	eggs	2	cups grated unpeeled zucchini
¾	cup oil	3	cups all-purpose flour
1⅔	cups sugar	1	teaspoon baking powder
2	teaspoons vanilla	½	teaspoon salt
½	teaspoon soda	2	teaspoons ground cinnamon
½	cup nuts		

Mix together eggs until light and foaming; add oil, sugar and vanilla. Mix, then add zucchini, flour, baking powder, salt, cinnamon, soda and nuts. Stir together. Grease and flour 2 loaf tins and bake in preheated 325° oven for 1 hour.

Pumpkin Bread

3	cups sugar	1	teaspoon ground nutmeg
1	cup Crisco	2	cups pumpkin meat, canned or fresh
4	eggs	2	teaspoons soda
⅔	cup water	1	teaspoon vanilla
3⅔	cups all-purpose flour	1	cup chopped nuts
1½	teaspoons salt		
1	teaspoon ground cinnamon		

Blend together sugar and Crisco. Add eggs, one at a time and water. Beat and add flour, mixed with spices, salt and soda. Add pumpkin, vanilla and nuts. Pour into 3 greased and floured loaf pans and bake in preheated 350° oven for 1 hour.

Orange Loaf

1	cup raisins	1	teaspoon vanilla
½	cup dark rum	1	egg, beaten
	Juice of 1 large orange	2	cups flour
	Hot water	¼	teaspoon ground cloves
	Rind of large orange		
1	teaspoon baking soda	1	teaspoon baking powder
1	cup white sugar		
2	tablespoons vegetable oil	¼	teaspoon salt
		1	cup chopped pecans

Preheat oven to 350°. Cover raisins with rum and simmer for a couple of minutes; then drain. Squeeze juice of the orange into measuring cup and fill with hot water to equal 1 cup.

Chop orange rind and add rind and raisins to the orange juice/ water mixture. Stir in baking soda. Add sugar, oil and vanilla. Add beaten egg; then add flour, ground cloves, baking powder and salt. Beat thoroughly and add nuts. Pour into a buttered and floured loaf pan. Bake for approximately 60 minutes or less, until a straw inserted into the middle comes out dry. Slice orange loaf and toast with butter or fry in pan with butter.

This freezes well; wrap in plastic wrap, then foil to freeze.

This Orange Loaf recipe comes from my friend David Grimes. It was his mother's recipe and has been passed down for many years.

Apple Bread

1	cup sugar	1	teaspoon baking soda
3	tablespoons Crisco shortening	1	teaspoon baking powder
2	eggs	1	cup unpeeled apples, grated
1	teaspoon vanilla		
3	tablespoons sour milk	½	cup raisins, optional
2	cups all-purpose flour	½	cup nuts, optional
½	teaspoon salt		

Blend together sugar and Crisco. Add eggs, one at a time, vanilla and milk. Add flour mixed with salt, soda and baking powder. Add the apples, and raisins and nuts if desired. Pour into 2 greased and floured loaf pans and bake in preheated 375° oven for 45 minutes.

This Blueberry Bread recipe was given to me by my friend Elizabeth Pitts nearly 20 years ago. It's a great house warming gift or a nice bread to take if staying with friends for the weekend.

Blueberry Bread

½	cup butter	¼	teaspoon salt
1	cup sugar	2	eggs, beaten
2	cups all-purpose flour	½	cup milk
1½	teaspoons baking powder	1½	cups fresh blueberries
		2	teaspoons lemon rind

Cream butter with sugar until light. Mix dry ingredients together and add to creamed butter. Add beaten eggs and milk, then lemon rind. Fold in blueberries last. Pour into greased and floured loaf pan, or 2 smaller loaf pans, and bake in preheated 350° oven for 45 minutes, or until center is set.

For Blueberry Muffins, spoon batter into regular muffin tins – it will make about 12 – and bake for 30-35 minutes.

Old-Fashioned Gingerbread

*The recipe for this was so old that
the parchment paper was brittle and tearing.*

2	eggs, beaten	1½	teaspoons ground cinnamon
¾	cup brown sugar	½	teaspoon ground cloves
¾	cup molasses	½	teaspoon ground nutmeg
¾	cup melted shortening	½	teaspoon baking powder
2½	cups Gold Medal flour	1	cup boiling water
2	teaspoons baking soda		
2	teaspoons ground ginger		

Add beaten eggs to sugar, molasses and melted shortening. Then add dry ingredients which have been sifted together twice. Lastly, add hot water and mix. Pour into square cake pan and bake in moderate oven (350°) for 50 minutes.

Variation: You can add ½ cup raisins and ½ cup coconut to the cake mixture if desired. If doing so, toss the raisins and coconut with 2 tablespoons of the flour and spice mixture to coat.

breads

Homemade English Muffins

1	cup milk	1	package active dry yeast
3	tablespoons butter, cut into pieces		Cornmeal
2	tablespoons honey	5½-6	cups all-purpose flour
1	cup warm water (110°)	1	teaspoon salt

Combine milk, butter and honey in a saucepan. Warm the mixture over low heat until butter starts to melt, then whisk it briskly. Remove the pan from the heat and allow liquid to cool until it is barely warm. While the milk cools, combine the warm water and yeast in a mixing bowl until the yeast becomes foamy.

Line 2 baking sheets with wax or parchment paper and sprinkle cornmeal on the paper.

Pour the cooled milk into the yeast/water and gently stir until well blended. Add 3 cups of flour and salt to the liquid and beat with a wooden spoon until smooth (about 100 strokes). Beat in enough remaining flour (about ½ cup at a time), so that the dough is firm enough to knead – you don't want it sticky.

Scrape the dough from the bowl and lay it out on a floured surface or dough board. Flour your hands and knead the dough for several minutes, sprinkling with flour when needed. Let dough rest for 5 minutes or so. Then roll out the dough until dough is about ½-inch thick. Cut dough into circles with a 3½-inch biscuit cutter. Gather and reroll the scraps. You can also cut the dough into shapes if desired.

Transfer the cut muffins to the lined baking sheets, keeping them far apart from each other. Sprinkle cornmeal on the tops. Cover the muffins with a lightweight kitchen towel and let them rise until they are doubled – about 45 minutes. When the muffins have risen, heat a large heavy (cast iron) ungreased skillet over medium heat. Or you can heat up a large electric griddle at about 300°. Carefully lift the muffins from the waxed paper and place them in the heated pan spacing them an inch or so apart. Cook the muffins for about 10 minutes on each side. Lower the heat if muffins brown too quickly. After cooking, transfer the muffins to a wire rack to cool before splitting them with a fork.

Scones

1⅔ cups whole wheat pastry flour

1⅔ cups unbleached white flour

2 teaspoons baking soda

2 teaspoons cream of tartar

Pinch of salt

1 stick butter, chilled

1 cup sour milk or buttermilk

½ cup brown sugar

1 tablespoon vanilla

Currants

In a large bowl mix the whole wheat pastry flour with the white unbleached flour, the baking soda, cream of tartar and salt and cut butter in with a pastry cutter for about 6 minutes. Stir in the milk, sugar, vanilla and currants until dough is formed. Shape into small rectangles or triangles and place on lined cookie sheet. Bake in preheated 400° oven for 10-15 minutes.

Toppings may include: brushing dough with garlic olive oil, ricotta or mozzarella cheese, adding any vegetables you like. Sprinkle top with Parmesan cheese.

Whole Wheat Pizza Dough

5	teaspoons active dry yeast	1½	teaspoons salt	
2	cups flour	¼	cup olive oil	
1½	cups whole wheat flour	½	teaspoon sugar	
		1½	cups lukewarm water	

In a mixing bowl, combine the yeast, sugar and ½ cup warm water. Combine this mixture with the rest of the ingredients until a rough dough is formed. Knead until dough is smooth – about 8-10 minutes. (Or you can put all this in a food processor and process for about 1-2 minutes. If using a processor, remove from processor and knead by hand until smooth.)

Place dough in a bowl that has been oiled and turn it around to coat the dough. Let it rise, covered, in a warm place for about 1½ hours. You can let it stay covered in the refrigerator overnight if you like.

Divide the dough into 4 pieces and roll out for pizza toppings. Place on nonstick pie sheet or pizza pan and bake pizza for 8-10 minutes in hot 450° oven.

Basic French Bread

This recipe also doubles for pizza dough.

1	teaspoon olive oil	1¼	cups warm water	
1	package dry active yeast	3	cups unbleached all-purpose flour	
½	teaspoon sugar	2	teaspoons salt	

Mix the yeast and sugar with the warm water until water becomes foamy. Put flour and salt in a bowl and gradually add the yeast mixture. When dough is too stiff to mix with a spoon, use your hands to knead in the rest of the flour. The dough should not be sticky – it should be smooth.

You can also make this up in a food processor. Put all dry ingredients in the processor along with the warm water and process for 30 seconds. It will be very sticky. Take out of processor and knead back and forth with the heel of your hand, using both hands, on a floured surface, keeping flour on your hands.

Put kneaded dough in a bowl and cover it with a clean dish towel. Put the bowl in a warm place and let rise for about an hour. Punch dough down and shape into loaves. Let loaves rise until they are doubled in size. Brush the top of the loaves with a beaten egg and bake in a preheated 350° oven for 25-30 minutes.

breads

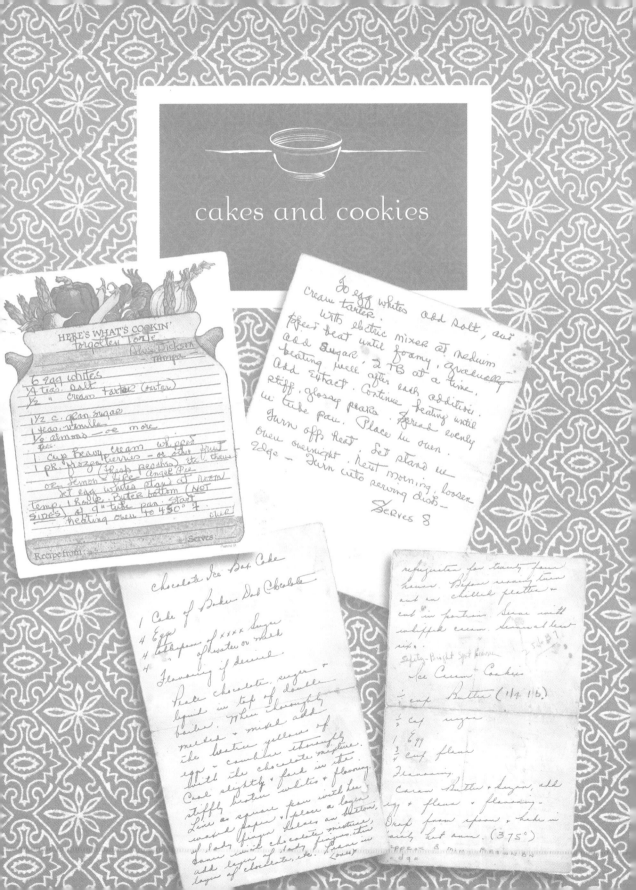

cakes and cookies

HERE'S WHAT'S COOKIN'
Forgotten Torte
Alice Dickson
— Tampa —

6 egg whites
1/4 teas. salt
1/2 " cream Tartar (tarter)

1 1/2 c. gran sugar
1 teas. vanilla
1/2 almonds — or more
teas.

1 cup heavy cream whipped
1 pk. frozen berries — or other fruit
(fresh peaches etc) thawed
or — lemon pie filling Angel Pie
let egg whites stand at room
temp. 1 hour. Butter bottom (NOT
SIDES) of 9" tube pan. start
heating oven to 450° f.

Recipe from

Serves:

To egg whites add salt, and
cream tarter.
With electric mixer at medium
speed beat until foamy, gradually
add sugar, 2 TB at a time,
beating well after each addition.
Add extract. Continue beating until
stiff, glossy peaks. Spread evenly
in tube pan. Place in oven.
Turn off heat. Let stand in
oven overnight. Next morning, loosen
edge — Turn onto serving dish —
Serves 8

Chocolate Ice Box Cake

1 Cake of Baker Dot Chocolate
4 Eggs
4 tablespoon of xxxx Sugar
4 " of water or milk
4 Flavoring if desired.

Place chocolate, sugar +
liquid in top of double
boiler. When thoroughly
melted + mixed add
the beaten yellow of
egg - combine thoroughly
with the chocolate mixture.
Cool slightly + fold in the
stiffly beaten whites + flavoring.
Line a square pan with lee
waxed paper + place a layer
of lady finger. Place a layer
down with chocolate mixture,
add layer of lady fingers, then
layer of chocolate, etc. Leave in

---

refrigerator for twenty four
hours. Before serving turn
out on chilled platter +
cut in portions. Serve with
whipped cream. Serves about
six.

Safety-Bright Spot heaven
Ice Cream Cookies
1/4 cup Butter (1/4 lb.)
1/2 cup sugar
1 Egg
3/4 cup flour
Flavoring.
Cream Butter + sugar, add
egg + flour + flavoring.
Drop from spoon + bake in
fairly hot oven. (375°)

cakes and cookies

---

white frosting

3 egg white
3/4 cups sugar
6 tablespoon light corn syrup
1/4 tsp cream tartar
1/4 tsp. salt
1/4 tsp vanilla

Combine egg whites, sugar, syrup cream of tartar + salt in top double boiler. Place pan over boiling water + beat until mixture stands in peaks.

coconut frosting

1-1/2 cups sugar
1/4 tsp. cream tartar
4 egg whites
1/2 cup water

Combine in saucepan. cook (stirring only until sugar dissolves) to very hard ball stage. Beat 4 egg white until stiff, not dry. pour syrup slowly over egg whites, beating constantly, add vanilla. beat until frosting holds in peaks. add coconut to frosting spread sides + top with shredded coconut

Icing for white Coconut Cake

2 cups white sugar, enough water to dissolve.
2 egg whites
1 coconut or 1 can
7 rakutied coconut
1 Vanilla

cook sugar + water until reaches soft ball stage. Pour over eggs then add Vanilla

---

A. G. BINGHAM ROOFING & SIDING CO.
PHONE 397   POST OFFICE BOX 547
THOMASVILLE, N. C.

Christmas Strawberry Cake

1 pkc. White cake mix
4 Eggs
1 cup vegetable oil
1 pkc. Strawberry jello
1 cup water
1/2 cup juice from a small pk frozen Strawberries

Soften jello in the halfcup water
Combine other ingredients and blend all together in Electric mixer for at least 4 min.
Bake in 9 in pans for 30 min. at 350°

Icing

1/2 stick butter
1 box sugar
1 small pkg frozen strawberries
Cream butter + sugar
add as much of the drained strawberries as the mixture will take

---

Devils Food Cake

Custard Part

1   Egg
1   C. Brown sugar
3 1/2 sq. Chocolate
1/2 C. Buttermilk or milk

Cook slowly over low flame until well mixed. Set aside + cool.

Cream together 1/2 c. Shortening + 1 c. brown sugar. Add 2 1/2 c. flour, 1/2 c. milk, 2 eggs, 1/2 tsp. sod—, — salt and vanilla. Pour in Custard part. Bake.

Bubba's Pound Cake

Try toasting pound cake with butter.

3¼	cups sugar	¾	teaspoon baking powder
2½	sticks butter	1½	cups whole milk
5	eggs	3	teaspoons lemon extract
¾	cup shortening	½	teaspoon vanilla extract
3½	cups all-purpose flour		

Cream sugar, butter and shortening. Add eggs one at a time. In a bowl, combine dry ingredients. Alternate milk with dry ingredients; Add lemon and vanilla extracts. Pour in large Bundt or tube pan – fill only ½ full. Bake in preheated 350° oven for 1 hour, 10 minutes or until set.

Marble Pound Cake

3	cups sugar	1	teaspoon vanilla
3	sticks butter, softened	1	teaspoon almond extract
6	eggs	2	squares baking chocolate, melted
3	cups flour, sifted		
1	cup evaporated milk		

Grease and flour angel food cake pan. In large mixing bowl, cream sugar and softened butter well. Add eggs, one at a time, mixing after each. Add sifted flour alternately with evaporated milk. Add vanilla and almond flavorings.

Divide batter in half. Add melted chocolate to one-half of batter. In greased tube pan, alternate spoonfuls of plain and spoonfuls of chocolate batter. Start cake in cold oven. Turn oven on to 300° and bake for 1½ hours. Use straw to test.

Southern cooks take pride in their heirloom pound cake recipes which have been passed down from generation to generation to generation ever since the first English colonists settled in Virginia. This was my grandmother's pound cake recipe, originally written down in pencil on the back of scrap paper and used for over 50 years.

My grandmother's files were full of different versions of pound cakes. The following recipes are versions of old pound cake recipes, some of them dating back at least 75 years.

This is the pound cake recipe that Lois Bradshaw, Bubba's best friend, prepared at all of my grandmother's birthday parties, even when Lois was in her 80's and 90's. She would painstakingly and meticulously assemble these beautiful cakes for Bubba's birthday parties that looked like wedding cakes, working on them for a week or more. Lois made my grandmother this special cake until Bubba's 98th birthday.

I found this Lemon Buttermilk Pound Cake recipe, after my cookbook was complete, in the back pages of a 1941 cookbook of my husband's grandmother. She had penciled it in between other recipes. I added it because it was different from the other pound cakes.

Lois Bradshaw's Famous Pound Cake

2	sticks butter	½	teaspoon baking powder
¼	cup Crisco shortening	¼	teaspoon salt
3	cups sugar	1	cup whole milk
5	eggs	1	teaspoon vanilla
3	cups all-purpose flour	1	tablespoon lemon juice

Cream butter, Crisco and sugar. Add eggs, one at a time and beat thoroughly. Add flour, which has been mixed with the baking powder and salt, and alternate with the milk. Blend in flavorings. Pour into greased and floured tube pan. Place in COLD oven at 350°. Bake 60-70 minutes (or until it leaves sides of pan).

Lemon Buttermilk Pound Cake

3	sticks butter or margarine	½	teaspoon soda
2½	cups sugar	1	cup buttermilk
4	eggs	1	teaspoon lemon extract or 2 tablespoons lemon juice
3½	cups all-purpose flour		
½	teaspoon salt		

Beat butter with sugar until light. Add eggs, one at a time. Beat in flour, which has been sifted with salt and soda, alternately with buttermilk. Add lemon flavoring or juice. Bake in a preheated 300° oven for 1 hour 15 minutes.

To make buttermilk:
Add 2 tablespoons vinegar to 1 cup regular milk.

cakes

Mrs. Snyder's Chocolate Pound Cake

2	sticks butter		¼	teaspoon salt
½	cup shortening		½	teaspoon baking powder
3	cups sugar		½	cup cocoa
5	eggs		1¼	cups whole milk
3	cups sifted all-purpose flour		1	teaspoon vanilla

Cream butter and shortening with sugar. Add eggs one at a time and blend well after each. Sift together dry ingredients and add alternately with milk. Add vanilla. Pour batter into greased and floured tube pan. Bake in a preheated 325° oven for 1 hour and 25 minutes. Cool and turn from pan.

Bubba's Cheesecake

This was my grandmother's cheesecake recipe, written on the back of a letter dated 1968.

1½	pounds cream cheese		1	teaspoon vanilla
1	(14-ounce) can sweetened condensed milk		1	teaspoon lemon or orange rind
4	large egg yolks		4	large egg whites
1	cup sour cream		½	teaspoon salt
1	tablespoon confectioners' sugar			Graham cracker crumbs

Beat together cream cheese with condensed milk. Keep beating, increasing the speed and add egg yolks one at a time, beating well after each addition, until mixture is very smooth.

Lower the speed slightly and add sour cream, confectioners' sugar, vanilla and lemon or orange rind. Beat egg whites with ½ teaspoon salt until stiff and fold them gently into the cheese mixture. Pour the batter in a 10-inch springform pan lined with your favorite cookie or graham cracker crumb crust.

Bake in slow oven – 275° for 1 hour. Turn off the heat, and do not open the door for at least 45 minutes. Let cake cook completely in the oven. Do not remove it from the pan until cake is cold.

This chocolate pound cake recipe came from a very old newspaper clipping, contributed from Mrs. Kenneth Synder of Reidsville, NC. She says, "This cake is real moist and gets better as the days go by. I have kept it for a week and it is still good but I usually freeze it after a few days."
My grandmother had it in her collection. Judging from the article, I'd say the recipe is at least 30-40 years old.

Graham Cracker Crust

1 cup graham cracker crumbs

¼ cup sugar

⅔ cup melted butter

Make graham cracker crust by mixing together the graham cracker crumbs, sugar and melted butter. Press firmly into a 10-inch springform pan that has been lightly sprayed with cooking spray.

Oreo Cheesecake

A nice alternative to the traditional plain cheesecake. Children will be particularly delighted.

1	cup graham cracker crumbs	4	eggs
¼	cup sugar	¾	tablespoon vanilla extract
⅔	cup melted butter	⅓	teaspoon salt
1⅓	pounds cream cheese, softened	4	cups sour cream
1⅓	cups sugar	7	ounces Oreo cookie crumbs
1⅓	tablespoons cornstarch		

Make graham cracker crust by mixing together the cracker crumbs, sugar and butter. Press into a 10-inch springform pan that has been sprayed with cooking spray.

Make filling by beating softened cream cheese on medium speed in a mixer until smooth; add sugar and cornstarch. Beat in eggs one at a time; mix thoroughly. Add vanilla, salt and sour cream. Beat thoroughly. Fold in cookie crumbs.

Pour into prepared springform pan. Set the filled cake pan inside a larger pan with a couple of inches of water around it to prevent the cake from cracking on the top, and place it all in the preheated 350° oven for 1-1½ hours. Pat the cake on top – it should not jiggle but should spring back. If the cake does not seem to be done and the top is as brown as you like it, lower the oven temperature to 325° and bake it another 15 minutes.

When done, remove the cake from the oven and allow to cool about 30 minutes before removing it from the pan. Run a knife around the sides before opening the pans, then run the knife under the bottom. You may need a large spatula to remove the cake to a plate.

Chocolate Cheesecake

18	chocolate wafers	1	cup sugar
¼	cup butter, melted	3	eggs
¼	teaspoon cinnamon	2	teaspoons cocoa
1	(8-ounce) package semi-sweet chocolate	1	teaspoon vanilla
		2	cups sour cream
3	(8-ounce) packages cream cheese, softened		

Preheat oven to 350°. Crush enough wafers with a rolling pin to make 1 cup of crumbs. Melt butter in saucepan. Mix in crumbs and cinnamon. Press the crumb mixture on bottom of an 8-inch springform pan, then buckle sides on. Chill.

Melt chocolate in top of double boiler. In a large bowl, beat the softened cream cheese until fluffy and smooth, using an electric mixer. Beat in sugar. Add eggs, one at a time, beating after each addition. Beat in melted chocolate, cocoa and vanilla, blending thoroughly. Beat in sour cream. Pour into springform pan. Bake 1 hour 10 minutes in the preheated 350° oven.

The cake will still be runny but will become firm as it chills. Cool at room temperature, then chill in refrigerator at least 5 hours before serving.

Lemon Delight Cake Sauce

¾ cup sugar

3 teaspoons cornstarch

½ teaspoon salt

¾ cup water

3 eggs, separated

1 tablespoon butter

⅓ cup lemon juice

¼ teaspoon cream of tartar

⅓ cup sugar

Mix sugar, cornstarch and salt in heavy pan and heat on medium heat. Gradually add water and continue cooking, stirring constantly. Boil 1 minute.

Beat egg yolks slightly and add half of the hot mixture to the egg yolks and then stir the yolk mixture back into the saucepan with the sugar mixture. Cook on medium heat until mixture boils. Add butter and lemon juice. If mixture is lumpy beat until smooth. Cool. When almost cold, add egg whites beaten to a meringue with the cream of tartar, folding in gently. Cut cake into 4 layers and spread lemon frosting between layers. Spread lemon frosting between layers and on top. Garnish with candied lemon and mint leaves. Chill until ready to use.

Yellow Angel Food Cake

Top this light cake with sugared strawberries or Lemon Delight Cake Sauce.

5	egg yolks	5	egg whites
½	cup cold water	½	teaspoon salt
1½	cups sugar	¾	teaspoon cream of tartar
1½	cups cake flour	1	teaspoon vanilla
½	teaspoon baking powder	1	tablespoon lemon juice

Beat egg yolks until light. Add cold water and sugar and beat well. Sift cake flour together with baking powder. Sift several times. Add flour to the egg yolk mixture.

Gently beat egg whites until stiff. Add salt, cream of tartar and continue beating. Add vanilla and lemon juice, then fold egg white mixture into the yolk/flour mixture. Pour into ungreased 10-inch angel food cake pan with removable bottom. Bake for 1 hour in a 300° oven, then 15 minutes longer at 325°. To release cake, insert knife between outer crust and the cake, pressing hard all around the sides of the pan. Enjoy the cake plain or top with Lemon Delight Cake Sauce or with strawberries and sugar.

Mother's Easy Coconut Cake

1 cup butter, softened
2 cups sugar
4 large eggs
1 teaspoon vanilla

½ teaspoon salt
3 teaspoons baking powder
3 cups sifted flour
1 cup milk

Beat the butter with the sugar until light and creamy. Add eggs one at a time and add vanilla. Mix the flour with baking powder and salt and add to the batter, alternating with the milk. Pour into 2 (8-inch or 9-inch) cake pans. Bake in a preheated 350° oven for 35-30 minutes. Cool on wire racks. When cool, slice layers in half to make 4 layers. Ice layers with Coconut Icing.

Lemon Cheesecake

1 cup graham cracker crumbs
4 tablespoons butter, melted
1 (3-ounce) package lemon Jell-O
1 cup boiling water

3 tablespoons lemon juice
1 (8-ounce) cream cheese
1 (3-ounce) cream cheese
1 teaspoon vanilla
1 cup sugar
1 large can Pet sweet milk

Crush graham cracker crumbs in bowl. Stir melted butter in the crumbs until mixed. Press in the bottom of a 9-inch springform pan until firm and bake in a 325° oven for 10 minutes. Remove from oven.

Dissolve lemon Jell-O with boiling water and lemon juice. Set aside. Cream together in large bowl the cream cheese, vanilla and sugar.

Pour 1 can of Pet sweet milk in a large bowl in refrigerator or freezer until ice crystals form around edge of bowl. Whip sweet milk until stiff. Add a few drops of lemon juice after milk has whipped up and begins to stiffen.

Combine Jell-O mixture and cheese mixture, blend well and add to whipped cream. Whip all well. Pour in graham cracker crust and chill until firm.

Coconut Icing

3 cups sour cream

2¼ cups granulated sugar

4½ cups frozen coconut

Mix icing with a spoon and spread between layers and on top. You can make 1 day before using and refrigerate. You can even freeze.

Coconut Cake Supreme

2¾	cups sifted cake flour	1½	cups sugar, divided
4	teaspoons baking powder	4	egg whites
¾	teaspoon salt	1	teaspoon vanilla extract
¾	cup butter	1	cup coconut milk or sweet milk

Sift cake flour, baking powder and salt 3 times. In separate bowl, cream butter well. Add 1 cup sugar and beat until fluffy and light. Beat egg whites at room temperature until frothy; gradually add ½ cup sugar and beat until stiff peaks form.

Combine liquids; add alternately with flour to creamed mixture. Beat well. Fold in egg whites. Pour into 3 greased and waxed paper lined 8-inch layer pans. Bake in moderate preheated oven, 350°, for 25-30 minutes. Cool on cake racks. Unfrosted layers will freeze. Frost with Snowy White Frosting.

Snowy White Frosting:

2	cups sugar	3	egg whites
1	cup water	½	teaspoon vanilla extract
⅛	teaspoon salt	½	pound fresh coconut, grated
1	teaspoon white vinegar		

Cook sugar, water, salt and vinegar in heavy saucepan over medium heat, stirring until clear. Without stirring, cook until mixture forms thin threads when dropped from a spoon.

Beat egg whites until stiff. Add hot syrup in a thin stream, beating constantly until frosting holds shape. Add vanilla. Spread on layers and sprinkle with coconut. Frost top and sides and sprinkle with coconut.

cakes

Coconut Poke Cake

1	white or yellow sheet cake	½	cup sugar
1	teaspoon coconut flavoring	2	(6-ounce) bags frozen coconut
1	cup milk		Cool Whip

Prepare one white or yellow sheet cake according to cake box directions in a 9x13-inch pan, but add 1 package coconut and coconut flavoring to the batter. After baking cake, while it is still warm, punch holes in it with a fork, then pour over it a syrup made with: 1 cup milk, ½ cup sugar and 6 ounces coconut. Boil the syrup just a couple of minutes. Let sit until cool. Add a layer of cool whip to the top of the cake and sprinkle coconut on the top. You can use more coconut if desired – up to 12 ounces frozen coconut works well. Recipe makes a rather thick cake and one that should be eaten with a fork.

Variation: For a different icing try mixing ¼ cup warm water with 1 cup confectioners' sugar and 1 can sweetened condensed milk. Pour over cake while it is still warm and follow rest of original recipe.

Easy Chocolate Bundt Cake

Semi-homemade, but passes for scratch every time!

1	box Duncan Hines yellow cake mix	1	teaspoon vanilla
2	(3-ounce) boxes Jell-O instant chocolate pudding	4	eggs
		1	(12-ounce) package chocolate chips
1½	cups water		White chocolate to drizzle on top
½	cup oil		

Mix above well and pour into greased and floured Bundt pan. Bake in preheated 350° oven for 1 hour. Drizzle with melted white chocolate.

Chocolate Butter Frosting

½ pound butter, softened

¾ box confectioners' sugar

6 tablespoons cocoa

¼ cup milk, hot

Pinch of salt

1 teaspoon vanilla

Beat together butter, sugar, cocoa, hot milk, pinch of salt and vanilla until creamy and light.

Deep Dark Chocolate Cake

1¾	cups unsifted flour	1	teaspoon salt
2	cups sugar	2	eggs
¾	cup cocoa	1	cup milk
1½	teaspoons baking soda	½	cup vegetable oil
1½	teaspoons baking powder	2	teaspoons vanilla
		1	cup boiling water

Combine dry ingredients in large mixer bowl. Add eggs, milk, oil and vanilla. Beat 2 minutes at medium speed. Remove bowl from mixer and stir in boiling water. Batter will be thin. Pour into 2 greased 9-inch or 3 (8-inch) layer pans or 1 (13x9x2-inch) pan. Bake 350° for 30-35 minutes. Cool on wire racks and ice with Chocolate Butter Frosting.

German Chocolate Cake

2	cups sugar	2½	cups cake flour
1	cup Crisco or butter	1	cup buttermilk, divided
4	eggs, separated	1	teaspoon baking soda
1	(4-ounce) bar Baker's German Chocolate	1	teaspoon vanilla
½	cup boiling water		Dash of salt

Cream shortening and sugar together. Separate eggs and add yolks one at a time to shortening and sugar mixture. Add Baker's chocolate which has been melted in the boiling water. Dissolve baking soda in ½ cup buttermilk. Add alternately the flour and ½ cup buttermilk (not soda/buttermilk mixture). Now add the buttermilk/soda mixture. Add vanilla and salt. Fold in stiffly beaten egg whites.

Grease and flour 4 (8-inch) cake pans. Line bottom of pans with wax or parchment paper. Bake 30 minutes in preheated 350° oven.

Coconut-Pecan Icing

1	cup sugar	3	beaten egg yolks
1	cup evaporated milk	1	can angel flake coconut
1	stick butter	½	cup chopped pecans
1	teaspoon vanilla		

Beat together sugar, milk, butter and egg yolks; cook in heavy double boiler until thick, stirring constantly. Add coconut and pecans. Add vanilla. Spread between layers and on top and sides of cake.

cakes

Decadent Fudge Cake

1	cup butter, softened
1½	cups sugar
4	eggs
1	cup buttermilk
½	teaspoon baking soda
2½	cups all-purpose flour
2	(4-ounce) bars sweet baking chocolate, melted and cooled
1	cup chocolate syrup
2	teaspoons vanilla extract
1½	cups semi-sweet chocolate mini-morsels, divided
4	ounces white chocolate, chopped
2	tablespoons plus 2 teaspoons shortening, divided
	Chocolate and white chocolate leaves (optional)

Cream butter in a large mixing bowl; gradually add sugar, beating well at medium speed of an electric mixer. Add eggs, one at a time, beating well after each addition. Combine buttermilk and soda, stirring well. Add to creamed mixture alternately with flour, beginning and ending with flour. Add 2 bars melted chocolate, chocolate syrup, and vanilla. Mix well. Stir in 1 cup mini-morsels.

Pour batter into a heavily greased and floured 10-inch Bundt pan. Bake in a preheated 300° oven for 1 hour and 20 minutes or until a wooden pick inserted in center comes out clean. Invert cake immediately onto a serving plate, and let cool completely.

To make icing drizzle for cake, combine white chocolate and 2 tablespoons shortening in top of a double boiler; bring water to a boil. Reduce heat to low; cook until melted and smooth. Remove from heat. Drizzle mixture over cooled cake. Melt remaining ½ cup mini-morsels and 2 teaspoons shortening in a small saucepan over low heat, stirring until smooth. Remove from heat, and let cool; drizzle over white chocolate. Garnish with chocolate and white chocolate leaves – optional. Makes 1 (10-inch) Bundt cake.

Chocolate Ice Box Cake

1 cake of Baker's chocolate

4 tablespoons confectioners' sugar

4 tablespoons water or milk

4 eggs, separated

Ladyfingers

Place chocolate, sugar and water or milk in top of double boiler. When mixture is thoroughly melted and mixed, add the beaten egg yolks and combine thoroughly with the chocolate mixture. Cool slightly and fold in the stiffly beaten egg whites and flavoring, if desired.

Line a square pan with heavy waxed paper and place a layer of ladyfinger halves on the bottom. Cover with chocolate mixture and add another layer of ladyfingers. Repeat with chocolate mixture and top with ladyfinger halves. Leave in the refrigerator for 24 hours. Before serving, turn out on chilled platter. Cut in portions. Serve with whipped cream. Serves at least 6.

Vanilla Cream Filling

1 cup cream

¼ cup confectioners' sugar

1 teaspoon vanilla

Whip cream with confectioners' sugar and vanilla. Refrigerate until ready to use.

Chocolate Frosting

6 ounces good quality chocolate chips

½ cup half-and-half or cream

1 cup unsalted butter

2½ cups confectioners' sugar

Combine chocolate chips, half-and-half and butter in a medium saucepan. Stir over medium heat until smooth. Remove from heat and blend in confectioners' sugar with wire whisk. Set saucepan over a bowl of ice and beat frosting until it thickens and holds its shape.

Chocolate Layered Cake

2¾	cups flour, sifted	1	cup salted butter, softened
2	teaspoons baking soda		
½	teaspoon salt	2½	cups sugar
½	teaspoon baking powder	4	eggs
1	cup cocoa	1½	teaspoons vanilla
2	cups boiling water		

Preheat oven to 350°. Spray 3 (9-inch) round cake pans with Baker's Joy or grease and flour.

In a bowl, combine cocoa and boiling water, whisking until smooth. Cool completely. Sift flour with soda, salt and baking powder. Set aside.

In a large bowl, beat butter, sugar, eggs and vanilla until light. At low speed, beat in flour mixture, alternating with cocoa mixture – about 4 times – beginning and ending with flour. Do not overbeat.

Divide evenly into 3 cake pans and bake in oven for 25-30 minutes. Cool 10 minutes. Loosen sides and remove from pans. Cool on racks. Fill layers with Vanilla Cream Filling and frost cake with Chocolate Frosting.

Holiday Cranberry Cake

1¼	cups ground frozen cranberries	4	eggs
		½	cup ground walnuts
1	(1-pound 3-ounce) package lemon cake mix	¼	cup sugar
		1	teaspoon mace (optional)
1	(3-ounce) package cream cheese, softened		Confectioners' sugar (optional)
¾	cup milk		

Run berries through food chopper while still frozen. This will save a lot of mess. Blend cake mix, cream cheese and milk and beat 2 minutes at medium speed. Add eggs, blend and beat for 2 more minutes. Combine cranberries, walnuts, sugar and mace; fold into cake batter. Pour into well greased and floured 10" tube or Bundt pan. Bake in preheated 350° oven for 1 hour or until done. Cool 15 minutes and remove from pan. Cool on wire rack. Dust with confectioners' sugar if desired.

Tipsy Cake

¾	cup slivered almonds		Sponge cake
	Apple brandy	1	pint whipping cream
	Boiled Egg Custard,		Sugar to taste
	recipe listed below		

In a small bowl, soak almonds with apple brandy until barely covered. Let almonds soak while you are preparing the Boiled Egg Custard.

Boiled Egg Custard:

1	quart whole milk	¼	teaspoon salt
1	tablespoon flour	4	eggs, beaten
1	cup sugar	2	teaspoons vanilla

To make the Boiled Egg Custard, first heat milk in top of a double boiler until hot. In a medium-sized bowl, mix together the flour, sugar and salt with the beaten eggs. Temper the egg mixture with a little hot milk, then slowly add all of the milk to the bowl. Immediately transfer the milk/egg mixture back to the double boiler, cooking on medium heat until custard is thick and smooth, about 20-25 minutes. Remove from heat and stir in vanilla.

To assemble Tipsy Cake, use your favorite sponge cake recipe or purchase a store bought brand. In a 4-quart dish, break up sponge cake into small (1 to 2-inch) pieces. Layer cake pieces in 3 layers, sprinkling about ¼ cup of the brandy-soaked almonds on each layer. (Reserve a few almonds to sprinkle on top of cake.) You may also drizzle each cake layer with apple brandy, using as much as you would like (a few tablespoons per layer might be adequate.)

Pour warm Egg Custard over entire layered cake and almonds.

Whip one pint of whipping cream, adding 1-2 tablespoons apple brandy and sugar to taste. Top the layered cake pieces and Egg Custard with whipped cream. Sprinkle reserved almonds on top. Cover and refrigerate overnight. The longer it sits, the better.

This recipe has been handed down for three generations in my cousin's family from Carrie Sparger Coon. My cousin Ann Hall Banks graciously shared it with me.

Strawberry Frosting

½ stick butter

1 box confectioners' sugar

1 small package frozen strawberries, juice reserved for cake

Cream butter and add confectioners' sugar. Add as much of the drained strawberries as the mixture will take.

Red Velvet Cake Frosting

1 cup milk

3 tablespoons flour

1 cup sugar

1 cup butter

1 cup pecans, chopped

1 cup flaked coconut

1 teaspoon vanilla

Cook milk and flour until thickened. Set aside to cool. Cream sugar and butter; add to cooled flour mixture. Add remaining ingredients, mixing well. Ice cake.

Christmas Strawberry Cake

My grandmother wrote this recipe in the pages of June Platt's 1941 Plain and Fancy Cookbook.

1	package white cake mix	½	cup water
4	eggs	½	cup juice from a small package of frozen strawberries
1	cup vegetable oil		
1	package strawberry Jell-O		

Soften Jell-O in the ½ cup water. Combine softened gelatin with cake mix, eggs, vegetable oil and strawberries and juice in electric mixer, beating for at least 4 minutes. Pour into 3 prepared (9-inch) pans and bake for 30 minutes in a preheated 350° oven. When cooled, frost cake with Strawberry Frosting.

Red Velvet Cake

2	cups sugar	2½	cups cake flour
1	cup butter	½	teaspoon salt
3	eggs	1½	teaspoons baking soda
1	tablespoon vinegar	¼	teaspoon baking powder
1	tablespoon cocoa	1	cup buttermilk
2	ounces red food coloring	1	teaspoon vanilla

Cream sugar and butter; add eggs. Make a paste of vinegar, cocoa and food coloring. Add to creamed mixture. Sift together dry ingredients. Add dry ingredients to the creamed mixture, alternating with buttermilk. Add vanilla and blend thoroughly. Pour into greased and floured layer pans. Bake in preheated 350° oven for 30 minutes. Frost cake once cooled.

Pumpkin Cake

*This was one of my mother-in-law's recipes, passed down
by her mother. It would be wonderful around Thanksgiving.*

2	cups sugar		3	cups self-rising flour
4	eggs		2	teaspoons allspice
1½	cups Wesson oil		2	teaspoons cinnamon
2	cups packed pumpkin			

Beat sugar and eggs. Add Wesson oil. Mix in flour and spice
which have been sifted together. Pour into greased and floured
loaf pans and bake in preheated 350° oven for 45-50 minutes.
Ice cake with Pumpkin Cake Icing once cooled.

Orange Cake

1	stick butter		1	teaspoon soda
1	cup sugar		⅔	cup buttermilk
2	eggs		½	cup dates or nut meats
2	cups flour (sifted before measuring)			(optional)

Cream butter and sugar together, add eggs one at a time, beating
thoroughly after addition of each egg. Add dry ingredients
alternately with buttermilk. Add dates or nut meat if desired. Pour
into greased and floured Bundt pan. Heat in preheated 350° oven
for 45 minutes.

Remove cake from pan while still hot. While cake is hot, pour
orange glaze over cake.

Pumpkin Cake Icing

1 box confectioners' sugar

1 stick butter

1 cup Crisco shortening

2 egg whites, stiffly beaten

1 cup chopped pecans

Cream sugar, butter
and Crisco. Fold in egg whites.
Ice cake and sprinkle pecans
on top of cake.

Orange Cake Topping

1 cup sugar

Juice and grated rind
of 2 oranges

1 teaspoon + lemon juice

To make topping, mix sugar,
orange juice, grated orange
rind and lemon juice together
until well blended.

Lemon Cake Squares

6 tablespoons butter

1 cup sugar

2 beaten eggs

1½ cups sifted flour

1½ teaspoons baking powder

¼ teaspoon salt

½ cup milk

Grated rind of 2 lemons

Glaze:

⅔ cup sugar

Juice of 2 lemons

Cream together the butter and sugar. Add eggs, one at a time. Then add the flour, which has been blended with the baking powder and salt. Lastly mix in the milk and grated lemon rinds. Pour the batter into a greased and floured 13x9x2-inch baking pan. Bake in 350° oven for 25 minutes. Spoon the glaze over the cake and return to oven for 5 more minutes. Cut into squares while still warm.

Snow Ball Cake

2	(3-ounce) boxes lemon Jell-O	1	(20-ounce) can crushed pineapple (not drained)
¼	cup cold water		
1	cup boiling water	1	angel food cake, large
1	cup sugar	3	boxes Dream Whip Frozen fresh coconut

Mix 2 boxes lemon Jell-O and cold water together. Add boiling water and sugar; stir until dissolved. Add the crushed pineapple, and set aside and chill until thickened. Fold in 2 boxes of Dream Whip (mixed according to directions on the box, omitting the vanilla). Line large mixing bowl with waxed paper.

In the meantime, break the angel food cake into small pieces. Place alternate layers of cake and filling in the bowl until used up, beginning and ending with the cake on top and bottom. Put in the refrigerator and chill until firm.

Unmold on plate and take off waxed paper. Ice with 1 box of Dream Whip (mixed again according to the directions, omitting the vanilla). Garnish with 1 package fresh frozen coconut.

Variation: Strawberries can be used in lieu of the crushed pineapple.

Patti's Orange Blossoms

½	cup margarine, softened	¾	cup milk
1½	cups sugar	1	teaspoon vanilla extract
3	eggs	½	teaspoon lemon extract
2	cups all-purpose flour	1	teaspoon grated lemon rind
1½	teaspoons baking powder	1	teaspoon grated orange rind
½	teaspoon salt		

Preheat oven to 350°. Lightly grease mini muffin tins with cooking spray. Cream margarine and sugar. Add eggs one at a time. Beat well after each. Combine flour with salt and baking powder. Add to batter, alternating with milk until well combined. Add extract, lemon rind and orange rind.

Fill muffin tins half way and bake 10-12 minutes. Dip warm muffins in glaze and let cool on wire racks.

Orange Blossom Glaze

Juice of 2 oranges

Juice of 2 lemons

⅛ teaspoon salt

1½ pounds confectioners' sugar

A little grated orange rind

A little grated lemon rind

Mix juices with a little grated lemon and orange rind, along with salt and confectioners' sugar.

Oatmeal Cake

1½	cups boiling water	1	teaspoon baking soda
1	cup quick oatmeal	½	teaspoon nutmeg
2	sticks butter	1	teaspoon cinnamon
1	cup brown sugar		Pinch salt
1	cup white sugar	1	teaspoon almond extract
2	eggs		
1½	cups all-purpose flour		

Pour boiling water on the oatmeal. Set aside to cook. Cream butter, brown sugar and white sugar. Add eggs, one at a time, and beat well after each. Sift together flour, baking soda, nutmeg, cinnamon and salt. Add to sugar and egg mixture. Beat oatmeal and add flour mixture and almond extract. Bake in long Pyrex dish for 40 minutes at 300°. Remove from oven, leave in dish and top with following Coconut Topping.

Coconut Topping

1 stick melted butter

1 cup brown sugar

1 box or can of Angel flake coconut

½ cup pecans

2 egg yolks

Sprinkle topping on warm cake and brown under broiler or bake 15 minutes in 350° oven.

Apple Cake Glaze

1 teaspoon vanilla

½ cup buttermilk

1 stick butter

1 cup white sugar

In a saucepan, bring all the ingredients to a boil, stirring constantly. Pour over hot apple cake while hot cake is still in the pan. Let stand for approximately 8 hours or overnight in the pan. Remove cake from pan and icing will have seeped to the top.

My mother makes this cake all the time. It's a staple when she needs a simple cake for company. It has been served at many a family or holiday dinner.

Mom's Fresh Apple Cake

1¼	cups oil		2	teaspoons vanilla, divided
2	cups sugar		3	cups peeled diced Granny Smith apples
3	eggs			
3	cups unsifted plain flour, divided		1	cup chopped pecans
1	teaspoon salt		1	cup white raisins
1	teaspoon baking soda		1	cup coconut

With an electric beater, blend oil and sugar. Add eggs and all dry ingredients except ½ cup flour and 1 teaspoon vanilla. In a separate bowl, mix together the apples, pecans, raisins, coconut, ½ cup flour and vanilla. Add this to the batter. Pour into a greased, floured tube pan. Bake at 325° for 1-1½ hours, depending on how hot your oven is. Top warm cake while it's still in the pan with Apple Cake Glaze.

Mom's Rum Cake

1	package Duncan Hines Deluxe Golden yellow cake mix		½	cup water
			½	cup rum
			½	cup vegetable oil
1	regular size instant vanilla pudding mix		4	eggs

Mix above and pour into greased and floured Bundt or tube pan. Bake for 45 minutes in preheated 350° oven. Glaze warm cake.

Rum Cake Glaze:

1½	cups sugar, divided		¼	cup light Rum
1	stick butter		¼	cup water

Boil 1 cup sugar, butter, Rum and water in a small saucepan for 2-3 minutes. Remove from heat. Before spooning glaze over warm cake, add another ½ cup sugar to glaze. After glazing cake, sprinkle additional sugar over glazed cake. This will produce a "crusty" sugar coating.

cakes

Gooey Butter Cake

1 egg, beaten
1 stick butter, softened
1 Betty Crocker Chocolate cake mix
2 eggs

1 (8-ounce) package cream cheese, softened
1 box confectioners' sugar

Mix together the beaten egg, butter, and cake mix. Press into the bottom of a 9x13-inch pan.

Beat eggs, cream cheese and confectioners' sugar together and pour over the pressed cake mixture.

Bake cake for 45 minutes in preheated 350° oven. Check after 35 minutes. Let it cool before trying to cut. It's a little messy and hard to cut squares but is good, nevertheless.

Variation: Use Duncan Hines Butter cake mix instead of chocolate for a "chess cake."

My husband's grandmother and mother both had this butter cake recipe in their files, but his grandmother's recipe was almost illegible. I found this one typed in mother-in-law's recipe files.

Rum Frosted Mince Cake

1 package apple spice cake mix
¾ cup water

2 eggs, unbeaten
1 cup moist mincemeat

Empty cake mix into bowl. Add water, eggs and mincemeat. Beat 3 minutes until batter is creamy. Pour into 2 round 9-inch cake pans which have been greased and floured. Bake in a 350° oven 35-40 minutes. Cool. Spread Rum Butter Frosting between layers and over top and sides.

Rum Butter Frosting:

½ cup butter
4 cups sifted confectioners' sugar

5 tablespoons milk
½ teaspoon rum extract

Cream butter; add salt and part of sugar gradually, blending after each addition. Add remaining sugar alternately with milk, until proper consistency to spread, beating after each addition until smooth. Add rum extract and blend. Makes about 2⅓ cups frosting.

This recipe was originally published in the *Greensboro News* around 1960-1970 by Martha Long. In the article Martha said this cake was just the right cake to offer holiday visitors along with a cup of coffee. The addition of the mincemeat keeps the cake moist.

Caramel Icing

1 stick butter

1 cup dark brown sugar

½ cup milk

1 teaspoon vanilla

1 teaspoon vinegar

½-⅔ box confectioners' sugar

Melt 1 stick butter in heavy saucepan. Add dark brown sugar and boil hard for 1 minute. Then add ½ cup milk and cook 2 minutes. Remove from heat and add 1 teaspoon vanilla and 1 teaspoon vinegar. Let cool. Then add confectioners' sugar until desired consistency is reached.

This is one of my daughter's favorites when we go to county and state fairs. I came across this recipe while looking through a batch of old family recipes. My daughter was thrilled.

1-2-3-4 Cake

This is a basic yellow cake
recipe that you can ice as you see fit.

1	cup butter, softened	2	teaspoons baking powder
2	cups sugar		
3	cups flour	2	teaspoons vanilla or 1 teaspoon lemon extract
4	eggs		
1	cup milk		

Cream butter and sugar and add eggs one at a time. Beat well and add milk and dry ingredients last, beating thoroughly. Bake in 2 greased and floured 8-inch round pans or 2 (8-inch) square pans. Bake at 350° for 30 minutes or until set. Ice with Caramel Icing or any other that you like.

Funnel Cakes

6	eggs	½	teaspoon baking soda
7	cups all-purpose flour	4	cups whole milk
4	teaspoons baking powder	½	cup sugar
			Pinch salt

Mix all ingredients. Pour through a funnel into skillet of lard (can use oil or shortening) which has been heated to approximately 350-375°. (My cast iron skillet works well.) Make design of your choice and fry until light brown. Sprinkle confectioners' sugar on top of funnel cake and serve while hot. Makes 12-15 medium funnel cakes.

cakes

Homemade Strawberry Shortcake

The contrast of hot and cold
makes this simple dessert outstanding.

1	quart strawberries, hulled and cut into halves	½	teaspoon salt
		1½	sticks unsalted butter
2	tablespoons orange liqueur (optional)	1	cup light cream or milk
			Additional sugar for sprinkling over shortcakes
½	cup granulated sugar, divided		
		1	cup heavy cream
3	cups sifted all-purpose flour	¼	cup confectioners' sugar
4	teaspoons baking powder	1	teaspoon vanilla

Mix halved berries with liqueur and ¼ cup granulated sugar. Chill for several hours.

Sift flour with baking powder, salt and ¼ cup sugar. Cut in butter until butter particles are the size of small peas. Add light cream or milk all at once. Stir just enough to moisten dry particles. Turn dough out on lightly floured board and knead just a few times to shape into smooth ball.

With rolling pin or with fingers shape the dough into an oblong disc about 6x9-inches. With sharp knife, cut oblong into 6 (3-inch) or 12 (1½-inch) squares. Put biscuits on a lightly greased cookie sheet. Sprinkle additional granulated sugar over top of shortcakes and bake in preheated hot oven (425°) for 15 to 20 minutes or until biscuits are deeply browned.

While biscuits are baking, whip heavy cream with confectioners' sugar and vanilla until stiff. When biscuits are ready, split them while hot into halves. Spoon berries over bottom half. Top with second half of biscuit. Add more berries and top with whipped cream. Serve immediately.

Fluffy Butter Icing

6	tablespoons butter	4	cups sifted confectioners' sugar
¼	teaspoon salt	2	egg whites, unbeaten
1	teaspoon vanilla	1	tablespoon milk (about)

Cream butter, salt and vanilla together. Add sugar alternately with egg whites. Beat. Add milk and beat until smooth and of spreading consistency. Makes 2¼ cups.

Creamy Butter Frosting

½	stick butter	1	(16-ounce) box confectioners' sugar
1	teaspoon vanilla	⅓-½ cup cream	
¼	teaspoon salt		

Cream butter, add vanilla, salt, sugar and cream. Beat until smooth and of spreading consistency. Makes about 2 cups.

Butter Cream Frosting

2	sticks butter	2	egg yolks, unbeaten (1 whole egg may be substituted)
⅛	teaspoon salt		
1	(16-ounce) box sifted confectioners' sugar	1	teaspoon vanilla
		2	tablespoons milk (about)

Cream butter until soft. Add salt and part of sugar gradually, blending after each addition. Add egg yolks and vanilla, blend well. Add remaining sugar, alternately with milk, until of correct spreading consistency. Makes 2½ cups.

White Frosting

3	egg whites	¼	teaspoon cream of tartar
¾	cups sugar		
6	tablespoons light corn syrup	¼	teaspoon salt
		¼	teaspoon vanilla

Combine egg whites, sugar, corn syrup, cream of tartar and salt in top of double boiler. Place pan over boiling water and beat until mixture stands in peaks.

# Seven Minute Icing

1	cup sugar	⅓	cup boiling water
	Pinch of salt	1	egg white
⅛	teaspoon cream of tartar	½	teaspoon flavoring

Combine sugar, salt, cream of tartar and boiling water. Pour into top of double boiler. Place over boiling water and add unbeaten egg white. Beat with rotary beater about 7 minutes or until icing is thick enough to spread. Add flavorings to suit. Spread over cake.

Coconut Seven Minute Frosting

2	egg whites, unbeaten	1	teaspoon vanilla
5	tablespoons water	1	can Baker's Southern Style coconut
1½	teaspoons corn syrup		

Combine egg whites, sugar, water and corn syrup in top of double boiler. Beat until thoroughly mixed. Place over rapidly boiling water, beat constantly with egg beater and cook 7 minutes, or until frosting will stand enough to spread. Spread on white cake, sprinkling with coconut while frosting is soft. Makes enough to cover tops and sides of 2 (9-inch) layers.

Coconut Cream Cheese Frosting

2 tablespoons butter

1⅓ cups Angel Flake coconut

⅓ cup butter or more

2 (3-ounce) packages cream cheese, softened

1 pound (about 4 cups) sifted confectioners' sugar

1 tablespoon milk (or more)

½ teaspoon vanilla

Melt butter in saucepan. Add ½ cup coconut, sauté until golden brown, stirring constantly. Remove from heat. Cream ⅓ cup butter and add cream cheese to blend. Add small amounts of sugar and milk alternately and beat. Add vanilla and ¾ cup of coconut. Spread on cake. Sprinkle with remaining coconut.

Easy Chocolate Frosting

4 squares unsweetened
chocolate

2 tablespoons butter

4 cups confectioners' sugar

½ cup whole milk

1 teaspoon vanilla

Microwave chocolate
squares and margarine in large
microwavable bowl on High
2 minutes or more, until
margarine is melted. Stir until
the chocolate is completely
melted. Beat in sugar and milk,
alternately, until well blended
and smooth. Add vanilla and
blend. If necessary, let stand
until mixture is of spreading
consistency. Spread quickly.
If mixture gets too thick, add
a little milk by teaspoonfuls.
Makes 2½ cups.

Fluffy Cocoa Frosting

¾	cup Hershey's cocoa		½	cup butter
4	cups confectioners' sugar		1	teaspoon vanilla
			½	cup evaporated milk

Mix cocoa and sugar. Cream butter with part of the cocoa/sugar
mixture and blend in vanilla and half of the milk. Add remaining
cocoa-sugar and blend well. Add remaining milk and beat to desired
spreading consistency. Additional milk may be added if needed.

Creamy Chocolate Frosting

2	tablespoons Crisco shortening		2	cups sifted confectioners' sugar
1	tablespoon butter		¼	teaspoon salt
3	ounces chocolate squares		1	teaspoon vanilla
½	cup hot milk		½	cup chopped nuts, optional

Melt shortening, butter and chocolate in small saucepan on low
heat. In separate mixing bowl, pour hot milk over sifted
confectioners' sugar and salt and stir until sugar is dissolved.
Add vanilla and chocolate mixture and beat until thick enough
to spread (up to 5 minutes). If desired, add ½ cup chopped nuts.

Orange Cream Icing

1	stick butter		3	cups confectioners' sugar
4	tablespoons cake flour			
¼	teaspoon salt		1	tablespoon grated orange rind
½	cup orange juice			

Melt 1 stick of butter in saucepan. Remove from heat. Blend in
cake flour and salt. Stir in slowly orange juice and bring to a boil,
stirring constantly. Boil 1 minute. Remove from heat. Stir in sifted
confectioners' sugar. Set saucepan in bowl of cold water. Beat
until consistency to spread. Stir in 1 tablespoon grated orange
rind. Spread over cake.

Martha Long's
Rum Butter Frosting

Serve this yummy frosting over
Martha's Mince Cake, listed in the cake section.

½	cup butter	5	tablespoons milk (about)
	Dash salt	½	teaspoon rum extract
1	pound (about 4 cups) sifted confectioners' sugar		

Cream butter; add salt and part of sugar gradually, blending after each addition. Add remaining sugar alternately with milk, until spreading consistency is achieved. Beat after each addition until smooth. Add rum extract and blend. Makes 2⅓ cups frosting.

Apple Cake Glaze

Serve this glaze over any apple or spice cake.

1	teaspoon vanilla	1	stick butter
½	cup buttermilk	1	cup granulated sugar

Bring to a boil, stirring constantly. Pour over hot apple cake while cake is still in the pan. Let stand approximately 8 hours or overnight in the pan. Remove from pan and serve.

Quick Caramel Frosting

1½	sticks butter	3-4	cups sifted confectioners' sugar
1½	cups light brown sugar		
⅓-½	cup milk or cream		

Melt butter in saucepan, add brown sugar and boil over low heat for 3 minutes stirring constantly. Add milk, continue stirring until mixture comes to a boil. Remove from heat and cool. Add confectioners' sugar, beating well after each addition, until frosting becomes spreading consistency. Add rum flavoring to taste, if desired.

Grandmother's
Old-Fashioned
Caramel Frosting

1 pound light brown sugar

1 stick sweet butter

1 cup thick cream

Pinch of salt

2 teaspoons vanilla

Put brown sugar in heavy pan and moisten with thick cream. Add tiny pinch of salt and 1 stick sweet butter. Boil until soft-ball stage, 234°-240° on a candy thermometer. Remove from heat and add vanilla and cool. Beat with a silver spoon until creamy and thick enough to spread.

To wash pan in which sugar was caramelized, fill pan with hot water and boil until caramel melts in the water.

This was my mother-in-law's standard chocolate chip cookie recipe, and it came from Mrs. Ruth McCoy from Louisiana. All my neighbors in Charlotte adopted this recipe, which uses no brown sugar. Be careful in storing these, they can become brittle.

This is an adaptation of Toll House Cookies. Every time I make this recipe, they fly off the plate. They're kind of flat, chewy and crunchy, not cakey. They secret is reducing the normal number of eggs, and not adding nuts!

Ruth's Chocolate Chip Cookies

2	cups flour	1	teaspoon vanilla extract
1	teaspoon baking soda	1	(12-ounce) package semi-sweet chocolate chips
1	teaspoon salt		
1	cup butter or margarine	1	cup chopped nuts, optional
1½	cups sugar		
1	egg		

Mix flour with soda and salt. In large mixing bowl, cream butter until fluffy. Beat in sugar until light. Add egg and vanilla. Stir in flour mixture. Add chocolate chips and nuts if desired. Make 2-inch balls and set 3 inches apart on ungreased baking pan. Bake in preheated 325° oven for 9-12 minutes.

Favorite Chocolate Chip Cookies

2¼	cups all-purpose flour	¾	cup brown sugar
1	heaping teaspoon baking soda	1	heaping teaspoon vanilla extract
1	heaping teaspoon salt	1	large egg
2	sticks margarine, softened	2	cups or more semi-sweet chocolate chips
¾	cup granulated sugar		

Preheat oven to 375°. In a small bowl, combine flour, baking soda and salt. In another large mixing bowl, beat margarine until soft and creamy. Gradually add granulated sugar, brown sugar and vanilla and beat until smooth. Add egg and beat until combined. Add flour gradually and beat until combined – mixture will appear dry. Mix the chocolate chips in with a wooden spoon until combined.

Drop by large teaspoons onto baking sheets lined with parchment paper. Keep cookies 2 inches apart or they will bake together. Bake for approximately 8-10 minutes. Watch at 8 minutes. 10 minutes will produce dark golden brown cookies. For slightly lighter and softer cookies, bake 8 minutes. Makes approximately 4-5 dozen cookies, depending on size.

cookies

Chocolate Chip Crispies

1	cup butter, softened	1	teaspoon salt
1	cup vegetable oil	1	teaspoon cream of tartar
1	cup firmly packed brown sugar	1	cup regular oats, uncooked
1	cup white sugar	1	cup crisp rice cereal
1	egg	1	(12-ounce) package semi-sweet chocolate chips
2	teaspoons vanilla extract		
3½	cups all-purpose flour	¾	cup chopped pecans
1	teaspoon baking soda		

Cream butter and oil; gradually add sugars, beating at medium speed. Add egg and vanilla. Combine flour, soda, salt and cream of tartar; gradually add to the creamed mixture, mixing well. Stir in oats, rice cereal, chocolate chips and pecans. Drop by rounded spoonfuls onto greased cookie sheets. Bake at 375° for 10 to 12 minutes. Cool on wire racks. Makes 10 dozen.

This recipe was my old neighbor Jeannie Fuller's and she served these after all our neighborhood dinners. Everyone particularly liked the crunchiness that the rice crispies provide.

Cowboy Cookie in a Jar

1¼	cups quick-cooking oats	½	cup chopped pecans
½	cup granulated sugar	1⅓	cups all-purpose flour
1	cup semi-sweet chocolate chips	¼	teaspoon salt
½	cup brown sugar, packed	1	teaspoon baking powder
		1	teaspoon baking soda

In a 1-quart jar, press each layer firmly in place. Include a gift card with the following instructions:

Preheat oven to 350°. Grease cookie sheets or line with parchment paper. In a medium bowl, cream together ½ cup butter, 1 egg and 1 teaspoon vanilla. Stir in contents of jar with a spoon or you may need to use your hands to mix thoroughly. Drop by rounded teaspoons 2 inches apart. Bake 11 minutes. Cool on wire racks. Makes about 3 dozen.

This recipe came from my cousin, Becky Anhold, in Virginia. This version makes for great Christmas, teacher or neighbor gifts, and is equally good made the traditional way using the same proportions.

This recipe was handwritten in the pages of June Platt's *Plain and Fancy Cookbook*, published in 1941. My husband remembered these crisp oatmeal cookies made by his grandmother in Salisbury, NC when he was a child. I was skeptical that the recipe did not call for any eggs. However, they turned out great and are so easy to make. I used the soft baking butter with canola oil instead of shortening.

Grandmother's Easy Oatmeal Crispies

1	cup shortening or 1 cup butter, softened	1	cup flour
1	cup brown sugar, firmly packed	½	teaspoon salt
		3	cups quick-cooking oats
½	teaspoon vanilla	½	teaspoon baking soda
		¼	cup water

Cream shortening or butter with brown sugar and vanilla until light and creamy. Dissolve the soda in ¼ cup water and blend into the butter mixture. Continuing to use the electric beater, beat in the flour until blended. With a spoon, add the oats until well mixed. Drop by large tablespoons onto cookie sheet and bake in a preheated 400° oven for about 10 minutes. Cool on wire racks.

Mother's Oatmeal Cookies

1¾	sticks butter, softened	¼	teaspoon nutmeg
¾	cup brown sugar	½	teaspoon salt
½	cup granulated sugar	1	teaspoon cinnamon
1	large egg	3	cups uncooked regular oats
1	teaspoon vanilla		
1½	cups all-purpose flour	1½	cups raisins
1	teaspoon baking soda		

Beat butter and sugar until creamy; add egg and vanilla to blend. Combine flour, salt, nutmeg, baking soda, cinnamon and add to butter mixture. Stir in oats and raisins. Drop by rounded teaspoons 2 inches apart on ungreased cookie sheet. Bake in preheated 375° oven for 9-11 minutes. Cool 1 minute on sheet and remove to wire racks. Makes about 5 dozen.

Chess Pie Cookies

1	stick butter			Pinch of salt
2	cups light brown sugar		1	teaspoon vanilla
2	eggs		1	cup chopped pecans
1½	cups plain flour		8	ounces chopped dates

Melt butter in heavy skillet. Add brown sugar. Stir until sugar melts. Let cool and pour into a bowl.

In a bowl, beat eggs, one at a time, into the sugar mixture. Beat until smooth. Add flour that has been sifted with baking powder and salt. Mix well. Add vanilla and nuts and dates and bake in a 8x12-inch pan at 350° for about 30 minutes. Cool and cut.

This can be made without the dates, but most say it is better with them.

Forgotten Cookies (Meringues)

2	egg whites		6	ounces butterscotch morsels
⅔	cup granulated sugar			
	Pinch of salt		1	cup chopped nuts

Preheat oven to 350°. Beat egg whites until stiff. Add sugar and salt. Blend until peaks form. Add butterscotch morsels and nuts. Drop from teaspoon onto ungreased (foil covered) cookie sheet. Put into preheated oven. Turn off the heat and leave in oven overnight. Carefully store these cookies as they will crumble if you're not careful.

Christmas Cookies

½ cup sugar

2 sticks butter

½ cup buttermilk

3½ cups sifted flour

½ teaspoon salt

1 teaspoon baking soda

1 teaspoon vanilla

Cream butter well and add sugar gradually. Put soda in buttermilk and add to first mixture alternately with flour and salt. Chill for at least 2 hours in refrigerator. Roll out and cut into desired shapes. Bake in 350° oven for scant 10 minutes.

After trying five different sugar cookie recipes, some of them dating back to the early 1900's, this sugar cookie recipe was by far the best. It was exactly what I was aiming for. Mrs. Margaret Isley used to bring these cookies to my grandmother in the nursing home and my mother begged her for the recipe.

The Best Ever Sugar Cookies

2	sticks butter	1	egg
1	cup sugar	2	teaspoons baking soda
1	cup brown sugar	2	teaspoons cream of tartar
2½	cups sifted all-purpose flour	2	teaspoons vanilla

Using an electric beater, mix all of the ingredients in a large bowl in the order written. Cover bowl and place dough in the refrigerator overnight or for several hours. Pinch dough to form medium sized balls – about the size of a walnut. Roll the balls in granulated sugar and place on cookie sheet. Bake for 10 minutes in a 350° oven. Cool on wire racks.

Old-Fashioned Ginger Cookies

1	cup granulated sugar	½	teaspoon each: ground cloves, cinnamon and ground ginger
1	cup shortening		
1	cup New Orleans molasses	5	cups sifted all-purpose flour
2	whole eggs		
2	teaspoons baking soda	2	teaspoons baking powder
½	cup boiling water		

Cream together the sugar, shortening, molasses and eggs. Add the baking soda which has been dissolved in ½ cup boiling water, stirring. Sift together the flour, cloves, baking powder, cinnamon and ginger and add the sugar/egg mixture. Blend well. Chill mixture in a bowl for at least 5 hours – best kept overnight. You can either drop cookie dough or roll out on well-floured board and cut. Bake in preheated 350° oven for about 12 minutes.

Peanut Butter Chocolate Chip Cookies

1	cup butter	1	small box light brown sugar
1	cup Crisco (can use Crisco sticks)	4	eggs
1	(16-ounce) jar of peanut butter (Arlene uses Smucker's Natural)	5	cups all-purpose flour
		1	tablespoon baking soda
		2	teaspoons baking powder
2	cups granulated sugar	1	(12-ounce) bag chocolate chips

Using an electric mixer, blend butter, Crisco, peanut butter, granulated sugar, brown sugar and eggs. Blend in remaining ingredients in order. Cover and chill at least 4 hours, better overnight. Heat oven to 375°. Shape dough into approximately 1-inch balls or by spoonfuls and roll in granulated sugar. Place on ungreased baking sheet 3 inches apart. Dip fork in sugar and press across each cookie in a criss-cross pattern to partially flatten. Bake about 10 minutes or until set, but not hard. After baking, promptly remove from baking sheet onto wire racks.

Gingersnaps

2	cups all-purpose flour	½	cup butter
¼	teaspoon salt	¼	cup Crisco shortening
3	teaspoons baking soda	1	cup granulated sugar
1	teaspoon each: ground ginger, ground cloves and cinnamon	1	egg, slightly beaten
		¼	cup Grandma's Molasses

Sift flour, salt, soda, cloves, ginger and cinnamon all together 3 times. Cream butter with Crisco until light and fluffy. Gradually add sugar. Blend in egg and molasses. Stir in flour mixture until well-blended. Dough will be moist. Drop by teaspoonful in pan of granulated sugar and roll until coated. Place on cookie sheet 2-3 inches apart. Bake in preheated 350° oven for 8-10 minutes. Let cool for a few minutes before removing from pan. Makes about 7 dozen cookies and your kitchen smells heavenly!

Our neighbor in Charlotte, Arlene Simonton, used to make these cookies whenever there was a need for food to be taken to someone and also for all of the family occasions on our street. When she moved, my next door neighbor and great friend, Sarah Jasperse, took over the tradition.

It is best to make these cookies a day before serving. They can be made to the point of baking and frozen. Freeze unbaked cookies on a cookie sheet and after they have frozen, store them in a freezer bag. Then, you can bake as few as you like.

Tipsies

1 (6-ounce) package
semi-sweet chocolate morsels

3 tablespoons light corn syrup

½ cup bourbon

2½ cups crushed
vanilla wafer crumbs

½ cup confectioners' sugar

1 cup finely chopped pecans

Granulated sugar to
roll cookies in

Melt chocolate over hot
water in a double boiler. Add
remaining ingredients and mix
well. Let stand for 30 minutes.
Form into balls. Roll in
granulated sugar and let ripen
in covered container for
several days.

Lace Cookies

1	stick butter	¾	cup flour
1	cup light brown sugar, packed	1	teaspoon baking powder
1	teaspoon vanilla	½	teaspoon salt
1	egg	½	cup finely chopped nuts

Cream butter and add sugar, vanilla and egg. Beat until light. Add sifted dry ingredients and nuts. Drop by scant teaspoonfuls into cookie sheets – Bake in hot oven, 400°, for about 5 minutes. Cool ½ minute on cookie sheet, remove and cool further on wire rack. These cookies store well in an airtight container. Freezes well.

Sandies

6	tablespoons shortening	½	teaspoon ice water
2½	tablespoons confectioners' sugar	½	cup chopped walnuts
		½	teaspoon vanilla
1	cup sifted cake flour	¼	cup confectioners' sugar
⅛	teaspoon salt		

Work shortening with spoon until fluffy and creamy. Add confectioners' sugar gradually while continuing to work mixture until light. Add flour, salt, water, walnuts and vanilla and mix well. Cover and chill about 2 hours in refrigerator. Shape into rolls 1-inch long by ½-inch wide. Place ½-inch apart on greased cookie sheets. Bake in slow oven at 300° for 30-35 minutes or until lightly browned. Remove from cookie sheets and shake immediately in a bag with confectioners' sugar. (Add a little cinnamon if desired.) Remove from bag. Makes about 20.

Oatmeal Carmelitas

1 cup flour
1 cup quick-cooking oats
¾ cup packed brown sugar
½ teaspoon baking soda
¼ teaspoon salt
¾ cup butter, melted
1 (6-ounce) package chocolate chips
½ cup chopped nuts
¾ cup caramel (ice cream) topping
3 tablespoons all-purpose flour

Combine flour, oats, sugar, soda, salt and melted butter in a large bowl to form crumbs. Press half of the crumbs into bottom and sides of greased 9-inch square baking dish. Bake at 350° for 10 minutes. Sprinkle the chocolate chips and nuts over the baked crust. Mix ¾ cup caramel topping with 3 tablespoons flour and drizzle over the chocolate chips and nuts. Sprinkle remaining crumbs over the caramel topping. Bake at 350° for 15-20 minutes until golden brown. Chill bars and cut. Makes about 24.

Blondies

1½ cups brown sugar, firmly packed
¾ cup granulated sugar
1 cup vegetable shortening
3 eggs
1 teaspoon vanilla
2¼ cups sifted all-purpose flour
1 teaspoon baking soda
1 teaspoon salt
1½ teaspoons ground cinnamon
¾ cup milk
4 cups quick-cooking oats, uncooked
1 (12-ounce) package semi-sweet chocolate pieces

Blend sugars into shortening gradually. Beat in eggs, vanilla. Sift flour, soda, salt and cinnamon together; add to batter along with milk. Stir in rest of ingredients. Spread batter in greased 15½x10½x1-inch jelly-roll pan. Bake in preheated 350° oven for about 30 minutes. Cut while warm, but cool completely in pan.

Frosted Date Balls

1¼ cups sifted flour

¼ teaspoon salt

⅓ cup sifted confectioners' sugar

½ cup butter

1 tablespoon milk

1 teaspoon vanilla

⅔ cup chopped dates

Extra confectioners' sugar

Combine flour and salt, sift twice. Cream the butter and gradually add the sugar. Add milk and vanilla, stir and mix in the sifted flour. Blend in dates and nuts. Roll in 1-inch balls. Place about 3 inches apart on ungreased baking sheet. Bake in moderate oven (300°) for about 20 minutes until light brown. While still warm, roll in confectioners' sugar. Makes about 3 dozen.

Double Delicious Halloween Bars

½ cup butter or margarine

1½ cups graham cracker crumbs

1 (14-ounce) can sweetened condensed milk

1 (12-ounce) package semi-sweet chocolate chips

1 cup peanut butter chips

Preheat oven to 350° (325° for a glass dish). In 13x9-inch baking pan, melt margarine or butter in oven. Sprinkle crumbs evenly over butter; pour sweetened condensed milk evenly over crumbs. Top with chips; press down firmly. Bake 25-30 minutes or until lightly browned. Cool. Cut into bars.

🏵 White Chocolate and Macadamia Brownies

1	cup all-purpose flour	1	stick unsalted butter, melted
¼	teaspoon salt	1	teaspoon vanilla
2	large eggs, room temperature	1	cup chopped toasted unsalted macadamia nuts
½	cup sugar	5	ounces imported white chocolate, coarsely chopped
7	ounces imported white chocolate, chopped and melted		Hot Fudge Sauce

Preheat oven 350°. Butter and flour a 9x13-inch baking pan. Sift flour with salt into bowl. Beat eggs in large bowl until frothy. Add sugar 1 tablespoon at a time and beat until pale yellow and slowly dissolving ribbon forms when beaters are lifted.

Gently fold in melted white chocolate (it may lose volume). Add melted butter and vanilla and stir well (it may look curdled). Fold in flour. Fold in nuts and chopped white chocolate. Pour mixture into prepared pan. Bake until toothpick comes out not quite clean – about 25 minutes. Do NOT overbake. Cool in pan on rack.

Pour Hot Fudge Sauce over brownies.

Hot Fudge Sauce:

¾	cup whipping cream	2	tablespoons unsalted butter
¼	cup sugar		
5	ounces bittersweet chocolate, chopped	2	tablespoons light corn syrup

Cook cream and sugar over low heat until sugar dissolves. Add chocolate and stir until melted and smooth. Add butter and corn syrup and stir until butter melts. (Can be prepared 1 day ahead.) Let stand at room temperature. Stir over low heat before serving with brownies.

cookies

Almond Macaroon Brownies

1 (3-ounce) package cream cheese, softened	1⅔ cups Baker's Angel Flake coconut
6 tablespoons butter	1 cup whole almonds
¾ cup sugar	6 squares semi-sweet chocolate
3 eggs	½ teaspoon vanilla
½ cup plus 1 tablespoon all-purpose flour	½ teaspoon baking powder
	¼ teaspoon salt

Beat cream cheese and 2 tablespoons butter until softened; beat in ¼ cup sugar. Stir in 1 egg, 1 tablespoon flour and coconut. Reserve 16 almonds for garnish; chop remaining. Stir in ⅓ cup of the chopped almonds. Set aside.

Stir 5 squares chocolate and remaining butter over low heat until melted. Remove from heat; stir in ½ cup sugar and vanilla. Beat in 2 eggs. Stir in ½ cup flour, baking powder and salt. Add remaining chopped almonds.

Spread chocolate batter in greased 8-inch square pan. Spread cheese batter on top. Garnish with whole almonds. Bake at 350° for 40 minutes or until cake tester inserted in center comes out clean. Don't overbake. Melt remaining chocolate, drizzle over brownies. Cool in pan. Cut into bars or squares. Makes about 16 brownies.

Fruit Bars

½ cup butter	2 eggs
1 cup all-purpose flour	2 tablespoons flour
2 teaspoons sugar	1 tablespoon melted butter
1 cup chopped nuts	1½ tablespoons fresh lemon juice
1 cup flaked coconut	¾ cup confectioners' sugar
4 ounces chopped candied cherries	
1½ cups brown sugar	

Mix butter, 1 cup flour and 2 teaspoons sugar. Spread in 13x18-inch pan and bake 325° for 10-12 minutes, until lightly browned. Mix the nuts, coconut, candied cherries, brown sugar, eggs, and 2 tablespoons flour together and spread on above crust. Bake 15-25 minutes until lightly browned. Mix 1 tablespoon melted butter, lemon juice and confectioners' sugar and spread on baked bars while still warm. Cut into squares.

Chocolate Brownies

2 squares unsweetened chocolate

1 stick butter

1 cup sugar

2 eggs, beaten

½ cup sifted all-purpose flour

Dash of salt

1 cup chopped nuts

½ teaspoon vanilla

Melt chocolate and butter over low heat in small saucepan. Add sugar and cool slightly. Add beaten eggs. Sift flour and add ½ cup flour to this mixture. Add dash of salt, nuts and vanilla. Stir well. Pour batter into greased 8x8-inch square pan and bake in preheated 350° oven for about 30 minutes. Set on rack to cool before cutting.

Butterscotch Squares

¼ cup butter

1 cup brown sugar

1 egg

¾ cup all-purpose flour

1 teaspoon baking powder

½ teaspoon vanilla

¼ cup chopped nuts

Cream butter and sugar together and add slightly beaten egg. Then add dry ingredients which have been sifted together. Stir until well mixed. Add vanilla and nuts. Line jelly-roll pan with waxed paper or grease and flour. Pour mixture in pan, but do not spread. Bake for 30 minutes in preheated 300° oven.

Seven-Layer Cookies

1	stick butter	1	cup chopped pecans, optional
1	package honey graham crackers, crushed (about 1½ cups)	1	cup coconut
1	cup chocolate chips	1	can condensed sweetened milk
1	cup butterscotch chips		

Preheat oven to 350°. Melt butter in a rectangular Pyrex dish. Place stick of butter in Pyrex dish and let butter melt, but not burn or brown. Take pan out of the oven and mix in the crushed graham crackers – stir together and then press down on bottom and slightly up sides. Sprinkle the chocolate chips over top across the dish, then the butterscotch chips. Next sprinkle the coconut so it nearly covers the top. You'll still be able to see the chips poking through.

Pour 1 can of sweetened milk over top slowly, drizzling back and forth until nearly covered. If desired, you may put chopped pecans after the chips and before the coconut.

Bake in 350° oven for 17 minutes – you want the mixture to be browning on the sides and slightly bubbly, but be careful, do not overcook. You don't want the chocolate chips to melt – they should still look whole.

It will take a while for this to cool and solidify. Sometimes I put it in the refrigerator for a while and then take out. Don't worry, it will eventually get hardened and you'll be able to cut these. Serve cold and preserve in an airtight container. They will last about 3 days.

Lemon Bars Deluxe

2¼	cups all-purpose flour, divided	2	cups granulated sugar
½	cup confectioners' sugar	⅓	cup fresh lemon juice
1	cup butter, softened	½	teaspoon baking powder
4	eggs, beaten		Additional confectioners' sugar

Sift together 2 cups flour and confectioners' sugar. Cut in butter until mixture clings together. Press into a greased 13x9x2-inch pan. Bake at 350° for 25 minutes or until light brown. Combine eggs, sugar and lemon juice; beat well. Sift together ¼ cup flour and baking powder; stir into the egg mixture. Pour over baked crust. Bake at 350° for 25-30 minutes or until lightly browned. Sprinkle with confectioners' sugar. Cool, cut into bars.

pies and desserts

Chocolate Pie

1 cup sugar
3 eggs
1/2 cup cocoa
1/2 cup butter
1 tsp. Vanilla
1 can evaporated milk, undiluted

Combine sugar & cocoa & mix well. Beat egg yolk, add to sugar & cocoa & mix thoroughly, then add milk, butter, salt & Vanilla. Pour into large pie plate & cook slowly until mixture is thick. Top with egg white well beaten with 1/8 tsp. cream of tartar & 6 tablesp. sugar.

Chocolate Pie

1 cup sugar
3 tablesp. flour
3 " Cocoa
1 cup milk
2 eggs
dash of salt
1 tsp. Vanilla

Combine first 3 ingredients, mix well. Separate eggs. Beat yolks, add milk gradually to yolks. Add first mixture. Pour into pastry pan. Bake slowly 375° until done. Add meringue made of egg white & 4 tablesp. sugar beaten stiff — reduce heat 350° Brown slightly

Dream Pie
Helen Meeks

1 No 2 can crushed Pineapple
1 No 2 can cherries
    Save juice
1 1/4 cups sugar
2 T flour
  Cook juice, sugar + flour until slightly thickened, remove from heat + pour in
1 pkg orange jello
  Cool slightly + add the pineapple cherries + 1 cup nuts + 4 bananas cut into pieces.
  Put mixture in 2 - 9 inch baked pie crust + chill.
  Makes 2 pies or 12 individual pies -
  Spread with thin layer of whipped cream few hours before serving

CAROLINA LADDER CO., INC.

TELEPHONE 803/554-8833

Charleston Heights, S. C.

P. O. BOX 4824

Manufacturers of Quality Ladders

This is an old recipt for fudge

---

3 cups sugar
3/4 cups milk
5 tablespoons butter or margarine
2 tablespoon dark corn syrup
1 – 3 cup unsweetened cocoa
1 tsp vanilla

In heavy 3 qt. saucepan turn the sugar, milk, butter, corn syrup and cocoa. Stirring constantly, ~~cook~~ cook over medium heat until mixture boils. Then cook, stirring, until softball stage (238 degrees on candy thermometer). Add vanilla and cool to lukewarm (110 deg) Beat until fudge begins to thicken and loses its gloss Pour into a buttered 8" square pan – Then when cool cut in squares.

Coconut Chess Pie

½	stick butter, softened	1	teaspoon vinegar
1½	cups sugar	1	tablespoon vanilla
3	eggs	1	teaspoon cornstarch
1	teaspoon cornmeal	1	cup flaked coconut

Cream butter and sugar until light. Add eggs one at a time, beating thoroughly. Add next 4 ingredients and beat well. Stir in coconut and pour into pie shell. Bake in slow oven (325°) for 1 hour or until firm.

Chess Pie with Raisins and Pecans

Crust:

1¼	cups sifted all-purpose flour	⅓	cup margarine
½	teaspoon salt	3	tablespoons cold water

Filling:

¾	cup margarine	1½	cups seedless raisins, plumped
1½	cups sugar		
3	eggs	1	cup chopped pecans
1	teaspoon vanilla		

Make crust: Combine flour and salt in mixing bowl. Add margarine and cut in with blender or 2 knives to make crumbs like course meal. Sprinkle in water, a tablespoon at a time, tossing with a fork until mixture begins to hold together. Press lightly to form a ball. Flatten on a square of floured waxed paper. Roll with floured rolling pin to make a 12-inch circle. Lift crust frequently as you work, and sprinkle flour under it to prevent sticking to paper. Line a 9-inch pan with the rolled crust. Chill while you prepare filling.

To make filling: Blend together ¾ cup margarine, sugar and eggs. Stir in vanilla, raisins and pecans. Spread in pastry-lined pan. Bake in preheated 425° oven 5 minutes. Reduce heat to 325° and bake 45-50 minutes longer, until filling is firm. Cool on rack. If desired, garnish pie with whipped cream.

To plump raisins, cover with water. Bring slowly to a boil. Take from heat. Let stand 5 minutes; drain and dry on paper towels.

Variation: To make a Japanese Pie, add 1 tablespoon vinegar and 1 cup coconut to pie filling.

Our grandmothers had so many pie and cake recipes. When they were young wives, desserts were served nearly every day. You couldn't buy pre-made cakes and pies like you can today. Nowadays, you can go into most any major grocery store and buy homemade bread, biscuits and pies. While these will do when you're in a hurry, there's no substitute for a hot, homemade pie.

I have never mastered the pie category myself. My husband likes to tell our friends that no matter what kind of pie I make, they all end up the same – cobbler! When was the last time you made a homemade pie for your family?

Chess pie was probably the pie that my mother made more than any other. It is also the one pie that I had more recipes for than any other. There are many variations – lemon, chocolate, coconut, plain or tarts – enjoy them all!

Fabulous Chocolate Chess Pie

1⅓ sticks butter

1⅓ squares unsweetened chocolate

1⅓ cups sugar

3 small eggs

⅓ teaspoon salt

1 teaspoon vanilla

1 (9-inch) pie crust, unbaked

Melt butter and chocolate over boiling water. Mix sugar, eggs, salt and vanilla; add to chocolate mixture. Pour into pie shell and bake at 375° for about 35 minutes.

Buttermilk Chess Pie

This is our family's favorite.

4	eggs	2⅔	tablespoons flour
2⅔	cups sugar	⅔	cup buttermilk
1⅓	sticks margarine	1⅓	teaspoons vanilla

Melt butter, add rest of ingredients. Mix with electric beater. Pour into 2 prepared uncooked pie shells and bake in preheated 350° oven for 45 minutes. Makes 2 pies.

Majelle's Lemon Chess Tarts

6	tablespoons margarine or butter	Juice of 4 lemons
6	eggs	Grated rind of 3 lemons
2½	cups sugar	Small tart shells

Melt margarine. In a medium bowl, beat eggs, sugar, lemon juice and grated lemon rind. Add this mixture to the margarine and blend well. Pour into small tart shells and bake for 30 minutes in a preheated 350° oven.

Jefferson Standard Lemon Chess Pie

This recipe was printed in the Jefferson Standard newsletter about 40-50 years ago.

2	cups sugar	¼	cup scalded milk
2	tablespoons cornmeal	¼	cup lemon juice
1	tablespoon flour	4	teaspoons grated lemon rind
4	eggs, unbeaten		
¼	cup melted butter	1	unbaked pie shell

Mix sugar, cornmeal, flour. Add eggs one at a time and beat well. Stir in butter, milk, lemon juice and rind and mix well. Pour in pastry shell and bake at 350° for 45 minutes or until done. Can be cut warm, but better to let cool and top with whipped cream.

Bubba's Famous Pecan Pie

1	cup sugar	1	cup pecan halves
1	stick butter	¼	teaspoon salt
3	eggs	1	teaspoon vanilla
1	cup light Karo syrup	1	unbaked 9-inch pie shell

Melt butter and sugar over heat until sugar is melted. Cool a bit. Add eggs, syrup, salt, vanilla and pecan halves. Pour into unbaked 9-inch pie shell and bake in 325° preheated oven for 50-55 minutes.

Variation: My friend Tim Goetz says to split the Karo syrup with ½ cup maple syrup and ½ cup Karo syrup and to add 2 tablespoons bourbon to pie for a delicious taste.

This is the best pecan pie! After a day, when it has set, it'll get chewy on the ends. Serve this delicious pie warmed with homemade whipped cream with a touch of vanilla. YUM.

Luscious Peach Pie

6-8	ripe fresh peaches	1	cup heavy cream, not whipped
1	cup sugar		
4	tablespoons flour		Unbaked 9-inch pie shell
	Dash or more of cinnamon and nutmeg		

Fill unbaked pie shell with sliced peaches. Mix sugar, flour, spices and cream together and pour over peaches. Bake at 350° for 1-1½ hours. Place a pan under the pie to catch drippings.

My next door neighbor in Charlotte, North Carolina, Betsy Hayes Gaefell, used to prepare this peach pie nearly 20 years ago and I still enjoy it today.

Mother's Easy Peach Pie

6-8	peaches, sliced	2	tablespoons butter
¼	teaspoon cinnamon	½-¾	cup sugar
⅛	teaspoon nutmeg	½	cup water
2	tablespoons flour	1	unbaked 9-inch pie shell

Slice peaches and put on bottom of pie shell. Mix sugar with flour, cinnamon and nutmeg and sprinkle over peaches. Slice butter and put on top. Pour water over. Bake at 350° for 45 minutes – 1 hour.

Plain Pastry

2 cups sifted all-purpose flour

1 teaspoon salt

⅔ cup shortening

5-7 tablespoons cold water

Sift together flour and salt; cut in shortening with pastry blender until mixture is size of small peas. Sprinkle water, 1 tablespoon at a time, over part of the mixture. Gently toss with fork; push to one side of bowl. Sprinkle next tablespoon of water over dry part; mix lightly and push to moistened side. Repeat until all is moistened.

Gather up dough with fingers and form into a ball. For double crust pie, divide dough for lower and upper crust. Form each into a ball. Flatten slightly and roll ⅛-inch thick on floured surface.

Perfect Apple Pie

5-7	tart apples	¼	teaspoon nutmeg
¾-1	cup sugar		Dash salt
2	tablespoons flour	1	recipe plain pastry
1	teaspoon cinnamon	2	tablespoons butter

Pare apples and slice thin. Combine sugar, flour, spices and salt, mix with apples. Put apple mixture in a 9-inch pastry lined pie pan; dot with butter. Adjust top crust. Sprinkle with sugar for sparkle and bake in 400° oven for 50 minutes or until done. A strip of aluminum foil around edge of crust will keep juices in pie instead of running over in oven.

Bubba's Apple Pie Fry

2½	cups canned sliced apples	2	cups all-purpose flour
¾	cup light brown sugar	2	tablespoons sugar
1	teaspoon nutmeg	½	teaspoon salt
¼	teaspoon allspice	⅔	cup shortening
1	tablespoon flour	¼	cup cold water
¼	cup seedless raisins		Powdered sugar

Drain apple slices. Add brown sugar, nutmeg, allspice, 1 tablespoon flour and raisins. Let stand until needed. In another bowl, sift together the 2 cups flour, sugar and salt. Cut in shortening and blend with cold water if needed. Roll out small pieces of dough to ⅛-inch thickness. Cut in 5-inch circles. Place apples on half of circle and moisten edge with water and fold over. Fry in deep fat at 350° for about 4 minutes until brown. Drain on paper towels. Sprinkle with powdered sugar and serve warm.

pies

Cherry-Ripe Pie

1	quart ripe red cherries	½	teaspoon almond flavoring
1	cup sugar		
2-3	tablespoons flour	1	(9-inch) pastry shell
¼	teaspoon salt	1	(9-inch) pastry for top

Wash and pit cherries. Mix sugar, salt and flour. Mix with cherries, then add almond flavoring. Fill pastry shell with cherries. Cover top with pastry – either criss-cross or plain – and dampen edges and crimp together. Bake in hot oven (450°) for 10 minutes. Lower heat to 350° and bake 20-25 more minutes. Serve with vanilla ice cream.

Strawberry Ice Cream Pie

1	(3-ounce) package lemon Jell-O	1	baked 8-inch pie shell, cooled
1¼	cups boiling strawberry juice plus water		Garnish of Cool Whip, strawberries and mint leaves
1	pint vanilla ice cream		
2	cups drained strawberry halves, juice reserved		

Dissolve Jell-O in boiling water with strawberry juice. Add ice cream by spoonfuls, stirring until melted. Chill ice cream mixture until thick, about 25 minutes. Fold in strawberries and pour into pie shell. Chill until firm, another 25 minutes or so. Garnish with whipped cream dollops, with strawberry halves on top of whipped cream.

This recipe was given to me many years ago by my best childhood friend, Beth Jones Carpenter from Charlotte, NC.

Beth's Blueberry Crunch Pie

Filling:

½	cup sugar	1	unbaked deep dish pie shell
⅓	cup flour		
3-4	cups fresh blueberries		Juice from ½ lemon

Topping:

1	cup flour	½	cup butter or margarine, melted
½	cup brown sugar		

Combine sugar, flour, berries and pour into pie shell. Sprinkle with lemon juice. Mix topping ingredients in a small bowl with a fork until combined. Sprinkle topping over and bake for 20 minutes in a 400° oven. Reduce heat and cover outside crust with foil. Bake for 20-25 additional minutes until pie is bubbling. Serve warm with vanilla ice cream.

This is a different version of an all-American classic. Martha Long published this recipe around 30 years ago.

Martha's Blueberry Pie

4	cups fresh blueberries	1½	tablespoons lemon juice
½	cup water		
1	cup sugar	1	tablespoon butter
2½	tablespoons cornstarch	1	baked pie crust

Wash and pick over blueberries. Crush 1 cup of the berries and combine with the water, lemon juice and the cornstarch and sugar which has been mixed together. Bring to a boil for 2 minutes. Add butter and cool slightly. Mix with remaining berries and pour into baked pie shell. Chill several hours. Serve topped with whipped cream.

Variation: This recipe can also be used with strawberries. Omit the lemon juice and add a little red food coloring if you like.

Pitt's Pumpkin Praline Pie

For Crust:

1	cup pecans	½	teaspoon salt
2	tablespoons sugar		Raw rice for weighting the shell
1¼	cups all-purpose flour		
¾	stick cold unsalted butter, cut into bits		

In a food processor, grind course the pecans with the sugar and transfer to mixing bowl. In processor, blend flour, butter and salt until mixture resembles meal and add it to pecan mixture. Add 3 tablespoons ice water, toss mixture until water in incorporated, and press dough into bottom and up the side of a 9-inch deep dish pie plate, crimping the edge decoratively. Prick crust with a fork and chill for 30 minutes. (The crust can be made 2 weeks in advance and kept wrapped well and frozen.)

Line crust with foil, and fill the foil with the rice. Bake crust in the middle of a preheated 425° oven for 7 minutes. Remove rice and foil carefully and bake crust in a reduced oven temperature of 350° for 5 minutes more and let it cool.

Filling:

2	cups canned solid pack pumpkin	½	teaspoon ground allspice
1¼	cups whipping cream	½	teaspoon ground nutmeg
¾	cup pure maple syrup	½	teaspoon ground ginger
3	large eggs	½	teaspoon ground cinnamon, optional
1	tablespoon brandy		
1	teaspoon vanilla		

Mix all ingredients in large bowl. Pour filling into prepared crust. Bake until edges are golden and center no longer moves when shaken, about 50 minutes. Cool on pie rack. Sprinkle Pecan Praline on top.

Pecan Praline

3 tablespoons sugar

1 tablespoon plus
1 teaspoon water

½ cup toasted pecans

⅛ teaspoon ground allspice

⅛ teaspoon cinnamon

Butter cookie sheet.
Cook sugar and water in heavy saucepan over low heat, stirring until sugar dissolves. Increase heat and boil without stirring until syrup turns deep golden brown, about 5 minutes. Stir in pecans and spices. Immediately transfer mix to cookie sheet. Cool completely. Break into pieces. Course grind in processor or crush with rolling pin. (Can be prepared 2 weeks ahead – refrigerate airtight.)

Martha Long says
that even children love
this pumpkin pie!

Old-Fashioned Pumpkin Pie

1	cup evaporated milk or light cream	¾	teaspoon ground cinnamon
¾	cup brown sugar	¼	teaspoon ground cloves
1½	cups cooked mashed pumpkin	¼	teaspoon ground mace
1	tablespoon molasses	¾	teaspoon salt
½	teaspoon ground ginger	2	eggs
		1	(9-inch) unbaked pie shell

Combine the evaporated milk or cream, sugar and pumpkin, mixing well. Add the molasses, spices and salt. Beat the eggs and add them to the pumpkin mixture. Pour the filling into the pie shell and bake in a very hot oven (450°) for 20 minutes. Reduce the heat to 325° and bake for 45 minutes longer or until a knife inserted in the center comes out clean. Top with dabs of whipped cream or arrange walnut halves around the outer edge of the pie.

Chocolate Cream Pie

1	cup sugar, divided	1¼	cups evaporated milk
6	tablespoons cocoa	1	cup water
2	tablespoons cornstarch	2	eggs, separated
½	teaspoon salt	1½	teaspoons vanilla
		1	baked 9-inch pie shell

Mix together ¾ sugar, cocoa, cornstarch and salt. Slowly stir in the evaporated milk which has been diluted with 1 cup water. Put in a double boiler over boiling water. Cook 20 minutes after water again comes to a boil, stirring frequently. Remove from heat and slowly stir into slightly beaten egg yolks. Return to heat and cook 2 minutes longer, stirring constantly. Cool, then add vanilla.

When cold, put in 9-inch baked pastry shell. Beat egg whites until stiff, but not dry. Continue beating while adding remaining ¼ cup sugar. Spread on top of pie, sealing edges. Bake in a 300° oven for 15 minutes or until brown. Cool thoroughly before serving.

Chocolate Silk Pie

2	(15-ounce) cans Eagle Brand milk	½	cup water
4	(1-ounce) squares unsweetened chocolate	1	teaspoon vanilla
		1	deep dish frozen pie shell
¼	teaspoon salt	1	cup whipping cream
		5	tablespoons sugar

Bake pie shell as directed. Melt chocolate with milk and salt in top of double boiler. When melted, add water and cook, stirring constantly until mixture is thick and glassy. Remove from heat and stir in vanilla. Pour into baked pie shell. Cool. Whip cream with sugar and add to top of chocolate pie.

Bubba's Chocolate Pie

1½	cups sugar	1	large can chocolate syrup
½	cup flour	1	large can evaporated milk
1	(15-ounce) can Eagle brand condensed milk		
		1	tablespoon vanilla
4	eggs	3	unbaked pie shells
½	cup water		

Beat all ingredients together and pour into 2 unbaked pie shells and bake in preheated 325° oven for 35 minutes.

Million Dollar Fruit Pie

1	cup Eagle brand sweet milk	½	cup chopped pecans
½	cup lemon juice	2	graham cracker pie shells
1	large carton Cool Whip		Maraschino cherries for garnish
1	(20-ounce) can crushed pineapple, drained		

Mix all ingredients and pour into 2 graham cracker pie shells and chill. Top with red maraschino cherries.

Fudge Pie

2 squares chocolate, melted

1 stick butter

3 eggs, beaten

1 cup sugar

¼ cup all-purpose flour

1 teaspoon vanilla

½ cup chopped nuts

Melt chocolate with butter.
Let cool slightly. Beat in
3 eggs, beaten, sugar, flour,
vanilla and nuts. Pour into a
greased 9-inch pan and bake
in a preheated 350° oven
for 20-24 minutes.

Crustless Brownie Pie

1	cup sugar			Pinch of salt
½	cup flour		½	cup chopped pecans or walnuts
¼	cup cocoa			Whipped cream or ice cream
½	cup butter, softened			
2	eggs			
1	teaspoon vanilla			

Combine first 7 ingredients; beat 4 minutes at medium speed of electric beater. Stir in nuts. Spread batter evenly in a buttered 9-inch pie plate. Bake at 325° for 40 minutes or until wooden pick inserted in center comes out clean. Pie will puff, then fall slightly. Serve with whipped cream or ice cream. Makes 1 (9-inch) pie.

Bourbon Walnut Butterscotch Tarts

1	package butterscotch pudding	6	tart shells
1½	cups milk		Walnut halves for garnish
¼	cup bourbon		Whipped cream for garnish
1	egg white		
¾	cup chopped walnuts		

Prepare 1 package of butterscotch pudding mix as directed on the package, using only 1½ cups milk. Remove from heat and stir in bourbon slowly. Beat egg white until it stands in peaks; fold in the hot pudding, blending until no trace of egg white remains. Fold in chopped walnuts. Pour into baked tart shells; cool thoroughly. Top with whipped cream and garnish each tart with a walnut half.

Rum Cream Pie

2	(9-inch) graham cracker crumb pie crusts	½	cup cold water
6	egg yolks	1	pint whipping cream
1	scant cup sugar	½	cup dark rum
1	envelope gelatin		Grated bittersweet chocolate

Make 2 graham cracker crumb pie shells or buy them already made. Beat egg yolks until light and add sugar. Soak gelatin in cold water. Heat gelatin and water over low heat until dissolved. Pour gelatin over egg mixture, stirring briskly. Whip cream until stiff. Fold whipped cream into egg mixture and flavor with dark rum. Cool until mixture begins to set. Pour into pie shells. Chill until firm. Sprinkle top of pie with grated bittersweet chocolate and serve cold. Each pie serves 6 generously.

 Grasshopper Pie

A famous classic!

1½	cups chocolate cookies, crushed	1	cup whipping cream, whipped
½	stick butter, melted	3	tablespoons green crème de menthe
32	marshmallows (big)	3	tablespoons white crème de coca
½	cup milk		

Make crust by combining crushed chocolate cookies with melted butter and press firmly into 8-inch glass pie plate and bake in 375° oven for approximately 5 minutes.

In a saucepan, melt marshmallows in milk over low heat. Cool until it congeals, but is not cold. Fold in whipped cream and add crème de menthe and crème de coca.

Refrigerate until set.

Coconut Cream Pie

2 egg yolks

2 level tablespoons cornstarch

1 cup milk

¾ cup sugar

1 can prepared coconut

1 (9-inch) baked pie shell

2 egg whites

2 tablespoons sugar

Beat 2 egg yolks, lightly with 2 tablespoons cornstarch and add 1 cup of milk. Dissolve ¾ cup sugar in 1 cup of the milk. Add the eggs to the milk and cook in a saucepan until thick. Add ⅔ can prepared coconut and pour into baked pie shell. Cover with beaten egg whites that have been sweetened with 2 tablespoons sugar. Sprinkle rest of coconut on top of meringue and make in 350° oven for 7-10 minutes until meringue and coconut are light brown.

This egg pie recipe comes from my husband's long time family housekeeper, Lois Hill.

Egg or Coconut Pie

4	eggs	1	stick butter, melted
2	cups sugar	1	teaspoon vanilla or
2	tablespoons flour		lemon extract
1	cup milk	1	cup coconut, optional

Beat eggs. Add sugar and flour. Beat until smooth and add milk and vanilla. Add melted butter and mix until smooth. Pour batter into 2 unbaked pie shells and bake for 45 minutes in preheated 350° oven.

Variation: To make a coconut pie, add about 1 cup flaked coconut to the mixture before pouring into shells.

Lime Chiffon Pie

4	egg yolks	6	egg whites
1	(15-ounce) can sweet condensed milk	½	cup sugar
½	cup lime juice	1	(9-inch) baked pastry shell
¼	teaspoon salt		

Beat 4 egg yolks until lemon colored; stir in milk, lime juice and salt, blending well. Beat 6 egg whites until foamy, gradually adding sugar and continue beating until meringue stands in peaks. Fold ¼ cup of meringue into egg yolk mixture and pour into baked pie shell. Top with additional meringue and bake in 400° oven 8-10 minutes or until lightly browned.

Key Lime Pie

4	eggs, separated	6	tablespoons sugar
1	can condensed sweetened milk	½	teaspoon cream of tartar
½	cup fresh Key Lime juice or Joe's Key Lime Juice in bottle	1	(9-inch) baked pastry pie shell or graham cracker crust

Combine condensed milk, 4 egg yolks and lime juice. Beat 1 egg white stiff and fold into mixture and pour into pie shell. Beat 3 egg whites until stiff and gradually add sugar and cream of tartar while beating. Cover top of pie with meringue. Bake at 350° for 20 minutes or until meringue is lightly browned. Chill overnight.

Bubba's Lemon Meringue Pie

1¼	cups sugar	3	egg yolks
⅛	teaspoon salt	⅔	cup fresh lemon juice
6	tablespoons cornstarch	3	egg whites, room
2	cups boiling water		temperature
1	teaspoon grated lemon rind	¼	teaspoon cream of tartar
¼	cup butter	6	tablespoons sugar

Mix sugar, salt and cornstarch in a small saucepan. Add 2 cups boiling water and 1 teaspoon grated lemon rind. Cook, stirring until thick. Cook an additional 20 minutes on low heat, stirring now and then. Add ¼ cup butter. Mix together 3 egg yolks and ⅔ cup lemon juice and add slowly to the egg mixture. Blend well and heat again until steaming.

Pour into baked shell and bake 5 minutes at 400°. Make meringue by beating egg whites. Add cream of tartar and beat until frothy. Then add very, very slowly 6 tablespoons sugar. Beat until glossy. Cover hot pie with meringue and bake on middle rack for 10-12 minutes at 350°.

Lemonade Meringue Pie

1	cup sour cream	⅓	cup frozen lemonade concentrate, thawed
3	slightly beaten egg yolks	1	(9-inch) baked pie shell
1	(4.6-ounce) package regular vanilla pudding mix	3	egg whites
		½	teaspoon vanilla
1¼	cups milk	¼	teaspoon cream of tartar
		6	tablespoons sugar

In small saucepan, combine sour cream with slightly beaten egg yolks. Stir in vanilla pudding mix, milk and frozen lemonade concentrate that has been thawed. Cook and stir until the mixture thickens and boils. Remove from heat; spoon into baked pastry shell. For meringue, beat egg whites, adding vanilla and cream of tartar until soft peaks form. Gradually add sugar, beating to stiff peaks.

Spread meringues atop HOT filling, sealing to edges of pastry. Bake in 350° oven for 12-15 minutes.

Lemon Cheesecake Pie

Graham Cracker Crust:

1	cup graham cracker crumbs	⅓	cup sugar
		⅓	cup melted butter

Filling:

2	(8-ounce) packages cream cheese	2	tablespoons flour
2	tablespoons butter	⅔	cup milk
½	cup sugar	¼	cup fresh lemon juice
1	egg	2	tablespoons lemon rind

Prepare crust by blending with a fork in a small bowl the cracker crumbs, sugar and melted butter until combined. Reserve a few crumbs. Press crumb mixture into pie plate that has been sprayed with cooking spray.

Prepare filling by beating softened cream cheese, butter with sugar, mixing well. Add egg and mix. Add flour and milk, blending well. Stir in lemon juice and rind. Sprinkle with crumbs. Bake in 350° oven for 30-35 minutes.

Dream Pie

1	(20-ounce) can crushed pineapple – save juice	2	tablespoons flour
		1	(3-ounce) package orange Jell-O
1	(20-ounce) can cherries – save juice	1	cup nuts
		4	bananas, cut into pieces
1¼	cups sugar		Whipped cream

Cook juice, sugar and flour until slightly thickened; remove from heat and pour in 1 package orange Jell-O. Cool slightly and add the pineapple, cherries and 1 cup nuts and sliced bananas. Put the mixture into 2 baked pie shells or 12 individual tarts. A few hours before serving, spread a thin layer of whipped cream on top of pies.

Banana Chocolate Cream Pie

1½	squares unsweetened chocolate	1	tablespoon butter
2	cups milk	½	teaspoon vanilla
¾	cup sugar	1	baked 9-inch pie shell
5	tablespoons flour	3	very ripe bananas
½	teaspoon salt		Egg white meringue or sweetened whipped cream
2	egg yolks, slightly beaten		

Add chocolate to milk in top of double boiler. Heat over rapidly boiling water until chocolate is melted. Beat with rotary egg beater until blended. Combine sugar, flour, and salt. Stir slowly into chocolate mixture. Cook until well thickened, stirring constantly. Cook 10 minutes longer, stirring occasionally

Stir small amount of hot mixture into egg yolks; then pour back into remaining hot mixture while beating vigorously. Cook 1 minute longer. Remove from heat and add butter and vanilla. Cool.

Cover bottom of pie shell with small amount of cooled filling. Peel bananas and slice into shell. Cover immediately with remaining filling. Top with egg white meringue or sweetened whipped cream.

Be sure the filling is thoroughly cool before pouring it over the bananas.

Apple Crisp Topping

1⅓ cups brown sugar

1 cup flour

1 cup oatmeal

1½ teaspoons cinnamon

1½ teaspoons nutmeg

⅔ cup melted butter

Prepare topping in a separate bowl by combining brown sugar, flour, oatmeal, cinnamon and nutmeg. Blend together and pour melted butter over and mix together.

Barbara Shank's Pie Pastry

2¼ cups flour

⅔ cup shortening, chilled

⅓ cup ice cold water

½ teaspoon salt

Mix salt into flour. Work shortening into flour with pastry cutter. Add cold water and work with a fork. Roll out on floured surface and place in pie pan. Bake at 375° until done, 20-25 minutes.

Apple Crisp

¾	cup brown sugar	½	teaspoon salt
¾	cup granulated sugar	10	cups fresh apple slices
4	tablespoons flour	2	teaspoons vanilla
1	teaspoon ground cinnamon	¼	cup water
		2	tablespoons butter

Mix together brown sugar, white sugar, flour, cinnamon and salt. Coat apple slices with this mixture and set aside.

Add vanilla and sprinkle on coated apple slices. Toss and add water and toss again. Pour mixture in greased 9x13-inch Pyrex pan. Dot top of apples with 2 tablespoons butter.

Sprinkle apple crisp topping over apples and bake for 45 minutes in a 375° oven until bubbly.

Peach Cobbler

1	quart (about 1½ pounds) sliced peeled fresh peaches	⅛	teaspoon salt
		¼	cup butter
1	cup sugar	1	large egg
1	cup sifted flour	3	tablespoons milk
1	teaspoon baking powder	¼	teaspoon vanilla

In a small glass baking dish, mix the peaches and ½ cup of the sugar. In a medium mixing bowl sift the flour, baking powder and salt. With a pastry blender, cut in butter until it is like coarse meal. In a small mixing bowl, beat the egg and remaining ½ cup sugar until thick and creamy. Beat in milk and vanilla and fold into flour mixture; do not stir smooth. Spread over peaches.

Bake in a preheated 375° oven for about 45 minutes. Serve hot or reheat. Top with whipped cream or ice cream if desired.

Variation: Substitute apple slices for the peach slices to make apple cobbler.

Apple Crumble

| 7-8 | apples sliced | ½ | teaspoon cinnamon |
| 1 | cup sugar | ½ | teaspoon nutmeg |

Mix all ingredients and let stand a few minutes. Then put in a greased casserole.

Prepare the following and pour over apples:

1	cup flour	⅛	teaspoon allspice
1¼	cups sugar	2	eggs, beaten
1½	teaspoons baking powder	2	tablespoons butter
½	teaspoon salt	1	tablespoon water

Bake in 350° oven for 30 minutes. Increase temperature to 400° and bake for additional 15-17 minutes.

Blueberry Cobbler

¼	cup butter	1	teaspoon lemon juice
1	cup sugar		Pinch of salt
1	cup Bisquick	2-3	cups fresh blueberries
¾	cup milk		

Melt butter in deep dish. Mix Bisquick with milk and sugar. Add lemon juice and pinch of salt. Stir and pour into casserole. Place blueberries on top and bake for 45 minutes in 350° oven. Batter will rise to the top

Variation: This cobbler recipe works for any fruit – try with peaches or apples.

Coconut Graham Cracker Crumb Crust

1	can flake coconut	¼	cup butter, melted
¼	cup Graham cracker crumbs	¼	teaspoon cinnamon
		¼	teaspoon nutmeg

Combine all of the above and press firmly to the bottom of a pie pan. Bake in 350° oven for 15 minutes to seal. Fill as usual.

Basic Cobbler Recipe

½ stick butter

1 cup sugar

1 cup Bisquick

¾ cup milk

1 tablespoon lemon juice

Pinch of salt

2-3 cups fruit

Melt butter in casserole dish. Mix in dry ingredients, then milk and lemon. Add fruit last. If fruit has not been sweetened, then add about ½ cup additional sugar. Bake in preheated 350° oven for 45 minutes.

If you don't have Bisquick, substitute 1 cup flour and 2 teaspoons baking powder for the Bisquick.

I grew up with my grandmother in our kitchen making this seafoam candy. She'd plop the candy all over the counter to dry. This is really an old fashioned dessert – one that your mother and grandmother would recognize.

This Apricot Balls recipe used to be served at the Governor's Mansion in Raleigh, North Carolina, thus it's name. My copy of the recipe says that Ruthy Cunningham paid 10 cents for this recipe years ago at a political tea in Raleigh at the Jack Blythe home.

Bubba's Seafoam Candy

3	cups granulated sugar	2	egg whites
½	cup dark corn syrup	1	teaspoon vanilla
⅔	cup water	1	cup chopped walnut pieces
½	teaspoon salt		

Combine sugar, syrup, water and salt in a 1½-quart saucepan. Cook over medium heat, stirring constantly until sugar dissolves. Put egg whites in electric mixer and beat.

Cook syrup now, without stirring until firm ball stage, when candy thermometer reaches 244-248 degrees. When ready, slowly pour syrup into egg whites. Continue beating at high speed until candy holds shape. Then with spoon, stir in vanilla and nuts. Drop meringues onto waxed paper to set.

This will not set as well if the humidity is high or if there's dampness in the air.

Mansion Apricot Balls

1	(12-ounce) package dried apricots		Juice of 1 orange
2	cups powdered sugar Grated rind of 1 orange	1	cup pecans, chopped fine

Grind apricots and add sugar and orange juice and rind. Cook for about 10 minutes in medium saucepan. Add nuts and cool. Form into balls, 1 teaspoon to a ball, and roll in powdered sugar. Makes about 100 balls.

desserts and candy

Chocolate Delight

1 cup all-purpose flour
1 stick margarine or butter, melted
1 cup chopped nuts
1 (8-ounce) package cream cheese, softened
1 cup powdered sugar
1 large container Cool Whip, divided
1 (3.4-ounce) box instant vanilla pudding
1½-2 cups whole milk
1 (3.4-ounce) box instant chocolate pudding
1½-2 cups whole milk
Grated sweet chocolate

Make a paste of 1 cup flour and 1 stick melted margarine or butter. Add 1 cup chopped nuts. Spread on bottom of baking dish. Bake at 350 degrees until golden brown. Cool.

Beat together softened cream cheese, softened, and 1 cup powdered sugar. Fold in ½ large Cool Whip. Spread on crust.

Mix 1 box instant vanilla pudding mix with 1½-2 cups milk. Spread over Cool Whip layer. Mix 1 box instant chocolate pudding mix with 1½-2 cups milk. Spread over vanilla layer.

Spread remaining Cool Whip on top. Sprinkle with grated sweet chocolate and serve.

Frozen Chocolate Dessert

14 Oreo cookies

1 quart coffee ice cream

Chocolate syrup

14 additional Oreo cookies

1 quart chocolate ice cream

Crushed Heath candy bar

Press crushed Oreo's to bottom of springform pan. Layer rest of ingredients in order as printed and freeze. Slice when ready to serve. Serve with additional chocolate syrup if desired.

Brittany Chocolate Dessert

4 ounces semi-sweet chocolate chips

4-5 tablespoons sugar

1 stick butter

Pinch salt

Pinch nutmeg

3 eggs, separated

Melt chocolate over boiling water; add sugar, butter, salt and nutmeg. Pour small amount of chocolate into beaten egg yolks. Return all to chocolate mixture. Allow to cook 2-3 minutes until thickened slightly. Remove from fire, cool; fold in stiffly beaten egg whites.

Mold or place in individual compotes. Sprinkle with chopped almonds. Serve chilled with whipped cream. Serves 8.

Creamy Chocolate Mousse

This creamy mousse can also be used in crêpes.

2	cups heavy cream, whipped until very stiff	3	tablespoons cocoa
⅓	cup sugar	¼	cup egg substitute (equivalent to 4 egg yolks)
1	(12-ounce) package semi-sweet chocolate chips	2	tablespoons Grand Marnier (or other type liqueur)
1½	sticks butter		Whipped or chantilly cream for garnish

Whip 2 cups heavy cream with ⅓ cup sugar until very stiff. Melt chocolate and butter together. Let cool slightly, add cocoa and egg substitute, then liqueur if you desire. Fold in whipped cream.

Place in large airtight container if using in crêpes, or in individual compotes if serving individually. Chill in refrigerator for at least 1-2 hours. If serving with crêpes, roll up crêpes, place on lined cookie sheet and freeze. Remove to thaw when ready to use.

Serve topped with whipped or chantilly cream. Garnish with a strawberry if desired.

Chantilly Cream:

1	cup whipping cream	2	teaspoons vanilla
¼	cup sugar		

Whip together the whipping cream, sugar and vanilla.

Pumpkin Mousse

2½	tablespoons unflavored gelatin	1	teaspoon ground ginger
⅔	cup cold water	1	cup sugar
6	eggs	2	cups light cream
1¾	cups canned pumpkin	2	teaspoons vanilla
1	teaspoon salt		

Soften gelatin in cold water. Beat eggs lightly and add canned pumpkin, salt, ginger and sugar. Scald cream in double boiler and slowly add to above mixture. Return to double boiler and cook over hot water until mixture thickens (about 10 minutes), stirring often.

Remove from heat and add softened gelatin and vanilla and stir until gelatin dissolves. Cool slightly and pour into a 1½-quart mold which has been rinsed in cold water. Chill until firm and unmold.

This can be frozen as well. Serves 8-10.

 Crème Brûlée

1	quart heavy whipping cream	6	egg yolks
1	cup sugar	1	whole egg
1	vanilla bean, split		Additional granulated sugar for topping

Heat cream and sugar in a saucepan with a split vanilla bean over low heat. Let vanilla bean separate and steep into the cream for about 15 minutes. Do not let cream get too hot and stick to the pan.

Lightly beat the egg yolks and whole egg in a bowl. Temper the eggs into the warm cream and mix well. Fill 6 (8-ounce) custard dishes ¾ full. Place custard dishes in a large baking or roasting pan and prepare a hot water bath for the custard dishes so that the water goes half way up the dishes.

Bake in a 300 degree oven for 25-30 minutes or until set. Check at 25 minutes – if custard is still too jiggly, bake a little longer. Take the custard dishes straight to the refrigerator to cool.

To prepare crème brûlée for serving, sprinkle additional sugar on top of the custard, so that custard is covered in a thin layer. Under the broiler or with a torch, brown the sugar until it's caramelized – several minutes with a torch or up to 5-7 minutes under a broiler. Do not let burn. Serve with a touch of whipped cream and a strawberry if desired.

Smore's Parfait

A dessert kids will love!

4 ounces chocolate ice cream

1 large graham cracker, crushed

3 ounces marshmallow cream

3 ounces chocolate sauce

1 whole graham cracker

Scoop ice cream into ball. Roll ice cream in crushed graham cracker and place in freezer. To serve, place ice cream in martini glass. Top with chocolate sauce then with the marshmallow cream.

Toast marshmallow cream with kitchen blowtorch (don't overheat!). Garnish with whole graham cracker on side.

Crème Brûlée is one of my favorite all-time desserts – the one most likely to turn my head after dinner. Mark Freedman, owner of Mark's on Westover in Greensboro, NC, makes an excellent version, which he graciously shared with me.

Grandest Batch of Fudge

This recipe was written as part of a letter in 1962, describing this as the grandest batch of fudge.

1 stick butter or margarine

3 squares Baker's bitter chocolate

1 pound powdered sugar

1 egg

2 tablespoons cream

Dash of salt

1 teaspoon vanilla

½ cup nuts, optional

Put chocolate and margarine in a saucepan and melt. In a bowl, put powdered sugar, 1 egg, cream, vanilla and salt. Mix together and pour the hot chocolate/butter into the sugar mixture. Mix well with an electric beater. Turn out in a buttered pan and put in refrigerator for 20 minutes. Take out and cut into squares.

Pet Milk Fabulous Fudge

The old torn advertisement for this recipe says, "Couldn't be creamier. Never fails...with blendable PET milk."

2¼	cups sugar	¼	teaspoon salt
¾	cup PET evaporated milk	1	(6-ounce) package semi-sweet chocolate chips
16	large marshmallows or 1 cup marshmallow crème	1	cup chopped pecans
¼	cup butter	1	teaspoon vanilla

Mix in a heavy saucepan sugar, evaporated milk, marshmallows or marshmallow crème, butter and salt. Cook, stirring constantly, over medium heat to a boil (mixture will be bubbling all over top). Boil and stir 5 minutes more. Take off heat.

Sir in chocolate chips until they are completely melted. Stir in pecans and vanilla. Spread in a buttered 8-inch square pan and cool. Cut into 30 pieces.

Eagle Brand Chocolate Fudge

The recipe says that even beginners will get a marvelous result from this recipe – a melt-in-your-mouth smoothness, a glorious creaminess!

2	cups sugar	3	squares unsweetened chocolate
1	cup water		
1	cup Eagle Sweetened condensed milk	1	cup nut meats (optional)

Mix sugar and water in large saucepan and bring to boil. Add condensed milk and boil over low heat until mixture will form a firm ball when tested in cold water (235-240 degrees on a candy thermometer). Stir mixture constantly to prevent burning. Remove from heat and add chocolate, which has been cut into small pieces. Chop nut meats and add. Beat until thick and creamy. Pour into buttered pan. When cool, cut into squares.

desserts and candy

Cherries Jubilee

A fabulous flaming dessert!

1	can black Bing cherries, juice reserved	1	tablespoon cornstarch Vanilla ice cream
1	tablespoon sugar	½-¼	cup 100 proof apple brandy

Drain juice from 1 can black Bing cherries. Mix together in a saucepan 1 tablespoon sugar and 1 tablespoon cornstarch and add the cherry juice a little at a time to the sugar and cornstarch. Cook gently for 3 minutes, stirring constantly. Add the cherries. Have the ice cream in the sherbet glasses or dishes. Pour over the cherries ¼-½ cup 100 proof apple brandy and light with match. Fire will quickly burn down. Spoon the sauce and cherries over the ice cream and serve immediately.

Peaches Flambé

6	fresh peach halves	2	tablespoons brandy (86 proof)
½	cup sugar		
½	cup water	6	servings vanilla ice cream
2	tablespoons Cointreau		

Dissolve sugar in water in a skillet, bring to a boil then lower heat and cook 10 minutes. Add peeled peaches, simmer 5 minutes. Remove peaches, continue cooking 5 minutes to reduce slightly. Remove mixture to a chafing dish pan and place in the chafing dish blazer over direct heat. Add the peaches and warm. Add Cointreau. Warm brandy in ladle, ignite. Lower ladle of flaming brandy as flame burns. When flaming ceases, serve over ice cream. Serves 6.

Simple Vanilla Ice Cream

1 tablespoon vanilla

5 eggs

2 tall cans evaporated milk

2 cups sugar

3 cups whole milk

Beat eggs well in large bowl of electric mixer at medium speed. Mix in all milk, sugar and vanilla until sugar is thoroughly dissolved. Pour into freezer can and freeze according to operating directions. Makes approximately 1 gallon.

Variation: You can make fresh peach or strawberry ice cream by adding 1-quart peaches or strawberries. After dissolving sugar, fold in fruit right before pouring into freezer can.

In some parts of the South, banana pudding ties with pecan pie as "the" dessert for Thanksgiving. It is always found on menus at Southern diners. Banana pudding is a part of Southern heritage and an integral part of Southern life. This recipe calls for a more traditional, homemade custard as its base.

Homemade Banana Pudding

1	cup sugar	1	tablespoon vanilla extract
¼	cup all-purpose flour		
	Pinch salt	1	box vanilla wafers
4	cups whole milk	8	bananas sliced
8	egg yolks	8	egg whites
		2	tablespoons sugar

To make the custard, mix the sugar, flour and salt in a bowl. Pour milk into a heavy saucepan and add dry ingredients. Heat but do not boil. Beat egg yolks and pour some of the hot milk mixture into egg yolks and beat briefly. Then add egg yolk mixture to the base mixture in the saucepan. Bring to a boil over low heat, stirring constantly and cook slowly until just thick enough to coat the back of a spoon. Be careful not to scorch. Add the vanilla and remove from heat. Cover with plastic wrap to prevent a skin from forming on top.

Line the bottom and sides of a 9x13-inch baking pan with vanilla wafers. Put a layer of bananas over the wafers, then another layer of vanilla wafers until you have used all of the wafers and bananas. Then pour in the custard, completely covering the bananas and wafers. Heat oven to 375 degrees.

Beat egg whites until they form soft peaks. Add 2 tablespoons sugar and beat to stiff peaks. Spread meringue fully over the top of the pudding and bake until browned, about 15-20 minutes.

Pronto Banana Pudding

Easy, but just as delicious as homemade!

	Vanilla wafers	1	medium container Cool Whip
4-6	bananas		
1	(5.1-ounce) instant Jell-O vanilla pudding	1	(8-ounce) container sour cream

In a large casserole dish layer vanilla wafers on bottom and sides of dish. Slice 4-6 bananas and layer on top of wafers. Prepare box of instant vanilla pudding according to directions on box and spread on top of bananas. Mix Cool Whip with sour cream and spread on top of pudding. Chill for several hours.

desserts and candy

Banana Split Dessert

One of my childhood favorites!

2	sticks butter, melted and divided	1	teaspoon vanilla
2	cups graham cracker crumbs	4	bananas, sliced
2	cups powdered sugar	1	(15-ounce) can crushed pineapple, drained
2	eggs	1	medium container Cool Whip

Mix 1 stick melted butter with graham crumbs and press in bottom of 9x13-inch Pyrex dish. Bake in preheated 375 degree oven for 5-6 minutes. Cool.

Mix 1 stick softened butter, powdered sugar, eggs and vanilla. Beat until smooth and creamy. Spread over crust. Slice 4 bananas long-wise and place over custard. Spread large can crushed pineapple, well drained, over bananas. Cover with carton of Cool Whip. Refrigerate and enjoy!

Be sure to use fresh eggs since they are not cooked.

Strawberry Delight

1	cup all-purpose flour	1	cup sugar
¼	cup firmly packed brown sugar	2	teaspoons freshly squeezed lemon juice
½	cup chopped pecans	2	egg whites
½	cup melted butter	1	cup whipping cream, whipped
1½	cups sliced fresh strawberries		

Combine flour, brown sugar, pecans, and butter. Bake at 350° for 20 minutes in a 9-inch square pan, stirring often. Let cool. Combine strawberries, sugar, lemon juice, and egg whites; beat at high speed of electric mixer about 20 minutes or until light and fluffy. Fold whipped cream into strawberry mixture.

Remove ⅓ of crumb mixture from pan; pat remaining crumbs into smooth layer. Pour strawberry mixture over crumbs in pan, and sprinkle reserved crumbs over top; freeze.

Orange Navels

2 small cans crushed pineapple

1 cup brown sugar

5-6 slices ginger, cut up

Vanilla ice cream

Navel oranges

Whipped cream

Grand Mariner

Mix crushed pineapple,
brown sugar and ginger.
Boil 15 minutes. (Can keep
in the refrigerator.) Put
layers of vanilla ice cream
and sauce in navel oranges
that have been scooped out.
Place in freezer until few
minutes before serving time.
Put whipped cream with
Grand Mariner on top.

Cold Lemon Soufflé
with Wine Sauce

1	package unflavored gelatin	1½	cups sugar, divided
¼	cup cold water	¾	cup lemon juice
5	eggs, separated	2	teaspoons lemon rind
		1	cup heavy cream

Sprinkle gelatin over water to soften. Mix 5 egg yolks with lemon juice and rind and ¾ cup sugar. Pour lemon mixture into the top of a double boiler, stirring constantly until lemon mixture is slightly thickened (about 8 minutes). Remove from heat and add gelatin until dissolved. Chill 30-40 minutes until mixture mounds when dropped from spoon.

Beat egg whites until stiff, gradually adding the other ¾ cup sugar. Beat cream until stiff. Fold whipped cream and egg whites into yolk mixture. Pour into a 2-quart soufflé dish and chill 4 hours or more. (Or pour into individual sherbet glasses.)

Wine Sauce for Soufflé:

½	cup sugar	½	cup dry white wine
¼	cup water	1	tablespoon cornstarch
1	teaspoon grated lemon rind	1	tablespoon lemon juice
		2	tablespoons butter

In small saucepan, mix sugar and cornstarch. Stir in water, lemon juice, and rind until smooth. Add butter. Bring to boil, then lower heat and cook until thickened. Add wine and blend. Chill, stirring occasionally.

desserts and candy

 # Caramel Pear Trifle

Pears:

6	cups water	½	teaspoon vanilla extract
1½	cups sugar		
1	(2-inch) strip lemon peel – or more	4	firm, but ripe Bartlett pears – peeled, halved and cored

Caramel:

1	cup sugar	1	cup warm whipping cream
¼	cup water		

Whipped Cream and Cake:

1½	cups chilled whipping cream	½	pound cake – can purchase from store, cut into ¼-inch slices
1½	tablespoons powdered sugar		
1½	teaspoons vanilla extract		Sliced, toasted almonds for garnish

For Pears: In large saucepan add 6 cups water, sugar, lemon peel and vanilla. Stir over medium heat until mixture starts to boil. Reduce to a simmer and add pear halves. Simmer until pears are tender, about 15 minutes. Cool pears in the syrup.

For Caramel: Stir 1 cup sugar and ½ cup water in heavy medium saucepan over low heat until the sugar dissolves. Increase heat and boil without stirring until the sugar mixture turns deep amber, occasionally swirling the pan or brushing the sides down with a wet brush, about 10 minutes. Remove from heat and add 1 cup warm cream – be careful, the mixture will bubble up. Return to very low heat and stir until smooth. Chill sauce uncovered in the refrigerator until sauce is cold, about 1 hour.

Beat chilled 1½ cups whipping cream, powdered sugar and vanilla in a large bowl until firm peaks form. Fold ½ cup cold caramel sauce into the whipped cream. Cover and chill remaining caramel sauce.

Drain the pears and cut crosswise into ½-inch thick slices.

To assemble dessert: Press a slice of pound cake into each bowl or 12 to 14-ounce goblets. Top each cake slice with 4-6 pear slices, 2 teaspoons reserved caramel sauce and spoonful of caramel cream. Repeat layers one more time. You can cover and chill this dessert and store in the refrigerator for up to 1 day. When serving, drizzle remaining caramel sauce over trifles and sprinkle with toasted almond slices. Serves 6.

I recently adapted this recipe for a dinner party my husband and I were having and received rave reviews on this delicious caramel and pear concoction. It looks filling but is actually very light. It takes a while to make so allow time accordingly. It's well worth it. The recipe doubles beautifully. Makes 6 servings.

Cream Puff Filling

1 cup milk

½ cup sugar

1 egg

3 tablespoons flour

2 tablespoons cream after mixture cools

1 teaspoon vanilla

In a small saucepan over low heat, make a paste of milk, sugar, flour and egg. Remove from stove and let cool. After paste cools, add 2 tablespoons cream and vanilla.

A traditional dessert, this is often brought to individuals who are sick or recuperating from hospital stays. B.J. Williams is known for her boiled custard, which has soothed many a sick individual in Greensboro, North Carolina. She graciously shared her recipe.

Cream Puffs

1	cup hot water	1	cup sifted flour
½	cup butter	3	eggs

Boil together hot water and butter. While boiling, stir in 1 cup sifted flour. Remove from stove, and stir to a smooth paste. After this cools, stir in 3 eggs, not beaten. Stir 5 minutes. Drop 1 tablespoon full on a buttered pan. Bake in quick oven (375 degrees) for about 25 minutes. Do not open oven door while baking. This makes 12 puffs. Do not let them touch in pan. After cream puffs and filling are cool, open puffs a little on one side with a sharp knife and fill with cream filling.

Boiled Custard

1	cup milk	¼	teaspoon vanilla (approximately 1 teaspoon for 3-4 cups milk)
1	egg		
2	tablespoons sugar to each cup of milk		

Measure amount of milk you want to prepare and add eggs, sugar, vanilla accordingly. We usually make a batch with 4 cups milk. Let milk get warm in a double boiler. Beat eggs, adding sugar slowly. Then pour the eggs/sugar mixture into the warm milk, stirring all the time. Stir until your spoon coats, the milk will feel a little thicker. Don't cook for too long.

When mixture is cool, add vanilla – 1 teaspoon for 4 cups milk. You will have a thin crust on the top after it cools. Stir this into the custard. Chill.

Pudding Éclairs

Who doesn't love éclairs?
These are simplified with Jell-O pudding.

6	tablespoons butter	½	cup whipped cream or Cool Whip
¾	cup water	2	squares unsweetened chocolate
¾	sifted all-purpose flour	2	tablespoons butter
3	eggs	1½	cups powdered sugar
1	(3-ounce) package Jell-O Vanilla Pudding and Pie Filling		Dash of salt
1½	cups milk	3	tablespoons milk

To Make Shells:

In a saucepan, melt butter and water, bringing to a boil. Reduce heat and quickly stir in flour. Cook and stir until the mixture leaves the sides of pan – about 2-3 minutes. Remove from heat and beat in eggs, one at a time. Beat until smooth. With a spoon, spread out dough on an ungreased baking sheet to form 5x1-inch strips of dough. Bake at 425 degrees for 20 minutes; reduce heat to 350 degrees and bake for 30 more minutes. Let éclairs cool.

To Make Filling:

Cook pudding mix as directed, but reduce milk to 1½ cups. Cover surface with wax paper and chill for 1 hour. Beat pudding with beat until smooth. Fold in the whipped cream or Cool Whip.

To Make Chocolate Glaze:

Melt chocolate with 2 tablespoons butter over low heat. Remove from heat and blend in powdered sugar, pinch of salt and milk. Immediately spread on top of éclairs after they have been assembled.

To Assemble Éclairs:

Cut tops off of shells and fill each éclair with pudding. Replace tops and glace with chocolate.

Lemon Torte

6 eggs, separated

4 lemons

1 package unflavored gelatin

¼ cup water

1½ cups sugar, divided

1 small angel cake

½ pint cream

Separate eggs. Grate rind of all lemons and juice and mix with the egg yolks. To this add ¾ cup sugar. Cook in double boiler until thick. Soak gelatin in ¼ cup water. Add to custard and cool. Whip egg whites until stiff. Add ¾ cup sugar. Fold into the custard gently. Add broken angel food pieces. After it sits, cut in slices. Serve with whipped cream.

Buck Eyes

1 (12-ounce) bag semi-sweet chocolate chips

¼ bar paraseal wax

2 cups chunky peanut butter

2 sticks butter or margarine

1½ pounds powdered sugar

Melt chips and wax in a double boiler. Cream peanut butter and butter. Add powdered sugar a little at a time. Use a mixer at first. Form into small balls – any size you want. Dip these balls into the chocolate/wax mixture with a toothpick. Don't cover very tip of ball. Set on wax paper to dry.

Peanut Brittle

This recipe of my mother's dates back to 1968.

3	cups white sugar	3	cups raw Spanish peanuts
½	cup water	3	teaspoons butter
1	cup white corn syrup (Karo)	2	teaspoons baking soda
		1	teaspoon salt

Boil sugar, syrup and water until a spun thread will crack, about 20 minutes on medium high heat. Add peanuts, cook until brownish gold color, about 20-25 minutes. Remove from heat and add rest of ingredients. Mix well. Pour onto 2 buttered cookie sheets. Work FAST when pouring on cookie sheet. Break into pieces when cool.

Caramels

1½	cups granulated sugar	1	cup evaporated milk
1½	cups strained honey	¼	teaspoon salt
½	cup light brown sugar	1	teaspoon vanilla
½	cup butter		

Blend sugar, honey, salt and boil until soft ball stage when tested in cold water. Slowly add milk (this is important) then pieces of butter so boiling does not stop. Cook to hard ball stage when tested in water or 254 degrees on candy thermometer. Remove from heat. Add vanilla and turn into buttered pan. When cold, cut in squares and wrap each piece in wax paper.

sauces and accompaniments

Pickle

4 qts. sliced cucumbers
6 med. onions, white, sliced
2 green peppers chopped
1/3 cup salt
1 1/2 ~~Turmeric~~ Turmeric (teaspoon)
1 1/2 Teas. celery seed
2 Tbls. mustard seed
3 cups vinegar
5 " " sugar

Slice cucumbers, add onions & peppers,
add salt, cover with crushed Ice, let
stand 3 hrs. cover - drain -
Combine rest of ingredients, add cu. heat
just to boiling point, put in Jars &
Seal.

Dill Sauce
(for vegetables, fish - Veal
served at room temperature) Pasta

1/2 C. Sour cream
(add mayo to make
1/2 C. plus)
2 tsp lemon juice
Fresh dill (or 1 tsp dillweed)
1/4 tsp salt
" " pepper   1/2 TSP
1 green onion minced (or less
1/2 tsp sugar   (dried)
1/4 C. buttermilk or 2 TB whole
milk
over

sauces and accompaniments

Back in the old days, a good white sauce was a staple in many Southern dishes. Every cook, young and old, should be able to easily whip up a white sauce. You may thicken or thin this as desired.

You can always season a white sauce with any sesonings you prefer or add cheese for a rich cheese sauce.

I often use two percent milk for my white sauce.

The following is my grandmother's white sauce from her recipe book she gave me.

"Basic White Sauce"
2 Tablp. Margarine 3 Tablep flour
2 cups milk, Salt to taste
melt Margarine, stir in flour add
Milk gradully, and simmer slowly
until thick. Makes 2 cups sauce

Dill Sauce

This is especially good for vegetables or fish –
serve at room temperature.

½	cup sour cream	¼	teaspoon salt
¼	cup mayonnaise	¼	teaspoon pepper
2	teaspoons lemon juice	1	green onion, minced
4	teaspoons fresh dill or 1 teaspoon dried dill weed	½	teaspoon sugar
		¼	cup buttermilk

Mix all of the above in a bowl and let rest at least 2 hours. This can be refrigerated up to 2 weeks in tightly sealed container.

Fruit Dip

½	cup sugar	½	cup unsweetened pineapple juice
1	teaspoon flour	1	cup whipped cream
1	egg yolk		
2½	tablespoons lemon juice		

Combine sugar, flour and egg yolk. Add fruit juices. Blend. Cook in double boiler until slightly thickened. Cool. Fold in whipped cream. Use for dipping fresh strawberries, melon or pineapple.

Ranch House Dressing for Baked Potatoes

1	pound cottage cheese	1	teaspoon Worcestershire sauce
1	cup heavy cream (whipped)	1	teaspoon Accent (optional)
1	teaspoon salt	1½	teaspoons paprika
¼	cup onion, chopped very fine or 3 drops onion juice	½	teaspoon garlic powder or granulated garlic

Whip the heavy cream. Mix other ingredients and fold into whipped cream. This has more flavor if the dressing stands overnight in the refrigerator. Spoon into hot baked potato.

Simple Marinades

Wine Marinade

1 tablespoon mixed herbs (rosemary, oregano, thyme, basil)

1 tablespoon Dijon mustard

1 cup dry red wine or white wine

½ cup olive oil

Oriental Marinade

½ cup naturally brewed soy sauce

¼ cup peanut or corn oil

1 tablespoon fresh grated ginger

2 cloves garlic, minced

Bourbon Marinade

1 cup bourbon whiskey

½ cup mild olive oil

1 teaspoon brown sugar

Pinch red pepper flakes

Fresh Tomato Barbeque Sauce

The fresh tomatoes make a difference!

¼ cup vegetable oil

3 cloves garlic, chopped

1 medium onion, chopped

¼ cup brown sugar

4 large ripe tomatoes, chopped

1 cup ketchup

1 teaspoon chili powder

Salt and pepper to taste

Heat oil in saucepan and sauté garlic and onion until soft. Do not brown or burn garlic. Add remaining ingredients and bring to boil. Simmer 30 minutes. Taste and adjust seasonings.

Châteaubriand Sauce for Steak

½	cup dry white wine	1	teaspoon finely chopped tarragon
1	shallot finely chopped		Pinch cayenne pepper
2	beef bouillon cubes		Dash lemon juice
1	tablespoon butter		

Simmer white wine with the chopped shallot. Simmer until wine is slightly reduced. Add the bouillon cubes, butter, tarragon, pinch of cayenne and dash of lemon juice. Simmer for a few minutes and pour over grilled steak.

Barbeque Sauce

This is the kind of barbeque sauce that kids will like!

1	cup tomato sauce	½	teaspoon liquid smoke flavor
¼	cup vinegar	1	teaspoon Worcestershire sauce
¼	cup brown sugar		
1	teaspoon salt		

Mix all of the above in a small saucepan and simmer for 15-20 minutes. It can easily be doubled.

Incredible Barbeque Sauce

1	cup ketchup		Salt and pepper to taste
1	sliced onion	5	drops Tabasco sauce
4	tablespoons dark brown sugar	½	cup water
		1	clove garlic, minced

Combine all ingredients in a saucepan. Cook over medium heat 30-45 minutes or until onion is tender. Strain the sauce and it's ready to use. Recipe may be doubled or tripled, and it freezes well.

Primm's London Broil Marinade

¾	cup soy sauce	½	teaspoon salt
½	cup salad oil	½	teaspoon pepper
1	tablespoon fresh or powdered ginger	½	teaspoon thyme
1	teaspoon dry mustard	½	teaspoon oregano
1	tablespoon sugar	½	teaspoon rosemary
3	cloves garlic, minced	2	tablespoons sherry
½	fresh lemon juice		Dash of Tabasco sauce
½	cup finely chopped onion		Sprinkling of sesame seed and chives

Mix all of the above together and use as a marinade for London Broil or flank steak. Score meat on both sides and marinate meat 8-12 hours in the refrigerator, turning several times. Use the sauce to baste while the steak is cooking on the grill.

Mel's Steak Marinade

¼	cup soy sauce	2	green onions, chopped
¾	cup vegetable oil	2	cloves garlic, crushed
¼	cup flour	¼	teaspoon pepper
½	cup sugar		

Mix all of the above and pour over any steak, London broil, or flank steak. Marinate for 4-8 hours, turning frequently.

Mel's Bourbon Meat Marinade

5	ounces soy sauce	1	tablespoon Worcestershire sauce
¼	cup brown sugar	½	cup water
¼	cup Bourbon	2	cloves garlic, minced
1	tablespoon lemon juice		Salt and pepper

Mix all of the above and marinate any favorite steak for 2-6 hours. Grill or prepare steak as desired.

Lee Ann's Beef Marinade

This recipe came from my cousin Lee Beam of Staunton, Virginia and has been used in our family for many years.

1 cup soy sauce

½ cup dry sherry

⅓ cup olive oil

3 cloves garlic, chopped

2 teaspoons ground ginger

Mix together and marinate steaks overnight or throughout the day.

London Broil Marinade

1	clove garlic	2	teaspoons dry mustard
1	cup corn oil	2	teaspoons Worcestershire sauce
½	cup vinegar		Dash cayenne pepper
1	teaspoon salt		Few drops Tabasco sauce
¼	teaspoon pepper		

Slice garlic in a large shallow casserole dish. Add remaining ingredients and stir until blended. Place London Broil in dish and pour marinade over it. Let stand, covered and refrigerated, at least 3 hours, overnight if possible. Remove from marinade and prepare as directed.

Flank Steak Marinade

1	cup red wine	1	bay leaf
2	cups balsamic vinegar	½	teaspoon pepper
⅓	cup soy sauce	3	tablespoons Dijon mustard
1	tablespoon Grated ginger	2	garlic cloves, minced
1	teaspoon dried thyme or 3 teaspoons fresh thyme		

Marinate flank steak 1 day and prepare as directed. This can be used on any steak.

Pork Marinade

This is a good marinade for a pork roast or ham.

3	tablespoons Dijon mustard	1	small can orange juice concentrate
1	can beer	1	teaspoon ground cloves
⅔	cup dark brown sugar		

Mix all of the above and pour over prepared ham or pork roast. Bake as directed.

Honey Soy Marinade for Chicken

1	cup soy sauce	2	tablespoons fresh ginger, minced	
1	cup honey			
2	tablespoons fresh garlic, minced		Salt and pepper to taste	

Mix all of the above in a jar with a tight fitting lid. Dip chicken in marinade right before grilling. Will keep for a while in the refrigerator.

To preserve ginger, process peeled sliced ginger with white wine in a food processor or blender until smooth. This will keep in the refrigerator for 1-2 weeks. Use this combination instead of chopped ginger in the above recipe if desired.

Special Mustard Sauce

The recipe said this is "food for the Gods!" It's good with shrimp, ham, turkey and even plain bread. Watch out, it's hot.

1	cup Coleman's dry mustard	2	eggs	
1	cup vinegar	1	cup sugar	
			Pinch of salt	

Mix the dry mustard and vinegar and let stand overnight. Beat 2 eggs and add to the sugar in top of a double boiler. Combine with the mustard-vinegar mixture which has sat overnight, and add pinch of salt. Boil until thick as a thin custard and coats the back of a spoon – about 10 minutes.

Spicy German Mustard

1 tin Coleman's dry mustard

1 cup balsamic vinegar

1 cup brown sugar

2 eggs, or the equivalent amount of egg substitute

Combine dry mustard and vinegar. Let stand 2 hours. Transfer to small saucepan. Add brown sugar and eggs. Cook over medium heat, stirring constantly until mixture has thickened. Let cool. Taste; if too spicy, add up to a tablespoon of Miracle Whip Salad Dressing.

Put the liquid into the eggs, not eggs into the liquid – until the egg mixture gets warm.

Tartar Sauce

½ cup mayonnaise

1 tablespoon minced
pickle relish

1 teaspoon minced capers

1 teaspoon minced chives

2 teaspoons minced parsley

Few drops onion juice

2 teaspoons plain
or tarragon vinegar

Combine all ingredients
and chill thoroughly. Serve
with fish or fried oysters.

Mayonnaise

1	egg yolk	1	tablespoon white-wine vinegar
	Salt and white pepper to taste	1	cup vegetable or olive oil, or a combination of both
1	tablespoon Dijon mustard		
1	tablespoon fresh lemon juice		

Place yolk in mixing bowl; add salt, pepper, mustard, lemon juice and vinegar. Beat with wire whisk or electric mixer. Add oil slowly, while using beater, until all of the oil is poured. Taste and adjust seasonings. Use immediately or store in refrigerator for a short time. Makes 1 cup.

Red Pepper Mayonnaise

1	roasted red pepper, finely chopped	2	cloves garlic, minced
1	cup mayonnaise	2	tablespoons fresh lemon juice
3	tablespoons chopped chives		Salt and freshly ground pepper to taste
	Pinch of cayenne pepper		

Mix all of above ingredients and chill.

Hollandaise Sauce

1	stick butter	¼	cup lemon juice
4	egg yolks	¼	cup half-and-half
¼	teaspoon salt		

Heat butter in top of double boiler until just melted. Set over boiling water. Separate 4 eggs. To the yolks, add salt and lemon juice. Mix well. The eggs are not beaten first.

Stir the egg mixture into the butter. Turn down the heat so the water underneath is just under boiling. Beat the egg mixture with a rotary beater until thickened. Add ¼ cup light cream or half-and-half and continue beating 2 minutes longer.

sauces and accompaniments

Satay Sauce

This is excellent with skewered chicken or shrimp.

1	clove garlic, minced	1	tablespoon soy sauce
1	cup shelled peanuts	½	teaspoon salt
½	teaspoon crushed hot red pepper	1	teaspoon turmeric
1	small onion, chopped		Juice of ½ lemon
2	pieces preserved or candied ginger	1	cup water (approximate)

In a mortar, crush the garlic, onion, peanuts, pepper and ginger. Stir in remaining ingredients or put all the ingredients in a blender and blend for about 30 seconds. Pour sauce into top part of a double boiler and place over direct heat. Bring to a boil, stirring often. Place over boiling water and cook 30 minutes, stirring occasionally. Thin to desired consistency with more water.

Roquefort Sauce

This is good for hot vegetables, tossed salad, dip – whatever you like.

1	(8-ounce) package cream cheese, softened	½	teaspoon salt
			Dash of pepper
1	large can evaporated milk	4	ounces Roquefort cheese, crumbled at room temperature

Beat cream cheese in a bowl with a beater. Gradually add evaporated milk, salt and dash of pepper. Place over low heat in a saucepan and add room temperature Roquefort cheese that has been crumbled. Stir fairly frequently and bring to soft boil. Serve immediately.

Shrimp Sauce

2 cups mayonnaise

¾ cup chili sauce

½ large onion, grated

2 tablespoons horseradish

1 tablespoon Worcestershire sauce

Dash Tabasco sauce

Crushed red pepper to taste

1-2 teaspoons curry powder (to taste)

Mix all of the ingredients in a bowl and chill. This is also a good vegetable dip.

Horseradish Sauce

½ cup heavy cream

4-6 tablespoons horseradish

½ teaspoon salt

Dash of pepper

Whip cream until stiff and add horseradish and seasonings.

Variation: One medium cucumber, chopped, may replace horseradish to make cucumber sauce for fish.

Rémoulade Sauce

This is perfect for crab cakes or fried oysters.

1	cup mayonnaise	⅓	cup green onions, minced
3	tablespoons Dijon mustard	⅓	cup celery, minced
2-3	tablespoons white wine vinegar	2	tablespoons finely chopped parsley
1	tablespoon paprika	2	tablespoons ketchup
2	tablespoons horseradish sauce		Salt and pepper to taste
1	clove garlic, minced		

Stir together and refrigerate.

Artichoke Butter Sauce

¼	stick butter	¼	teaspoon minced lemon zest
¼	cup olive oil or juice from marinated artichoke hearts	1½	teaspoons fresh minced thyme or ½ teaspoon dried thyme
¼	cup roughly chopped, drained marinated artichoke hearts		

In a medium skillet, melt butter over medium heat. Add oil and artichokes and sauté on high heat for 3 minutes. Remove from heat and toss with lemon zest and thyme.

Variation: For a spicier taste, add a dash of crushed red pepper along with the salt and pepper. Use this sauce over hot pasta and top with Parmesan cheese and fresh chopped thyme.

Medium White Sauce

3	tablespoons butter	¾	teaspoon salt
3	tablespoons flour	2	cups milk, scaled

Melt butter in top of double boiler over low heat. Blend in flour and salt; cook over low heat, stirring constantly, for 5 minutes. Gradually add hot milk, stirring constantly, until all liquid has been added and sauce is smooth. Place over simmering water and cook for 30 minutes, or until thickened, stirring frequently. Makes about 2 cups. Flavor or season white sauce any way you desire – add wine, Sherry or Vermouth, herbs or other seasonings.

Tomato Coulis

Serve this relish-like dish over fish, shrimp or pasta. It's obviously better in the summer with fresh tomatoes and it freezes well!

8	large ripe tomatoes, peeled, seeded and chopped	7	sprigs parsley, chopped, divided
1	tablespoon sugar	7	sprigs fresh basil, chopped, divided
2	medium onions, minced	2	tablespoons olive oil
2	teaspoon fresh minced garlic		Salt, pepper and cayenne pepper to taste

In a large pot, bring water and sugar and tomatoes to a boil and cook for 5-10 minutes. Strain tomatoes and reserve while they cool. In a large non-stick skillet, sauté onions, garlic and half of basil and parsley in 2 tablespoons olive oil. Do not brown.

Peel the tomatoes and cut in half width wise. Put your fingers in the holes and squeeze seeds out. Chop tomatoes and stir into the onion mixture. Season to taste with the salt, pepper and cayenne pepper. This will keep nearly a week in the refrigerator. Bring to room temperature before serving.

You may add chopped fresh oregano or other summer herbs if you desire.

Clarified Butter

Clarified butter is great for sautéing. It doesn't burn. It's also wonderful in sauces.

Place 1 stick butter in top of a double boiler over hot water or microwave covered on high for 1 minute. When butter is melted, pour off clear layer and discard milky sediment that is left. Makes about 5 tablespoons.

Icebox Strawberry Jam

2 cups crushed strawberries

4 cups sugar

¾ cup water

1 box powdered pectin
(sure-jell)

Stir strawberries and sugar together in bowl. Let stand 10 minutes. Bring water and pectin to a boil and boil 1 minute, stirring constantly. Add pectin mixture to fruit and stir 3 minutes. Put in jars, screw tops on tight. Let stand at room temperature for 24 hours or until set. Then freeze. Makes 6 half-pint jars.

Chow-Chow

A spicy relish served on many a Southern plate.

1	peck (8 quarts) green tomatoes	2	quarts vinegar
10	onions	2	pounds brown sugar
1½	pounds cabbage	1	cup salt
3	green peppers	2	teaspoons turmeric
3	red peppers	2	teaspoons dry mustard

Cut up green tomatoes and peppers and sprinkle ⅔ cup salt over. Let stand overnight or for several hours. Rinse, drain and chop vegetables. Cook tomatoes and cabbage in vinegar and brown sugar for 10 minutes or so before adding peppers and onions. Cook until thick or cabbage turns colors. Can in mason jars and store until ready to use.

Bread and Butter Pickles

12	medium cucumbers	2	tablespoons flour
2-3	medium onions	1	teaspoon dry mustard
¾	cup sugar	½	tablespoon turmeric
1	cup vinegar	½	teaspoon celery seed

Slice cucumbers and onions and soak separately in salt and water for 2 hours. Make sauce of sugar, vinegar, flour and dry mustard. Drain cucumbers and onions and add vinegar sauce in saucepan. Cook on medium heat until thick, 5-6 minutes. Remove and add ½ tablespoon turmeric and ½ teaspoon celery seed. Store in refrigerator until ready to serve.

Cranberry Relish

2	cups cranberries	2	tablespoons crystallized ginger, chopped
1	large orange and peeling		
¾	cup sugar	¾	cup raisins

In a blender on low speed, blend about ¼ each of the berries and oranges until coarsely chopped. Spoon into medium size bowl. Stir in raisins, sugar and ginger and mix. Refrigerate and serve with turkey or ham.

Mother's Cranberry Chutney

We use this cranberry chutney at
every Thanksgiving, with our turkey.

1	(24-ounce) bottle maple flavored pancake syrup	1½	cups raisins
		1	cup chopped walnuts
1	(16-ounce) package cranberries	⅓	cup lemon juice
		2	teaspoons salt
5	cups peeled, chopped apples	2	teaspoons finely chopped onion
		¼-½	teaspoon ground cloves

Combine all ingredients in a large saucepan or Dutch oven. Bring mixture to a boil, stirring often. Reduce heat and simmer, uncovered 40-50 minutes or until thick, stirring frequently as mixture thickens. Spoon hot mixture into hot, sterilized jars and seal. Or store in airtight containers in the refrigerator. Makes about 7 cups.

Watermelon Preserves

1	watermelon	2	lemons
	Salt		Sugar
	Alum (dissolved)		Spices

Peel and cut into slices the rind of 1 watermelon. Soak slices in a weak salt solution (1 teaspoon salt to 1 quart water) overnight. Drain off the water and parboil the watermelon rind for a few minutes in water containing a pinch of dissolved alum. Drain the slices again. Make a heavy syrup using 3 parts sugar to 1 part water.

Add 2 lemons, sliced thin, and add whatever spices are desired, cinnamon, allspice, ginger or cloves. Place watermelon in the boiling syrup and boil slowly until tender. Pack into clean hot jars and seal immediately.

Strawberry Preserves

2 quarts strawberries

4 cups sugar

½ teaspoon butter

2 cups sugar

Cap and wash 2 quarts strawberries; drain and put in container. Cover with boiling water and let stand 5 minutes. Drain and place in saucepan. After water comes to a boil, add 4 cups of sugar and ½ teaspoon butter. Let boil 7 minutes. Take off stove and add 2 cups sugar. Let boil 5 more minutes. While hot, pour into a flat dish, let stand until cool, for 5 hours or overnight. Put in jars and seal as usual.

Spiced Peaches

2 large cans peach halves

¾ cup brown sugar

½ cup vinegar

2 (3-inch) cinnamon sticks

1 tablespoon whole cloves

1 tablespoon whole allspice

Drain peaches, reserving liquid. Boil syrup with brown sugar, vinegar, cinnamon sticks, cloves and allspice for 5 minutes. Add peach halves one by one and cool. Put in refrigerator until ready to serve.

Hot Fruit Casserole

1	large can (16-ounce) each:	1	large jar Maraschino cherries
	Sliced pineapple	2	tablespoons flour
	Peach halves	½	cup light brown sugar
	Pear halves	1	stick butter
	Apricot halves	1	cup Bacardi Rum
	Green seedless grapes		

Drain all fruit thoroughly. Cut pineapple slices in halves as well as other fruit, if needed. Arrange fruit in layers in large casserole dish, leaving grapes and cherries for garnish on top.

In double boiler, melt butter, then mix with sugar, flour and rum. Cook over hot water stirring and cooking until smooth. Thickness should be like cream. Pour over fruit and let stand refrigerated overnight. Heat in a 350° oven until bubbly – about 20-30 minutes.

Pineapple Casserole

1½	cups sugar	1	pound pineapple chunks, drained
1	cup margarine		
3	eggs	4	cups bread crumbs – soft with crusts removed

Cream sugar and margarine. Add eggs, one at a time and beat well. Fold in the pineapple and bread crumbs. Pour into greased 9x12-inch or 12-inch square pan. Bake for 30-45 minutes in a 350° oven.

sauces and accompaniments

index

Someone's in the Kitchen with *Melanie*

621 Woodland Drive
Greensboro, North Carolina 27408
336-378-1700 Cookbook Office • www.melanies-kitchen.com

Please send me _____ copies of

Someone's in the Kitchen with Melanie   @ $24.95 each _____

North Carolina residents add 7% sales tax   @   1.75 each _____

Priority Postage and Handling   @   5.00 each _____

Total Amount: $ _____

Name_____

Address_____

City _____State _____Zip _____

Daytime phone number _____ email _____

Would you like book signed? _____ To whom? _____

Make checks payable to: Melanie's Kitchen

Or include your credit card information as follows: (circle one)   Visa   MasterCard

Card number _____ Expiration Date _____

Signature of Authorization _____

- -

Someone's in the Kitchen with *Melanie*

621 Woodland Drive
Greensboro, North Carolina 27408
336-378-1700 Cookbook Office • www.melanies-kitchen.com

Please send me _____ copies of

Someone's in the Kitchen with Melanie   @ $24.95 each _____

North Carolina residents add 7% sales tax   @   1.75 each _____

Priority Postage and Handling   @   5.00 each _____

Total Amount: $ _____

Name_____

Address_____

City _____State _____Zip _____

Daytime phone number _____ email _____

Would you like book signed? _____ To whom? _____

Make checks payable to: Melanie's Kitchen

Or include your credit card information as follows: (circle one)   Visa   MasterCard

Card number _____ Expiration Date _____

Signature of Authorization _____